WHO SAYS LIFE IS FAIR?

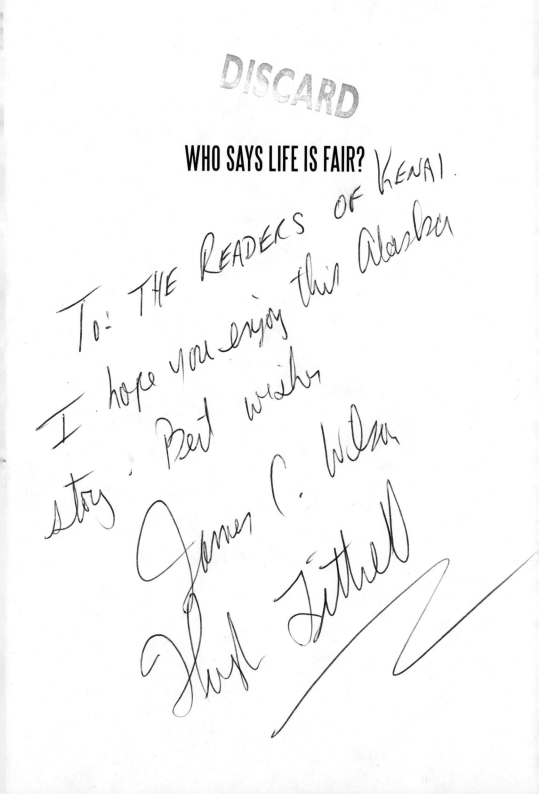

To: THE READERS OF KENAI.

I hope you enjoy this Alaska story. Best wishes

James C. Wilson

Floyd Littlell

WHO SAYS LIFE IS FAIR?

The Story of a Loving Dad. His Life, His Losses, and How He Came Out a Winner.

JAMES C. WILSON

authorHOUSE®

AuthorHouse™
1663 Liberty Drive
Bloomington, IN 47403
www.authorhouse.com
Phone: 1-800-839-8640

This book is a work of fiction. People, places, events, and situations are the product of the author's imagination. Any resemblance to actual persons, living or dead, or historical events, is purely coincidental.

First published by AuthorHouse 2/18/2010

ISBN: 978-1-4490-7642-9 (e)
ISBN: 978-1-4490-7641-2 (sc)
ISBN: 978-1-4490-7640-5 (hc)

Library of Congress Control Number: 2010900633

Printed in the United States of America
Bloomington, Indiana

This book is printed on acid-free paper.

DEDICATION

I dedicate this book to my beloved wife, who provides to me the light and love that make me the richest man in the world. God has truly blessed me with the gift of my life mate.

My Tribute to her:

> And yes, I know how lonely life can be,
> The shadows follow me,
> And the night won't set me free,
> But I don't let the evening get me down,
> Now that you're around — me.
>
> Don McLean, "And I Love You So"

ACKNOWLEDGEMENTS

I wish to thank the Sherwood Star, the Castle Rock Flash and Big T-Rex for their valuable and generous help.

INTRODUCTION

My name is Jim Wilson. I make my living as a technical writer, am happily married and am the proud father of three children. I became friends with Jack Hamilton a few years ago when we met at a weekend retreat for men. At that retreat, Jack made a presentation of his theories on how to live happily. What I heard from him moved me and inspired me to engage him further when we got together after the retreat and became better acquainted. I found the "Principles for Successful Living" as presented by Jack to be a worthy concept, and I was interested to realize that this is a man who really believes what he says about how to live honorably and joyfully and who makes a sincere effort to live what he advertises.

Jack and I became friends, and as our friendship grew, I learned of a sad loss that this decent and kindly man has experienced through his estrangement from his adult children. I was impressed by the fact that, despite this tragic feature of his world, Jack was clearly leading a joyful and rewarding life, and that he knew exactly why he was having such success despite what had happened with his family. This struck me as a topic worthy of further examination, and as I gained more knowledge of his life, the writer in me was inspired to get into the details of what had gone on with Jack and to get it down on paper for others to read about. We spent many hours together at my request as he told me the story of his life. The result is this book.

I have created a fictional rendering which uses as its inspiration what was told to me by Jack Hamilton about his life. It is an everyman's story which has within it joy and sorrow, victory and tragedy, ugliness and comedy and plenty of compelling drama. The story as presented is make-believe, and any resemblance to actual persons living or dead is because many people live similar lives. Names and places are made up, but the story told is enough like thousands of real-life experiences in thousands of families to have a lot of common ground to which others can easily relate.

Included at the end of the book are the principles that are active features of Jack Hamilton's daily life and which provide the basis for the wonderful enjoyment of living that he is grateful to experience. These concepts work very well for Jack and both he and I are hopeful that what is presented here can be of value to others. Jack has particular concern for other parents whose children are estranged from them, as is true with him. He hopes that other honorable and loving parents who have experienced a loss similar to his can gain help in living well and happily in spite of the loss. I find these concepts are also most efficacious for someone such as I, who has undergone no such mishap as family destruction, but who gets the benefit of this wisdom even in the absence of such tragedy.

I have written this fictional life story because I was inspired by what Jack has shared, and what is depicted is the life of someone with whom many will be able to closely identify. Jack has complimented me on my ability to get it down in a way that he finds interesting and fun to read. I have shared this literary undertaking with friends who are not acquainted with Jack, and they say that they find it very engaging. They describe it as a good read.

As a majority of those who have experienced parenthood can attest, one of the most amazing, beautiful, and wonderful things that can happen to a person is to be a parent. In the lives of his two children, there are many moments that remain cherished treasures of memory to Jack Hamilton, and to which he mentally refers whenever he wishes to relive some of the sweetest and most perfectly pure moments of his life.

He recalls for us the experience of standing over the crib of his twelve-month-old son while the child slept, and of being swept up in the sense of the miracle and the privilege of having had a part in the creation of that precious little person. He tells of laying eyes for the first time, just minutes after her birth, on his baby daughter and finding her to be the most utterly beautiful sight he had ever seen.

He speaks of the time at his daughter's fifth birthday party while, as she played with her friends, he found himself being profoundly struck by what a thoughtful, loving, special child she was, and how fortunate he was to be the father of that little angel.

He thinks of an occasion when he was observing his twelve year-old son as the boy performed some yard work his dad had assigned him. The youngster had a rich and powerful imagination, and was completely carried away in it as he slowly shoveled the dirt he was tasked with moving. His mind was far away as he did his work, and Jack remembers himself being transported, in a way not unlike what was happening to his son, with the love in his heart for this funny, sweet boy, well on his way to manhood, as he experienced spectacular mental adventures bearing no relationship to the work he was doing, in a plane of existence very far away from where his physical body could be found at that moment.

Jack holds in his heart an abundance of memories such as these. They are too numerous to count and too personal and mundane to be of abiding interest to strangers, but they are a part of who he is and he counts them among the great gifts of his life. He loves his children, and he loves his memories of them.

Sadly, Jack Hamilton's relationships with his children have ended. When speaking of people whose children have died, it is commonly said that there is nothing worse that can happen to a person than the death of his or her child. Estrangement from one's children, as complete as is true within the Hamilton family, is almost as bad as, or in at least one respect even worse than, the deaths of children. It can be seen as worse because there is no choice but for people to abide by the rules of death. Complete estrangement, on the other hand, involves just as much separation as death, but is, for some of those involved, voluntary. That can generate a unique kind of loss concerning someone who is still alive and who could change things if he or she chose to. The sting of such a circumstance is enormous.

Survivors of a loss by death can go through the stages of the grief process, and life can go on successfully in spite of the loss, but because estrangement does not include the ultimate finality of death, and because it can contain so much ugliness, it has the potential of remaining fresh, hanging on persistently, and doing its harm in insidious ways that don't necessarily attend a death.

This discussion is in no way an attempt to minimize the experience of one's child dying. As said before, the death of a child is as bad a thing as can happen. Loss of a child, whether by death or estrangement, is something best never experienced by anybody. It does happen, however, and must be dealt with. We can leave it to psychologists and philosophers to sort out the fine points of difference. Certainly, the loss of a child by whichever means is a sad and troubling occurrence, and dealing with either can be enormously difficult.

The reason for publishing this book is that, in spite of what has happened with his children, Jack Hamilton loves the life he leads. He enjoys a rich, rewarding, and happy existence, and affirms that he looks forward eagerly to each new day. He is profoundly grateful for the good fortune he enjoys, and oddly enough, he says that he sees a positive side to this sorry situation with his children. This thing is just about the only part of his life that he doesn't think of as good, great, lucky, fine, positive, wonderful, terrific, excellent, or at least okay. He offers the opinion that some adversity may be desirable in life just to give us perspective and to help us appreciate more fully that which is not adverse. If everything were great, it might be harder to perceive how beautiful life is without the contrast of how bad it can sometimes be. With a disagreeable circumstance or two in the picture, the good fortune is easier to recognize, contrast, and enjoy.

Jack suggests that it might be better if his dose of adversity were somewhat more minor in character, but he is doing very well, and he describes the sense of pleasure he has in facing each new day as "sweet indeed". He says that he recognizes that perhaps not all the people who have experienced the loss of their children are able to enjoy life as much as he does, but he believes that they would like to. This book is the collaborative effort of two friends, one a writer and the other a regular guy whose experiences have given him a lot of real treasures to share. Our hope is that this offering might be helpful in someone's journey to a happier life.

The help available in this book is not intended for those whose children have escaped from them because of physical, emotional, or sexual abuse or violence in the home. It could be said that in cases where children genuinely needed to flee from the terrible treatment inflicted upon them, or who did not flee as children but who separated themselves from their parents as adults because of abuse during childhood, the parents probably deserve the abandonment. The objective here is to communicate with those parents who, as Jack Hamilton did, loved and cherished their children, guided and nurtured them, and regarded the parental role they held as a sacred mission and a genuine privilege. These folks probably find themselves wondering how it could be that parents who loved so tenderly, valued so highly, and extended themselves so willingly for the benefit of the children whom they have lost could end up in a situation wherein they are treated so badly and discarded like so much trash by the very people they cared for so much.

Unfortunately, there are many such rejected parents, people whose goodness and devotion to duty and responsibility make them deserving of the appreciation and gratitude of their children. These parents should be honored by their children, but they do not get the loving recognition they are due. It is to these parents we say that such a state of affairs is disagreeable, to be sure, but it does not have to wreck your life. Life is wonderful and enjoyable, and you have a right to the best of it, even though what has happened to you may seem worse than most of what we humans are asked to endure in this world. Your life is a beautiful gift, but if you have a hard time making that true for yourself, then you need some new ways of looking at the world and of doing things, so that you can make it real for you.

The truth is that living happily and successfully is a skill. Accept that, learn it, and believe it. It is a fact. Living joyfully and well takes knowledge, understanding, competence, effort, determination, and, I repeat, skill. This book will provide some crucial knowledge. It is up to you to provide the understanding, the competence, the effort, and the determination, and through practice, develop the skill.

No parent does a perfect job. No human is capable of that. Both Jack Hamilton and Jim Wilson know that we made plenty of mistakes, as did our parents. But the Bible commands us to honor our parents. Good health and good sense dictate that we acknowledge the debt we owe to our parents. This is particularly true for children whose parents made a strong effort to love and raise their children properly and to give them the tools they need to be good citizens and respectable people, whether the children used those tools or not. Those parents deserve a happy life, and we mean for them to have it.

In the succeeding pages, we will share with you a look at the life of someone we call Phil Temple. Everyone has a story to tell, and you may find some commonality with the experiences related here in your own life. Perhaps we can all accompany one another in the "same boat." After the story, we will offer what Jack Hamilton has learned about making the most out of life. There are some basic principles of successful living, which he applies daily and which work astonishingly well. They are actually quite simple and straightforward. They are not necessarily easy, but they really are simple.

Most of this book is the fictional story of the life of Phillip Temple. It is inspired to a substantial degree by what Jack Hamilton has told Jim Wilson about what he has been through, but is a made-up story. The hope is that the account of Phil's life is presented interestingly enough to be enjoyable, and that the commonality of human experience strikes a chord in the reader. What is more important than this life story, however, is the help we hope to impart about how to enjoy a great life in spite of misfortune concerning estranged children.

This book is not about getting back together with your children, although that should always remain a possibility in your heart of hearts. Reconciliation can occur and can be a beautiful thing, but sometimes it is just not in the cards. A big mistake would be not to have a happy and rewarding life just because no reconciliation takes place. There is a lot more to life than suffering about people to whom it doesn't matter whether you suffer or not. To any parent who has experienced what our character named Phil Temple has been through concerning their children and who are having trouble enjoying life because of it, we say that we respect and admire you for being the loving and dutiful person that you are, and we hope that this offering can be helpful to you. You deserve the best.

Here is the story of Phil Temple. We hope you enjoy it.

1

MOM AND DAD

Phil Temple was born in January of 1944, three months after his father, Loren Temple, left home to do his part for America in World War II. Loren had been in the U.S. Navy for four years prior to the war, and had received his discharge in May of 1941. Loren and Phil's mother, Molly Raymond, met in January 1941 while Loren's ship was in dry dock at the Mare Island Navy Yard at Vallejo, California, adjacent to San Francisco Bay. Molly worked in a Navy Department office there, and the two of them were introduced by a mutual acquaintance. They liked each other, and their courtship developed thoughtfully and happily. They fell in love, and in May they decided that after his discharge from the Navy, they would get married. There is a photograph of the young lovers, taken in the spring of 1941 on the sidewalks of San Francisco by one of those street photographers who pops up, takes your picture as you walk along, and offers to sell it to you. Loren and Molly were courting, young, in love, brimming with fun and energy, and clearly showing the joy and excitement they felt. They look like they were meant for each other, and the picture shows a lovely start to their life together.

In late May 1941, Loren received his Navy discharge and left California for Cheyenne, Wyoming, to where several members of his family had moved from his childhood home in Oklahoma. The family move took place while Loren was in the service, so Cheyenne was new to him. He found living quarters for himself and his bride-to-be near Cheyenne's City

Center, and took a job driving a cab, a good way to learn his way around Cheyenne. When he had established circumstances to that extent, they set the date and arranged for her travel to Cheyenne.

Molly flew from Oakland to Cheyenne on June 16, 1941, the first plane ride of her life. Loren greeted her when her flight landed, and they spent the next two days getting ready for the wedding. Being proper young people of the time, they stayed in separate quarters until the ceremony. On June 19, they were married in a relative's home, and those in attendance included Loren's parents, his two older brothers and two older sisters and their families. There were no members of Molly's family, most of whom lived in Oregon and Washington, in attendance at the wedding.

What a brave, or perhaps naive, young woman Molly must have been to go to a strange city where she knew not a soul, to meet a large group, never before seen, of in-laws-to-be, and to marry a man whom she had known for five months. When Loren died in March of 2002, the two of them were approaching their sixty-first anniversary, so it seems that there may have been some wisdom included in her naiveté. They passed away within ten months of each other, with Molly following him in January of 2003. She missed him very much and did not wait long to join him.

Loren kept the cab-driving job for a short time after their marriage until he was able, through family connections, to get into the Iron Workers' Union, at which time he began doing construction work for good pay. The newlyweds had fun playing tennis together and attending pinochle parties at the homes of his family. They made friends around town and did some notable nightclubbing at some of the more well-known night spots in Cheyenne. They danced to the big band sounds of Les Brown, Eddie Howard, Ozzie Nelson, and Tommy and Jimmy Dorsey, to name a few. They smoked and drank with enthusiasm, as young people sometimes do, without much thought for the future consequences of such habits, and settled, with the normal adjustment struggles, into their new life together.

The December 7, 1941, Japanese attack on Pearl Harbor took place when fewer than six months had passed since the Temple's wedding. The lives of all Americans changed dramatically as a result of that attack, no less so for them, and Loren continued in construction for a while. As 1942 went by, the country transitioned into wartime configuration, and Loren went to work in essential defense employment, taking a job manufacturing military ammunition at the Remington Arms Co. plant west of Cheyenne. During 1942 and 1943, Molly suffered two miscarriages, which began to call into question the likelihood of their being able to have children, but in the summer of 1943, they learned that she was again pregnant, and they were determined that this one would make it.

Not long after they got the news that a baby was on the way, Loren began to get indications that despite his defense-related job, he was likely, before long, to be inducted into the Army by the Selective Service System. He and Molly discussed it and came to the conclusion that reenlisting in the Navy at an advanced pay rate made more sense than waiting to be drafted. So he rejoined the Navy at the end of the summer, and in September 1943, he boarded a train bound for San Diego. They would not see each other again for two years.

Loren went through an accelerated reorientation program for prior service personnel, and then, probably because of his iron working experience, he received orders to duty with Seabees, the Navy's combat construction arm. By November of 1943, he was in the South Pacific, working on the construction and maintenance of air strips, port facilities, and military camps on the islands captured in the American advance toward Japan. Loren's name and history can now be found, along with those of millions of his fellow Americans who served during that time, at the World War II Memorial in Washington, D.C., entered there for him by his son. Unfortunately, Loren saw neither the Memorial nor his history contained therein, because he died in March of 2002, before the Memorial was dedicated. Loren came home to Molly and their twenty month-old son in September 1945, having helped make the world safer for all Americans.

Loren had two to come home to instead of one because Molly's third pregnancy had reached full term, and their son, Phillip Loren Temple, was born alive. The decision was made, because of Molly's history of unsuccessful pregnancies, to deliver the baby by Caesarian section, and young Phillip emerged, to use Molly's words, as a big, bright, beautiful, bouncing baby boy. Phillip weighed in at more than 9 pounds, and grew up to reach six and a half feet in height and 240 pounds in weight. Both Molly and Loren were tall, five-eight and six-two and a half, respectively, but Phil grew up to be so tall just as much because Molly was a nutrition enthusiast. Phil never had a choice about eating right and was seldom allowed access to the kinds of food that Molly referred to as "junk." Phil grew up grateful to his mother for her insistence on a healthy diet. It is likely that, in large part, Phil's excellent health, as well as much of his advantageous size, is due to that.

Phil was twenty months old when his dad came home from the war. The story of what happened at the railroad station when Molly and little Phillip greeted Loren upon his return, and then later at home, is one that Loren enjoyed telling. Phillip's maternal grandmother had been living with Molly and Phillip since Phillip's birth, and the grandmother had left a few days before Loren's arrival. Maybe she considered it prudent to be gone from the small house in Northeast Cheyenne, to which Molly had moved while Loren was overseas, so that the reunited couple could, without extra personnel around, get reacquainted after two years of separation. The prompt arrival, nine months later, of Phillip's little sister Amy would seem to indicate that they did pretty well at reacquainting.

Young Phil was already dealing with the departure of his grandmother, who had been present for his whole life. The sudden entry of this large, exuberant, forceful man into the domain in which little Phil had been the only male, with his every need seen to by two doting women, was apparently a shock to the child, and he was extremely standoffish. He huddled on the opposite side of the car from his father, exhibiting body language that vigorously expressed suspicion, unfriendliness, and unwillingness to be open to Loren's fatherly advances. Even after they arrived at the house, it took a few days of coaxing and patience before Loren was able to penetrate his son's resistance. He ultimately did so, however, and thus began the relationship between father and son that went on, with mostly ups, but some downs, for the next fifty-six and one half years.

Loren was a very affectionate man, whose overt demonstrations of love for and devotion to his wife provided some of Phil's favorite childhood memories. Loren also enjoyed lots of hugging, gentle horseplay, and wholesome physical interaction with his two children. Phil has many happy memories of how safe and loved he felt with Loren's shows of affection. Phil especially treasures the recollection of the way his father tucked him into bed at night with a big snuggle while Phil said his prayers. Molly was more prim and proper about bedtime, sitting on the edge of the bed with her hands folded while Phil said his prayers, and then saying good night with a kiss on the forehead and a gentle pat. Phil liked the bedtime techniques of both parents, but preferred being pinned under the blankets with this giant hug from his dad while the boy said his prayers. Remembering his preference for this massive bedtime hug, Phil deliberately borrowed it from his dad in doing the same for his own children. Phil took great pleasure in imagining that he was able to make them feel as safe and loved by this as his father was able to do for Phil. There was never a time while Phil was growing up that he ever felt unloved by either of his parents, although feeling inadequate and disapproved of, particularly by his father, was something that was familiar to Phil.

Shortly after his arrival home from the Navy, Loren bought a military surplus truck with which he intended to open up a trash hauling and general conveyance business. As his fledgling enterprise began to take shape and he began to gather customers, he became aware that some pretty nasty people had a strong hold on that business around Cheyenne, and that he and his family could be in peril if he insisted on continuing his efforts in that direction. Loren did not like to talk about what happened or exactly how this information was presented to him, but by the beginning of 1946, he had obtained employment as a firefighter at the Federal Medical Depot in East Cheyenne and had left the hauling business permanently.

Loren worked in that U.S. government job long enough to learn that he liked being a firefighter, and in May 1947, he was hired by the Cheyenne Fire Department, where he remained until his retirement in 1978. He loved his job as a fireman, and the pride young Phil felt at being the son of such a person knew no bounds. Phillip's favorite thing that could happen during times when Molly, Phil and Amy were visiting Loren while he was on duty at the firehouse was when the firehouse alarm sounded. This brought the firemen hurrying, Loren's family would get out of the way and observe, and the visit was at an end.

The intense pitch of the fire bells, and in later years the electronic claxons, as they reechoed in the great sound chamber of the firehouse; the bustle of the firemen from all parts of the building, some sliding the poles, then donning their helmets and jackets, thus to mount the fire trucks; the deafening clamor as the mighty diesel engines roared to life in the trucks and the huge bay doors were cranked open by powerful electric motors; the incredible wail of the sirens, activated as the great vehicles began to move out the doors with their deep, nautical-sounding horns blaring; and the crackle and boom of the firehouse public address systems and the on-board truck radios as they broadcast information about where the rigs were headed and what the firefighters should anticipate when they got there all combined to create a fantastic atmosphere of wonder and action that still sends a furious storm of excitement through Phil as an adult as he recalls it. And, oh! the unbelievable thrill for young Phil of witnessing all this as his own dad took part was beyond expression. The rakish posture of the firemen as they mounted and rode the back steps, often still donning their gear, bespoke the pride they themselves felt about what they were doing.

Above all, for his own dad to be there, alas, mere words can't do justice to the feeling in a boy about all this.

As the years went on, the back-step riders began to be required to hook on to the trucks with safety lanyards, and even later yet, they were required to ride inside. Fire trucks with anyplace to ride outside the protection of the cab stopped being built because so many firemen were injured or killed in crashes and falls while riding the back step. Thus, some of the mystique and macho demeanor of riding to fires in that fashion may be gone, but firemen are still Phil's heroes. Loren used to say that more firemen died on the way to and from fires than actually died in fires. That is no longer true.

After several years as a fireman first grade, Loren achieved the rank of engineer, which is what the person is called who drives the pumper and operates and monitors the pumps and the delivery of water to the hoses handled by his colleagues. It was just as thrilling then, for Phil, to watch as his dad horsed the gigantic steering wheel, muscled the gearshift, and operated the siren, horn, and bells of the great fire engine, as it was to see him mount the step. The pride and competence that radiated from Loren could easily be seen as he drove that beautiful thing, and it was sweet for his son to behold. Loren retired after thirty-one years "on the job," as it was known to those fortunate enough to be employed there, and the presence of the Fire Department Honor Guard, along with the shroud-draped, historic 1953 Seagrave fire engine, restored and designated specifically for carrying the remains of firefighters who have passed on, added a very special touch to his funeral in 2002, following twenty-four years of retirement.

A powerful memory of something that happened on New Year's Day, 1950, just weeks before Phil's sixth birthday, stays with him as a part of the history of his father's career as a Cheyenne fireman. Loren and Molly had left Phillip and Amy to stay overnight at an aunt and uncle's house on New Year's Eve, while the couple went out to celebrate. They did not stay out too late, because Loren had to be on duty at 7:30 AM on January 1 for a twenty-four-hour shift. The department had a policy of allowing the men, one at a time from each rig, to go home from the firehouse for two hours on the main holidays to get in a little time with their families. During the mid-afternoon of the first, Loren showed up, at the beginning of his two hours off, to pick up Phillip and Amy where they had spent the night. It was clear to all that he was upset. Hugging his son fiercely and holding on tight as he related the story, Loren told the children's aunt and uncle of what had happened after he reported for work that morning.

Loren's unit had been first responders to an emergency involving three boys about Phil's age who had been playing with matches near some barrels containing gasoline. The fuel had been ignited and the boys were terribly burned. One was dead at the scene, another died at the hospital, and a third lived in a severely disfigured and disabled state until he, too, died a few years later. Phil was old enough to perceive how shaken his dad was by this and to detect how strongly he connected this sad event to his feelings for his boy. Firemen and other emergency workers have occasion to see many terrible things happen to people, and to survive emotionally, the workers must harden themselves to the effects of witnessing such pain and tragedy. In later years, Loren would say that this was the only time he was impacted so severely by such an occurrence. He was only two and one half years into his career, so he was still learning how to deal with such things. But it affected him the way it did because the children involved were so close in age and description to his son. In later times, even when Phil found himself experiencing some resentment toward his father for what he perceived as the harshness Loren often directed at him, Phil never lost the sense of how much his dad cared for him. Part of that was due to the memory of this episode.

After the birth of Amy in May, 1946, the Temple family was as big as it was going to be. Because of her history, doctors recommended that Molly not have any more children, so Loren underwent a vasectomy to ensure that this would be the case.

Phillip's memories of his growing-up years seem to fall into three categories as they relate to his parents. The first is that he felt much loved. The second is that he had great difficulty pleasing his parents, particularly his father, despite how much they loved him, and the third is the sense that his parents argued a lot. Phil was a loving child and can recall episodes of feeling so much love for his parents that he was almost overcome by the emotion of it. Phil also remembers hearing Loren speaking loudly and angrily, and hearing Molly responding in muffled tones in the other room after Phil had gone to bed. Phil does not recall knowing at the time what the issues between his parents were, although Molly revealed some of those facts to him after he was grown. Phil remembers that early on, his impression of the situation was that because Loren spent so much time being angry, Molly must be doing something really bad to make him that mad, that often. As the years went by, that anger became increasingly directed at young Phil, and his sense of things changed. He came to believe that Loren used anger as a tool of control, and that the loud voice, fearsomely glowering facial expression, and intimidating aura were his means to get Molly and Phil to behave as Loren wanted. Loren was not physically abusive, although Phil got his share of ordinary spankings from both parents. Phil is certain that Loren never hit Molly.

Once, when Phil was about five or six, he punched his sister and knocked her down. Loren soon learned of what had happened, and he sat his son down for some serious talk. He looked Phil in the eye and said calmly but seriously, "That is the last time you ever, and I mean ever, hit your sister, or any girl, or any woman. Do you understand that?" Phil nodded that he understood, and Loren said, "I had better never hear of you doing that again. Clear?" It was very clear to young Phil, and he has never hit a girl, except for a very few gentle spankings on the fanny of his daughter when she was small, all the rest of his life. This is the evidence that proves for Phil that Loren never hit Molly.

Phil came to be in dread of his dad's coming home from work in the mornings after his twenty-four-hour shift because he would often enter the house angry, and the anger would come out at the boy. When Phil was in his forties, there was an occasion when he told Loren about the fear he felt as a child about his dad's coming home from work, and this made Loren angry all over again. It was a strange moment, and Loren did not see the irony of it. Amy says that when they were children, she often felt sorry for poor Phillip because he was getting it so much from their dad. Phil was a compliant child with no inclination in him toward rebellion, and he had little need of harsh treatment to get him to behave. His greatest wish was to be pleasing to his parents.

Examples of this unpleasant pattern of paternal disapproval included Loren's impatience with Phillip in dealing with mechanical things, his responses to the boy's performance in sports, and his anger toward Phil just because he was around when Loren was in a bad mood, even though Phil had done nothing to merit the ire. Phil hated it when something went wrong with his bicycle, because he was expected to work on it, often with his dad's supervision or final inspection. Normally, that would be a good thing, because from it, a kid can learn mechanical fundamentals and personal responsibility. But for Phil, the trouble was that he only got only one chance to get it right. If Phil had a hard time threading a nut onto a bolt, or if he began turning a screw the wrong way, or some other, seemingly minor child's mistake, Loren would begin snarling things like, "Goddammit, that's the wrong way," or "What the hell is wrong with you, can't you do anything right?" or "How many times do I have to tell you how to do something, what is it with you?" Phil had to learn to make a point of going easy on himself, because his automatic reaction became to expect himself to get everything right on the first try or think of it as a failure if he didn't. This can cause an adult all sorts of problems and Phil believes that it has done so for him.

Phillip played quite a bit of baseball and basketball while he was growing up, and because Loren had been a good athlete in his day, he was hopeful that his son would be one, too. Loren showed his support of Phil's efforts in this direction by coming to as many of the boy's games as he could, given his fire department work schedule. He even took time off work for games once in a while. That was fine, and Phil liked the support, but some of the strongest memories he has of his playing career are of times when he booted a ground ball, or misplayed a fly ball, or made a bad pass on the basketball court, or some other goof-up, which happened fairly often because he was only a fair athlete, at best. Loren would grimace and shake his head or look at the sky in disgust, and a few times, he actually swore and shouted and told the coach to get Phil the hell out of there if he couldn't do any better than that. It was humiliating for Phil, he was embarrassed for his dad, and others witnessing this must have been embarrassed by it, as well. There were many more games at which Loren did not make such a display, but for Phil, once felt like too many, and it happened more than once.

As Phil's career in interscholastic athletics approached its end in high school, the inverse of this began to be the rule. He was a bench rider in varsity sports and did not get a lot of playing time. When he did get in, he still did his share of not playing so well, but he didn't hear about it anymore from his dad. When Phil succeeded in making a good catch or scoring a basket or getting on base, Loren was thrilled and let Phil know it. Phil turned out to have a real fireball throwing arm and was able to do well in throw-for-distance competition, which made Loren very happy. As Phil got older, that flame-thrower left arm came to be a source of amazement to himself and to others. Phil could scarcely believe how fast he could throw a baseball. He could not, however, get it over the plate very consistently, so he didn't turn out to be a pitcher, but it was fun for him to amaze his dad with how hard he could throw. Phil appreciated his dad's kindness and the absence of the harshness from Phil's younger days, but the damage was done. Phil's natural abilities were not that much poorer than those of his father, but Phil very definitely did not have the heart for competition that Loren did. Phil's competitive spirit may have been squelched by his father's angry reactions to Phil's earlier goof-ups. It is said that people born by Caesarean section, as Phil was, who do not have to experience the usual struggle at birth, are often less aggressive and more peaceful by nature than most of the general population. This is true of Phil, whether that is the reason or not.

Phil learned to read his father's demeanor when he came in the door from work, and Phil could tell by the way his dad looked if he was in for it or not. If Loren was having a bad day, nothing Phil could do was right, and he just had to hope that he did not have to be around his dad much that day. An indication of the amount of forgiveness present in the heart of a child is how happy and elated Phil was able to feel on those days when Loren was in a good mood and seemed to demonstrate no inclination to criticize or pick on his son. Then the dad would share jokes, kid around, sometimes play catch or shoot baskets with him, or just be nice, and, for the boy it was great. But then the next time, Loren might be back in his angry mode, and Phil needed to look out. Phil knew how much his dad loved his job, but sometimes the boy wondered what must go on there to make Loren so volatile and unpredictable when he got off work. Maybe Loren had not succeeded as much in hardening himself to the things he witnessed as a fireman as he thought he had.

Phil was not the only one who had to deal with these temper problems. Molly lived with them, too, and to a large extent, her life was shaped by this fact. In 1952, after considerable consultation with physicians, psychiatrists, counselors, healers, and anybody else who dealt with health issues, Molly was diagnosed with multiple sclerosis, a serious and troublesome autoimmune disease. She had begun, a year or two earlier, experiencing unrelenting, severe back pain, along with intermittent vision problems, and her desperation in trying to find relief was apparent in the number of different sources from which she sought help. Her MS did not present itself in classic form, which is slow, often steady loss of physical function, sometimes going into remission, then resuming its progress through ever-increasing disability and decline of physical capacity, until the victim becomes completely immobile and helpless, and eventually dies. In those days, ten or twenty years was not an unusual time period for MS to run its course to ultimate death. Instead of her disease taking that form, Molly suffered the back pain, at more or less the same serious level, with not much change in her other abilities to perform normal life functions, until she died of other causes more than fifty years after diagnosis.

A possibly valid observation is that Molly did not have MS. Instead, it may be that her life with Loren, a decent, loving, faithful, responsible man, but also one who used anger as a weapon of control in the household, caused her to experience resentment, tension, and fear of incurring that anger. Those feelings were harmful to her because she internalized and suppressed them in a way that caused them to come out sideways in the form of disabling pain. She was told by a psychiatrist that her symptoms were psychosomatic, which she interpreted to mean that he thought she was imagining everything. She was quite angry about what he said, but he did not mean to accuse her of faking. There is no doubt that her pain was genuine.

As the years went by, Molly became increasingly dependent on painkillers in her efforts to hurt less. She took so many aspirin and aspirin-related pills for such a long period that she developed an allergic reaction to such pharmaceuticals and had to stop taking them. After Phil and Amy left home in the early and mid-sixties, their mother became addicted to prescription painkillers, and in the seventies, Molly got into trouble with the police for taking prescription pads from several doctors and writing phony prescriptions for a medication call Percodan, a predecessor to today's well-known drug Percocet. Also, after the children left home, Molly began using alcohol to excess. She was never drunk or chemically impaired at home during her children's growing-up years, and she waited until she was done with her job raising her kids to become an addicted person. The

Temples would occasionally have friends over for an evening, and things would sometimes get a bit loud and unusually cheerful after everybody had a couple of drinks. Once, when he was about ten, Phillip saw his mother really sloshed at a fire department picnic. He was very angry at her for that, but it was the only time he ever saw either of his parents drunk during his childhood. Apart from the elevated level of laughter resulting from the liquid hospitality that flowed only now and then, Phil never saw in that home any behavior, harmful or otherwise, that was related to alcohol.

Loren's two brothers both died in middle age due to alcoholism and drug abuse. It was after an especially bad experience with one of those siblings that Loren apparently discontinued any use of alcohol whatsoever. The elder of Loren's brothers was creating a disturbance while on a codeine cough syrup- and booze-induced jag in a fleabag Cheyenne hotel. Loren and his nephew Ron, another firefighter, were summoned by the hotel proprietor to deal with the problem. When they arrived there, Phil's uncle pulled a knife and threatened to cut them, and they had to forcibly subdue him. He was committed to a mental health facility following that episode and died a short time later. Phil never saw his dad take a drink in the last forty or more years of Loren's life, and between what went on with Loren's brothers and then his own wife's dependence on alcohol, Phil believes that his father was a total or near-total abstainer. Loren's angry behavior stemmed from sources other than alcohol.

Phil came to believe that his mother's reliance on alcohol for relief came about as she learned that not only was the pain reduced, but it was easier to deal with her temperamental husband's angrier moments if she used beer or liquor for sedation. After her brush with the law, Molly made a conscientious effort to limit her use of prescription drugs to what could be regarded as medically appropriate, but she had become an alcoholic, and alcohol remained her chemical of choice.

Phil became aware of his mother's alcoholism while he was in the Navy after he finished college. Phil was an Air Intelligence officer in a naval aviation attack squadron based at Moses Lake, Washington, and his parents had come there to visit Phil and his family prior to his departure for the Western Pacific on a combat deployment during the Vietnam War. It was during that visit that Loren told Phil, with heart-breaking sadness, that Molly was spending a lot of time drunk, and that he was finding caches of liquor hidden around the house. About the same time, Phil received a letter from one of his folks' dear friends, one of the laughing visitors of his childhood, saying that she was terribly worried about Molly's drinking.

It was disturbing to Phil to learn this, but he had little knowledge of alcoholism, having been shielded during his childhood from most of its manifestations among their relatives, so he was actually more troubled by the sadness demonstrated by his dad about this.

Phil learned more about alcoholism in later years and came to know that he had more to worry about concerning his mother than he knew at the time. Phil has lived far away from his parents since becoming an adult, but he visited them often and never saw his mother drunk, although there was always beer in the refrigerator. She remained, in Phil's eyes, the sweet, thoughtful, loving mother he had always known and appreciated.

Molly went through drug rehabilitation after the Percodan incident and stopped abusing drugs, but her use of alcohol probably did not lessen until she went through alcohol rehab at the age of eighty. She had begun experiencing frequent falls many years earlier, probably caused by a combination of her painful disability and her drinking, and had survived all but two or three of the falls without serious injury. The times she broke bones were not enough to get her to change her ways until she suffered, not long after her eightieth birthday, a very serious and painful bone fracture by falling in the bathroom while drunk. That one caused her the most pain and embarrassment of any of her falls, and she apparently decided that enough was enough. She entered an in-patient rehabilitation program, and as far as is known, she never took another drink after that for as long as she lived. She was almost eighty-eight when she died.

By the time Molly took the cure at eighty, Loren, very near in age to Molly, had declined enough in vigor and energy that perhaps his anger was less aggravating to her, or maybe the rehab taught her some skills that made her better able to deal with him. Loren was easily angered right to the end, never realizing the harm it did. In the last two or three years before she died, Molly began to suffer from mild dementia, and her short-term memory became increasingly faulty. When Loren would get obstreperous, she probably just instantly forgot. Anyway, the rehab seemed to take. Although there have, no doubt, been older alcohol rehab patients, Phil never heard of one who was older than his mother.

Loren spent the last ten or so years of his life dependent on supplemental oxygen because of his smoking. He quit cigarettes at age fifty-five, because emphysema, a direct result of his tobacco use, was in its early stages in his lungs, and he could tell what was coming. But then, he took up pipe smoking, even inhaling the unfiltered pipe smoke in almost the same way as he had inhaled with the cigarettes, so quitting was not really quitting, at all. It was no surprise when it finally became medically necessary for him to quit smoking altogether and to carry the little oxygen tank with the plastic pipes in his nose. Having been a vigorous, able, and active man all his life, Loren felt a lot of discouragement as the result of the physical decline he experienced in old age. It did nothing to improve his disposition.

As a loyal and loving son, Phil made it his business to visit his parents at least once, and often twice, a year, throughout the period after he grew up and left home. He spent several years in the state of Washington while in college and in the Navy, lived a few years in California, and most of his adult life was spent in Alaska. He therefore always had to come quite a distance to visit them, but he loved them and felt that it was his duty to show that to be true by spending time with them, so he made sure to continue doing it. They had put a lot of time, effort, and love into raising their son, and he wanted to be certain that they were aware of his gratitude and appreciation.

Phil always thought that it was a bit odd that both he and his sister ended up living far away from their parents. After moving around quite a bit, Amy settled in Kentucky, where she remains. Phil was aware of no deliberate intent to separate himself from his folks, and he fell in love with Alaska with a passion that is unending. There was probably some unconscious motivation going on with Phil to put some distance between himself and all that anger. He learned that if he came alone to visit, with no grandkids or no daughter-in-law to provide a distraction for his dad from him, Phil could only visit for two or three days before he would start to get on Loren's nerves and Loren would begin making trouble and trying to strike up arguments with Phil. When that became a pattern, Phil scheduled short visits and realized that the distance had value and importance for him.

Amy never married, and she adopted a life-style much different from the traditional family pattern of marriage, career, children, house, and so on in which she grew up and which Phil adopted for his life. Phil disliked and disapproved of the liberal, Boulder, Colorado/Berkeley, California, hate-America, no-boundaries kind of life Amy chose, and this is part of why they are not close. Phil interpreted Amy's rejection of traditional American family life as the result of her spending her childhood witnessing what has been described as having gone on around their house. It may be that she made the decision that she did not want some man ruling her roost with scowls and sharp remarks, no matter how otherwise decent and loving he might be. She made sure that such a thing never happened to her. Because she was a girl, Amy was spared the experience of having Loren's anger directed at her, but she got plenty of opportunities to see it come to Molly and Phil.

Molly took another fall in the summer of 2001 at the age of eighty-six, this time just because she was more feeble and unsteady than ever, and not as a result of anything to do with alcohol. She fractured an upper thigh bone and, after that, was able to get around only with a wheelchair or, after a few months, occasionally with a walker for short distances. Later that summer, Loren suffered a spinal fracture while lifting Molly's wheelchair out of the trunk of their car, so he became unable to serve as her attendant as he had been doing for a number of years. They could no longer safely see to their own needs and had to move into an assisted living facility. Loren hated it there, and his decline became more rapid. He also got meaner, which made clear to all what his feelings were about how things were going.

It was necessary for Phil to go to Cheyenne fairly often to tend to them, although a lot of day-to-day stuff was seen to by Phil's cousin Ron, who was a dear kinsman and friend to Loren for all of Ron's life. Ron was a real God-send during this time. Phil took over managing his parents' affairs and paying their bills, and he put a lot of effort into making sure that they were aware of how much he loved them and how grateful he was to them for bringing him up to be, as each of them was, an honorable person of responsible character and with good values. Phil regarded it as his privilege and his duty to be helpful and supportive to them. Molly seemed to get the message Phil was trying to convey, and both Loren and Molly expressed appreciation when Phil told them how grateful he was to have had them as parents and how much he loved them. Phil never got the sense that his dad was really feeling all this. Loren was too caught up in how much he disliked what was happening to his life to relate happily.

Loren and Molly lived in the assisted living facility for almost six months before Loren died, and although he disliked it there intensely, he sure had a merciful passing. The two of them had just arisen from a night's sleep and were sitting in their bedroom talking about the activities of the coming day, when Loren stopped speaking in mid-sentence and tipped over on the bed, dead. It was just that quick. The death certificate gave "chronic, obstructive, pulmonary disease," or COPD, as the cause of death, but Loren had been diagnosed with an aortic aneurism, which probably burst and which would explain the amazing suddenness of his passing. It was a good way to go. Molly had a stroke ten months later and died in the hospital while the family was on their way to her bedside. She very much missed her lifelong partner, idiosyncrasies and all, and joined him with little delay.

Loren and Molly Temple were good and loving people who had their faults and weaknesses, as everyone does, but they made a positive and admirable mark on the world they left behind, and Phil considers himself fortunate to have been their son. Even yet, when Phil hears that wonderful song, "Stardust," by Hoagy Carmichael, which was "their song," or when he hears the unmistakable sounds of the Glenn Miller Orchestra, of Les Brown and His Band of Renown, or of other big bands from that era, Loren and Molly, with their love of dancing and good music, come to Phil's mind and a lump will often come to his throat. He cherishes that photo of them in San Francisco during their courtship, and it is a wonderful picture. Phil likes to think of them like that again, young, joyful, excited, full of fun, and together, in love, forever.

2

THE GROWING UP YEARS

An interesting feature about Phil's childhood is the fact that he was in love with one girl or another, almost continuously, from the very earliest times that exist in his memory. The object of his affection was someone different just about every year of his time growing up. When he was three or four, there was a neighbor girl of about six named Diane, who was fond of toddlers, so she came around to spend time with Phil's little sister. He was there, too, so she interacted with him, and he developed a big crush on her. She was older, little Phil thought she was beautiful, and she owned his heart, at least until he started kindergarten. Then, there was a pretty girl in his class named Donna, to whom he transferred his crush. Diane was forgotten. Phil's love for Donna lasted until he started first grade, when someone else became proprietress of his heart. That's how it went, year to year, all the way through junior high school.

None of these love interests ever knew of Phil's feelings for them. He was too shy to let anyone know about what was going on inside of him, so no one knew, not even his friends or family. Even when he got into junior high school, when some of his male contemporaries were starting to get into cultivating girlfriends, as in "going steady" or "hustling chicks," Phil stayed out of the action. He had been teased about his buck teeth, his big ears, his skinny frame, his funny name, and any number of other features of his upon which the cruelty of kids can be focused, and it may be that this fact, coupled with how much trouble he had in getting his father's approval on performance issues, caused Phil to lack the confidence needed to enter the treacherous territory of romance. He probably wasn't any more freakish than the average, but he took to heart the criticism about his appearance and kept out of the race. Phil had been advanced one grade at the age of six because of his unusual height and his high aptitude test and intelligence test scores, and as a result, was younger than 99 percent of his classmates—more than a year younger, in many cases. Being so much younger than everyone was another reason for his faint-heartedness with girls.

Phil spent part of the summer of 1958, when he was fourteen, in Oregon and Washington with some of his mother's relatives, and that was where he met Tammy, the girl who was the secret object of his affection until he was out of high school. Tammy never knew about the feelings Phil had for her, and he did not see her again for years, but she was where his romantic attachment remained, unrequited, for a long time. Phil continued to admire the girls while he was in high school, but his heart remained in the Northwest, and he never dated at all during those years. Phil's timidity with girls, even though he loved them dearly, was probably a strong contributing factor in his poor choice of the person he eventually married. A little more experience might have given him better information to use in making that choice.

When Phil was a small child, his favorite part about going to the movies, with the possible exception of the cartoons, was the pretty women. He always enjoyed seeing the beautiful ladies, especially in their strapless gowns and bathing suits, and from his earliest life, there was no doubt about his heterosexuality. He just lacked the boldness to do anything about it. He had no inclination to compel people to do anything they did not want to do, and in those days, he reckoned that romancing with a funny looker like he thought he was would not be anything a girl would want to do, so he just waited.

Fairly early on, it turned out that Phil was motivated by sympathetic feelings for children who were victims of bullies. On four or five occasions, starting in the third grade and continuing through junior high, He found himself coming to the aid of kids who were being bullied. Phil had no wish to fight and had no knowledge of how to do it effectively, but he experienced a strong sense of the need for justice and of compassion for smaller and weaker kids who could not defend themselves. When he intervened, the bullies would invariably turn their attentions to him, and so his objective of being helpful to the victims was accomplished, but then Phil had the problem.

For some reason, Phil never suffered any damage at the hands of the redirected bullies, which might explain why he continued to intervene like that, as it never cost him much in the way of pain. The troublemakers would cuss him and threaten him, and even push him around a little bit, but no one ever hurt him. Perhaps because he was tall, it represented more of a job to try to damage him than it was worth. Maybe, even though he was not showing a lot of fight, his size represented enough of a potential threat that bullies were discouraged from seriously exploring his abilities. A troublemaker feebly punched Phil in the jaw on one occasion, and it surprised him so much that he suddenly found himself chasing the kid down the street in anger. The coward fled into the arms of several of his friends, who kept him away from Phil, who eventually cooled off and left, but that guy never bothered him again. Phil probably never got hurt because bullies are just phonies and cowards. They are easy to despise.

The week he graduated from high school, Phil ended up in jail. This was unexpected, not only by Phil, for he had no intention of pursuing a life of crime, but also by his parents, who knew that he was a good kid. There was no one who thought of young Phil as troublesome, a problem child, a criminal type, or anyone who was likely to be doing stuff that lands people in jail. He had always abstained when his friends tipped over trash cans, went knocking on doors and running away before the people answered, threw water balloons at cars, stole apples out of neighbors' yards, or threw M-80 firecrackers on lawns. As Phil grew older, he had friends who liked to go on organized shoplifting excursions to get candy, food, and novelties from stores, and others who stole stuff out of parked cars, set fires on people's porches, threw eggs or rocks at cars, and performed other mischief. Phil never did any of those things because he just did not like being bad. There are a million things kids can do to get into trouble, and Phil did almost none of them. It could be argued that he was just chicken, and that he did not have the guts to get in on the risky fun, but it was just not fun to Phil, and he just didn't want to do what he knew to be wrong.

Every now and then, however, one of those million opportunities to goof up gets to even a good kid like Phil, and that happened on the Saturday night before high school graduation. Phil found Himself at a party with a couple of his friends, one of whom, Jackie Warren, was another good guy. Jackie was six months younger than Phil and had just completed his junior year at Central Cheyenne High, where Phil attended.

The other guy, Mitch Mauro, was a year and a half older than Phil and had graduated the year before. Mitch was a good-hearted nut case who placed no limits on himself about what risks he was willing to take, or about what kinds of mischief he would try just for kicks. Up to that time, he was the craziest person Phil had ever known. Mitch was a fun but dangerous guy to be friends with, but more importantly to Phil, he was a marvelously loyal friend.

One episode points out the fact of Mitch's friendship and explains why Phil carries such loyalty for him. While Phil was in high school, he had an after-school job at a Safeway store, and one day he arrived at work to find that a new grocery sacker, which was also the job Phil did, had been hired. This individual initiated their acquaintance by snarling at Phil and threatening him, to which Phil's response was to tell the guy where he could stick that attitude. A little later, when the new guy got ready to leave work (he was a school dropout whose work day ended when the after-school workers arrived), he stopped to talk to Phil. What the fellow said was that he was going to kick Phil's ass and that he would be there to do it when Phil got off work at nine o'clock, some five hours later. A short time after that exchange ended, just by chance, Mitch Mauro showed up at the store. He had formerly worked there, and that was how he and Phil had met. Mitch had been fired for some shenanigan involving running around with a girl while he was still on the time clock at work, but he still liked to come around to visit with Phil and his other former coworkers.

When Phil told Mitch what was happening, he offered the opinion that Phil had a real problem. Mitch knew that the new employee in question was a member of a notorious Cheyenne gang of hoodlums, and he guessed that some of the gang could be expected to be present to back up their guy in his fight with Phil. Phil knew of the gang, and he knew that the jerk who had punched him in the jaw and whom he had chased down the street a few years earlier was in that gang. Mitch said that there was no way Phil was going to have any luck in this situation by himself, so he volunteered to be there for Phil. Mitch said he would be back before closing time.

Around 8:30, Mitch showed up with a friend of his, who lived near him and whom Phil knew slightly, in tow. These guys both loved to fight, and they regarded this as a chance for some fun, as well as for Mitch to support a pal. Phil, on the other hand, was filled with apprehension and regarded the whole thing as no fun at all. When fight time came, there was no sign of Phil's opponent or his friends, and it was later learned that the troublemaker had quit his new job and never came back to work after that day. Mitch and his friend were disappointed that there was to be no action, but Phil was extremely glad about it. This demonstration by Mitch of that kind of loyalty, support, and friendship in Phil's time of danger stuck with Phil, and his love for his friend is lifelong. This explains why a level-headed kid like Phil could be found hanging around with a wild man like Mitch. He was a true friend, crazy or not.

Returning to the story of going to jail, Mitch, Jackie, and Phil went to this graduation party on the Saturday night before commencement ceremonies. The party was at the home of a girl whom Phil did not know and who went to a different high school than the one Jackie and Phil attended. Wild and crazy Mitch knew the girl; he always knew where there was a party, including this one, and so the other two just tagged along. The girl's parents were there and were observing the consumption of beer by underage people without objection. Mitch was eighteen, Phil was seventeen, Jackie was sixteen, and they should not have been drinking.

The three showed up in Phil's car, and Phil had several beers, which was something he was not accustomed to. When they left the party after midnight, Phil asked Jackie to drive, since Phil believed that Jackie had consumed very little alcohol. Mitch, who had a reputation for guzzling copious amounts of beer, had done exactly that and was not a good candidate for "designated driver." This was in the days before that term or the concept were popular. Phil was ahead of his time in making that request.

It was soon discovered that the gas tank on Phil's car was nearly empty, so Phil told Jackie to find a gas station. Phil was riding in the back seat, and Mitch was "shotgun." Instead of going to a gas station, Mitch instructed Jackie to let him out of the car on a residential street and to go around the block. When Jackie and Phil came back around to pick him up, Mitch was in possession of a length of garden hose, which he had cut off outside of somebody's house. They were already out of Phil's league for criminal activity. Mitch said, "We are going to get some free gas." Phil had had too much to drink for his good judgment to kick in, and he must have been mistaken about Jackie having not had much, because neither of them objected, even though they both knew better.

Shortly, they came upon a one-year-old 1960 Pontiac Bonneville parked at the curb on a North Cheyenne street, and Mitch said, "This is it; this is where we get our gas." One of the features proudly advertised about new cars of the day was their low, sleek styling. The idea of quickly siphoning fuel from that low-slung car, parked down against the curb, into the tank of Phil's high-riding 1948 Chevy Fleetside, sitting tall in the middle of the street, showed a serious shortage of understanding about the physics of fluid transfer, and right away, things were not going especially well. Jackie and Phil initially got out of the car to observe what Mitch was doing and possibly to help him with his task. Phil soon realized how much he hated what was going on, so got back in the car and began woozily praying that they would hurry up.

They had apparently been making a fair amount of noise, because after a few minutes of fruitless effort, the next sounds they heard were gunshots and somebody yelling, "Stay where you are, nobody move." Phil was sitting in the back seat, and when the gunshots sounded, his friends saw him tip over in the seat, and they both thought he had been shot. What Phil was really doing was reacting in despair to developments and calling out, "Oh, crap," or something to that effect, as he lay over in the car.

Phil was uninjured, because the shots had been fired in the air. The car owner told the boys that his wife had called the police, and that they were going nowhere until the police came. The cops quickly arrived and off they went to jail, Jackie and Phil for the first time, Mitch for about the third or fourth time. Because both Phil's dad and Mitch's dad were Cheyenne firemen, the boys spent about six hours in jail instead of having to stay until at least Monday morning, which would have been usual. Their dads were allowed to come to the jail early Sunday morning to pick the three of them up. No mention was made by the police of the boys' alcohol consumption, which they thought would have been apparent, and the arrest was reported as having only been because of the property offense. Firemen and policemen have a fellowship that allows for such special consideration under circumstances like this, and the boys felt a real thankfulness for that fact. Phil really disliked jail. He met a couple of guys in there who expressed the feeling that "it beats working." Phil did not agree.

One of the strangest things about this experience was the reaction of Phil's father to what had happened. When the two dads came to get them all out, Loren demonstrated no anger. He was not happy about this, but he was civil and calm with his son. Phil was, of course, grounded, with no driving his car or going anyplace except to work for two months, but all he said about what Phil had done was, "Well, you've got me beat. I've never been in jail." That was it. No anger, no recrimination, no chewing out. Phil appreciated it, but it was sure unexpected.

It turned out that the boys' victim was the owner of a local olive oil importing business who had reputed underworld connections. The police said that if he did not press charges, they could escape legal troubles, so they called him and asked for a meeting. He was very understanding, appeared quite amused by their shenanigans, and said that he, too, had done a few foolish things as a youngster. He told them that he would forgive them if they promised to leave his stuff alone forevermore. They promised to do exactly that, and thus concluded the adventure, except for Phil's grounding. He learned a lesson he never forgot, and that was the end of his life of crime. As much as his natural inclination led him away from behaving badly, this experience caused him to be even more determined to follow a righteous path.

During Phil's high school years, he had several friends who were interested in guitars, folk music, and rock music, and in performing publicly with their music. He was somewhat musical, having had a mother who was a fairly accomplished pianist and who taught piano to children, and so Phil was happy to join his friends in their musical endeavors. He played guitar, not well, and piano, also not well, but he loved to sing and has participated in choruses and choirs for much of his life. The late 1950s and early 1960s were a time when someone who knew one or two dozen guitar chords could play accompaniment to most of the popular tunes of the day, and that included Phil. By the fall of 1961, the year he finished high school, Phil was in a rock band with two school friends named Bob Cordes and Dan Warren. Dan was the brother of Jackie Warren, who went with Phil for his one and only night in jail. Dan was a classmate of Phil's throughout junior high school, when he and Phil were among the low performers in the smart kids' class. They continued to hang around together through high school, and Phil is still in touch with the Warren brothers all these years later.

Phil played rhythm and bass guitar and sang harmony and backup. Bob played guitar but did not sing, and Dan was the lead singer and lead guitarist in the group. Dan was one of Phil's friends who had been making time with girls since junior high school. That had a different meaning in the 1950s than it does now, what with today's internet porn, MTV, condoms and birth control pills handed out by the school nurse to eleven-year-olds, and the general raunchiness of popular culture. But Dan was a pretty successful ladies' man, fifties and early sixties style.

During the time Dan and Phil were performing together in the band, Dan had acquired a girlfriend named Laurie who liked to watch them practice and perform. This was how Phil met his first girlfriend. Her name was Kara, she was a friend of Laurie's, and Phil met her on a blind date on New Year's Eve to welcome the year 1962. The band had a gig at a party that night and the girls came along. Phil finally had a real date with a real girl, and within a few weeks they were "going steady," something that most of Phil's buddies had experienced years earlier. After a few months had gone by, Phil was "engaged to be engaged" to the first girl he had ever gone out with. He thought that his status as a rock and roll performer had provided him with an interesting enough persona that he didn't have to do much to overcome his backwardness with this girl.

To round out their combo, Dan dug up a guy from somewhere whose name was Leon Holder and who was a fairly good drummer. They called themselves "The Injectors," and thanks to Dan's ambition to be in the music business and his aggressive search for ways to realize his ambition, they got more and more jobs. By the time Phil reached age eighteen a few weeks after that New Year's party, the band had a steady gig at Buck's, a dance hall outside of town a few miles west of Cheyenne, and his short career as a professional rock and roller had begun. Phil had a day job as a delivery driver, which required him to be at work at 8 AM, and because of getting home from the band job at 2 AM, he was getting pretty tired from lack of sleep. He was also not getting to see Kara very much.

Phil considered himself to be a poor bet for big success in the rock star business, and he really did not enjoy watching people as they acted up at the dance hall, so after a few months of this way of living, he made the choice to quit the band. This way he could do better at his day job, get to see his girl more often, and be spared the need to watch night owls in action so much. By this time, Kara had figured out that Phil was a good person and a nice guy, and she liked him well enough to keep going out with him even though he was not a rocker any more.

After a year of working in not-very-promising jobs and finding out that he was not cut out to be a rock star, and with some strong nudging from his parents, Phil decided to go to college. He left Cheyenne in September 1962 to attend Western State College of Colorado in Gunnison, a cow town in a very rural mountain valley in the southwestern part of Colorado. Kara had problems at home with a stepparent, and not long after Phil left for Gunnison, she decided to go live with relatives in another state, so Phil was back to his no-dates status. Phil and Kara agreed to keep in touch and not date anyone else without telling each other. Phil learned that Kara went out with others behind his back before he left for college, so he had little confidence in her pledge.

Phil did not go out with anyone while he was in Gunnison for his freshman year, although he met a girl at a party in Cheyenne in the spring of 1963 and went out with her a couple of times. That did not develop into anything, and keeping his part of the bargain with Kara made it easier for Phil to stay out of the date market without reinforcing his sense that he was a no-success-with-girls kind of guy. Having a girlfriend whom he never saw and who almost never wrote to him was more palatable for Phil than having no girlfriend at all, although there wasn't that much difference.

Phil pursued his old pastimes of basketball and baseball while in Gunnison, in addition to which he got into fishing, skiing, hunting, and archery, and in general, had a pretty good time, despite not having experienced these more outdoorsy activities much while growing up. As a town kid from Cheyenne, Phil felt like he was really in the boondocks out there in the Colorado mountains, and trying some of the more backwoods diversions helped with adjusting to that. Phil still fishes and continued with winter sports during his years in Alaska. He still enjoys guns, although he's not a good marksman. He has never developed a taste for hunting, and is more of a collector.

Perhaps the most memorable thing that happened to Phil while he was at Western State was that he got into the one and only real fistfight of his life, not counting the scuffles and confrontations he had as a little kid. Phil had spent an evening with friends at the only dance hall/beer joint in Gunnison where people under age twenty-one could go, and he had downed a few brews. As the place was closing up at midnight, as required by law, he observed a guy looking at him in a benign, inoffensive sort of way, but holding his eyes on Phil, for whatever reason.

Phil said, "What are you looking at?" and he said, "You; what about it?" And in short order, the two of them were in the parking lot, punching and swinging away at one another. Phil caught the guy a good one above his eye, which opened up a big cut, and they found themselves getting seriously smeared with blood. Then Phil's opponent got Phil with a pretty good one on the side of his face, although without the blood factor being included. The rest of the fight was mostly body punches, light jabs, and missed swings. Pretty soon, they were both getting tired of this foolishness, and in a moment of reduced action, they agreed to quit fighting. Phil saw the other contender on campus the following week, and although Phil thought that he had won the fight because of all the bleeding the other guy did, Phil looked the worst of the two when a few days had passed. The big cut was healing and looked insignificant. Phil had a pretty good shiner where he took the punch beside his eye. They both agreed that it was all very stupid, and they parted not as enemies. Memories of these two experiences with finding his good-sense, upstanding-citizen self getting into these kinds of booze-affected scrapes helped, in part, with Phil's making a decision in later years not to use alcohol.

3

MOVING AWAY FOR GOOD

Despite learning some new recreational pursuits while in Gunnison, Phil was not fond of the place and decided not to return to Western State after his freshman year. Thanks to an offer from an uncle who lived in the Pacific Northwest and who was an accounting and business instructor at Columbia Community College in Kalama, Washington, Phil was able to find an advantageous way to continue his college education. Phil's uncle and aunt offered to let him live with them and to attend school at Columbia Community College. All Phil's credits from Western State transferred, so off he went to the green state of Washington.

Upon moving to Kalama, Phil began his full-time studies at the college and found a job working evenings and Saturdays for a janitorial contractor. A sixteen-credit-hour course load and twenty-eight hours a week of work kept Phil plenty busy. The magnificent Pacific Coast was not far away, the mighty Columbia River flowed past Kalama with great, seagoing ships plying its waters, and incredible greenery was everywhere. Washington is a beautiful state, providing an exciting new look at the world for a kid raised on the high plains.. At first, Phil was severely bothered by the acrid pulp and paper mill fragrances that permeated the atmosphere around Kalama. He found that even his sleep was affected by the smell, and he had nightmares about the burning that lingered in his nose, and which would not go away. After a couple of months, Phil finally became accustomed to the smell and stopped dreaming about it. He enjoyed his year in Kalama, and even today, he finds the still-present aroma there, now considerably lessened by the evolving efforts by the government and the wood pulp industry, not to be so bad. It brings back nice memories of his happy time in that place. Phil made some good friends there who remain important people in his life today. Living in the Northwest, Phil also had the opportunity to get better acquainted with some of his mother's relatives, with whom he had had limited or no contact during his growing-up years in Cheyenne.

Phil's Uncle Phillip, his mother's brother after whom he was named, and his wife, Phil's Aunt Carey, were very good to Phil while he was with them, and he came to love them both very much. They were kindly and loving people who shared their home and their hearts with their nephew, to his great benefit. They earned in the process Phil's everlasting gratitude and respect. It may be that a measure of their regard for their experience with Phil is that, following Phil's graduation from Columbia Community College after one year there, they invited two young cousins on Aunt Carey's side of the family to come live with them and attend Columbia Community College after Phil left. Uncle Phillip died suddenly in 1972 at the age of sixty-seven, and Aunt Carey died in 1986 at age eighty-one. Phil remembers them both with love.

By coincidence, Phil's erstwhile girlfriend Kara had a former stepfather living in Woodland, Washington, a town near Kalama. Kara arranged with this ex-step-father and his current wife to come and live with them so she could be nearer Phil, so Phil and Kara started going out again for a while. It was soon apparent that the arrangement Kara had made with the people who took her in was not one about which they were particularly happy, so it did not last very long. Kara got a low-paying job, which did not provide enough income for her to live out on her own, so she ended up going back to Cheyenne, and her relationship with Phil, which found the two of them apart during most of its life, finally came to an end. One main effect it had on Phil was to delay even further the time when he was to begin experiencing the world of dating at large. He had a couple of dates each with three girls in Kalama, but was soon gone and barely got to know any of them.

Phil worked during the summer of 1964 for the Weyerhaeuser Timber Company Railroad in Longview, not far from Kalama and had a good time maintaining, dismantling, and rebuilding railroad log-hauling cars. Later, he worked in the loading sheds, filling rail cars with lumber. It was all hard work, but Phil was proud to be a productive member of America's labor force. He really enjoyed the work, but also acquired a sense that he did not want to do that kind of work all his life. At summer's end, Phil headed for Ellensburg, the home of Central Washington State College, known today as Central Washington University. Thus began the last phase of Phil's pursuit of a bachelor's degree. He was unaware that he was also beginning the series of life experiences that would lead to the surprising circumstances yet to be revealed in this book.

The city of Ellensburg is located about a hundred miles east of Seattle in beautiful central Washington, is near to both wide-open farm country and deep forests, and is as agreeable a place as there is in lovely Washington State. When Phil arrived in Ellensburg he enrolled for classes, declared business administration as his major, got a room in a cheap hotel, and started looking around for a better living arrangement.

Phil soon ran into a guy with whom he had worked in the Weyerhaeuser loading sheds and who was also living in a hotel and looking for a better situation. They encountered another recent transferee to Central who was in a similar circumstance, and the three of them decided to room together. They found a pretty nice furnished apartment and moved in. Later, Phil's two roommates decided to move on campus and two other Kalama guys, Keith Strong and Kevin Gregory, moved into the apartment with Phil.

This was Phil's first time living in a place that was not his parents' home, the home of relatives, or a college dorm, and it was fun for him to be freer. It was a good thing that the roommates Phil acquired were all responsible people, because they had a pretty good environment for pursuing their studies. The other four were serious students, and Phil was also a serious, if somewhat lazy, student. He had always been a good reader with high rates of comprehension, and this allowed him to get good grades in subjects involving mostly reading and writing. Subjects like math, science, and business, which required a lot more study instead of just reading, were ones in which Phil had less success because he tried to apply his cramming skills to them, and this strategy did not work so well. As a result, Phil's grades in those subjects were more average than he was used to in history, English, philosophy, literature, and such.

Life in Ellensburg was soon proceeding well. It turned out that quite a number of friends and acquaintances from Columbia Community College in Kalama had transferred to Central, so Phil had a ready-made social circle in which to function. He found a pretty good part-time job on a clean-up crew in a cold storage and food processing plant, and was making more money at that than at any other part-time job he'd had up to that time, so Phil little to complain about. The apartment was a pretty good party pad and Phil and his roommates began having a few functions on weekends. Several months had passed since Phil's one and only girlfriend had gone away, and he was developing a stronger sense that a little female companionship was a suitable idea for him.

One day, while Phil was in the student center, he observed a female acquaintance of his from Kalama as she talked to a girl whom he found interesting. The girl who caught Phil's eye was attractive in a wholesome, clean-cut sort of way. She was not pretty, having a somewhat long nose, a receding chin, and irregular teeth. She had a reasonably good figure; thick, dark hair; almost Asian, almond-shaped brown eyes; and a pleasant and engaging demeanor as she interacted with the girl from Kalama.

As Phil observed the young women visiting, he was impressed with this stranger's animated yet conservative persona. She seemed to Phil to be the kind of girl he might have a chance with. Phil had no interest in pursuing fast, flirtatious, worldly girls, and he had the sense that, even if he wanted to go after girls of that type, his low skill level would not stand him in good stead with them. It seemed to Phil that a moderately attractive girl who appeared to be among the less sophisticated women in sight and who seemed to have a nice personality was as high as it made sense for him to shoot. The idea of dating a lot of girls at the same time and exploring the sea for a variety of fish was daunting to the shy Phil. One at a time was all he had the inclination or courage to check out. He encountered this girl one day in a classroom building, and as Phil tried to catch her eye, she ignored him vigorously, as though he were not there. This was a positive sign to Phil, confirming his sense that she was not a fast mover or a flirt.

Phil found out through mutual friends how to contact the Kalama girl and called her to ask about the other girl. It turned out that the girls lived in the same off-campus boarding house, and they knew each other slightly as residents of the same building. It was agreed that word of Phil's interest in her would be passed to the dark-haired girl, and Phil would be informed as to whether or not she would be willing to connect with him over the phone to discuss the possibility of a meeting. Sometime later, Phil was notified that a get-together was agreeable to the girl and phone number information was passed. The girl's name was Darla Oldburg, she was from Alaska, and she was a freshman. The two connected over the phone, met at the student center, shared a soft drink, made a date for the weekend, and the relationship began. Phil and Darla found out that they were two nice, inexperienced, decent kids who had their severe clean-cut status in common, and that they were comfortable spending time together as the America of the 1960's swirled around and beyond them, pretty much leaving them behind.

In later years, Phil developed the theory that he and Darla found refuge in each other from the frightening world of the sixties. The free speech movement, the sexual revolution, and the emerging overhaul of American culture and mores were strange and fearsome to them, and it may be that they found safety in each other, even though they did not have a great deal else in common. They went to movies, dances, the beach, and church together, and spent time necking in Phil's car between the end of the evening's activities and either ten, twelve, or one o'clock, depending on the day of the week and the time Darla was required by college curfew rules to be inside the boarding house.

Phil came to regard Darla as a decent, pleasant person with good morals, good values, and a cheerful outlook, who was a good student and an agreeable companion whose company he enjoyed. He was not in love with her, but didn't need to be. they were not having sex, which meant that nobody was owned by anybody and there were none of the obligations some people feel when sex is in the picture. During spring term, Phil met and went out a few times with another girl to whom he was much more strongly attracted, but he learned that she had been around quite a bit and seen a lot of action with guys on campus, and Phil did not like that. Phil felt a little guilty about being a bit disloyal to Darla, who had come to count on him for companionship. A point arrived when Phil was compelled to make a choice about whom to take to the spring prom, featuring Martin Denny and his Orchestra, of "Quiet Village" fame, and he found himself choosing not to go to the prom at all and he ended up spending the evening at a movie with Darla, even though he liked the fast girl better. The fast girl was pretty frosted about Phil's decision, and that was the end of her and Phil. He felt the loss, but believed that he had made a more practical and prudent choice for himself.

A feature of Darla's character that Phil found interesting, and of which he approved, was her search for truth concerning God and religion. She had been baptized into the Church of Christ as a small child, and had attended a Methodist church on her own, without her parents, during high school. She was sincerely seeking satisfying answers to questions of spirituality, and Phil liked that about her.

Phil grew up attending Sunday school, first at a nondenominational, evangelical church, and later at a "Friends," also known as Quaker, church.

He was exposed to the Bible in a moderately substantial way, having been very good at the competitive exercise in which the Sunday school teacher announced a scriptural reference, such as "John, Chapter 3, verse 16." The first kid to find that verse in the Bible, raise his or her hand, and, when called upon, read the verse, was the winner of that round. Phil won more than his share of those contests, as a result of which he knew the sequence of the books in the Bible very well. He did not memorize much scripture. Memorization was not as much fun as Bible verse competition. He did, however, know a lot of Bible stories because of his years in Sunday school.

Phil's mother made a practice of attending Sunday school with Amy and Phillip about half the time. The rest of the time the two children were required to walk on their own to church, not far away from the family home. The kids' dad never went. Molly was not a devout believer, and Loren was not even interested in the subject, but Molly felt that exposure to Godly people and concepts was appropriate for growing children, and Loren went along with her on that. In all the years Phil attended religious gatherings during his time growing up, all the adults he ever met in that connection left the impression on him that they were good, caring, honest, decent, loving, admirable people who made the world safe and positive for children. The children at church were like children anywhere, some were good and kind and some were rotten, but the overall sense Phil gained from his days in church-influenced living was that the adults were the sort of people who are the salt of the earth, are to be admired, and their children mostly grow up to be the same. Today, when it is possible to witness all the hatred and poison directed a Christians by the popular culture, a shake of the head in disbelief is what one has to do. Anyone who had the experience that young Phillip Temple did with folks at church could never believe or say the ugly stuff one hears so broadly in America today.

Phil was rather frightened as a child by the concept of hell and, as an adult, even resenting a bit having been caused to feel that fear when he was so young. Despite that feeling, Phil still regards the people who exposed him to that as loving and sincere, and as having had his best interest at heart.

Phil's approval of Darla's spiritual search stemmed from the upbringing he had, and even though he was not on a spiritual search himself, he supported her quest. Phil continued to believe in God and preferred being around the kind of people who can be found at church, but his own view of the subject of religion included a mixture of skepticism, unconcern, and relaxed acceptance.

It developed that the luck of the draw brought into Darla's life a roommate named Sylvia who was a lifelong and very devout member of the Alladist faith. As the two girls became close friends, Darla became increasingly interested in that religion and began attending the open meetings the group held to allow interested persons to become familiar with facts about the faith. This religion is an offshoot of Islam and proclaims that the founding prophet, who appeared in the mid-fifteenth century in what, in ancient days, had been the kingdom of Babylon, has revealed the latest word of God. This prophet is regarded by Alladists as the return of Christ, the Final Imam promised by Mohammed, the re-appearance of the Buddha, and the manifestation of any number of prophesied beings who are expected by their faithful to come and bring about the new world, the end of the world, the last days, or what have you. Alladism has a number of basic tenets, most of which are reasonable enough and which Phil found interesting, as he occasionally accompanied Darla to Alladist gatherings as she pursued God's truth. These precepts include such ideas as the following:

1. Equality of men and women.
2. Science and religion must agree. If they do not, then one or the other, or both, are false.
3. Use of alcohol and mind-altering chemicals is forbidden.
4. Seek to create a one-world government administered according to Alladist principles.
5. Back-biting is forbidden.
6. Universal education for all persons.
7. Activist, adversarial politics are harmful to social morals and are forbidden.
8. Honest work, performed in a spirit of service, is equal, in God's eyes, to worship of him.

There are other precepts of the faith, but these are some of the most important ones. Darla's interest in this religion grew steadily during the first year she and Phil went out together.

At the end of spring term, 1965, Phil departed Ellensburg for Seattle, where he found summer work unloading rail cars in the Associated Grocers warehouse. Darla, along with several other girls from her boarding house, was invited by one of the residents there to go home with that girl to Hawaii. Phil's summer was interesting, but lonely. He explored Seattle, went to a few church picnics, found extra work loading freight into trucks bound for Alaska, and went on one weekend trip to Kalama to visit his aunt and uncle. He had almost no social life at all and certainly no dates.

Darla and Phil had agreed to keep in touch, but she scarcely crossed his mind, and he only wrote to her once while she was in Hawaii. Phil rented a room in Seattle in the basement of an apartment building managed by some elderly relatives of his Aunt Carey, so he had some nice people to interact with. Phil's jobs involved vigorous physical labor, so he was tired enough at the end of each day not to feel a great need to go out. He read a lot and visited with the kindly people in whose building he roomed. He was making money in amounts sufficient, in conjunction with his part-time work in Ellensburg and some help from his parents, to cover his financial needs for the coming school term, so that, if he were thrifty, he could get by and did not have any major worries in that department. For Phil, it was just an okay summer.

After about two thirds of the summer had gone by, Phil got a letter from Darla saying that she was returning to Alaska from Hawaii for the remainder of the summer, and that she would be passing through Seattle and spending a couple of days en route. Her mother had a cousin in Seattle who worked for Boeing and with whom she could stay while in town. Darla contacted Phil from her cousin's home after her arrival, and the two of them made a date for a Saturday. Darla was rather miffed at Phil for not writing to her, but he said that he had been very busy, and she seemed to forgive him. Their date ended up being a trip to one of the public lake parks in Seattle, and Phil was completely thunderstruck when Darla appeared from the dressing room in a Hawaiian bikini she had acquired during the summer. Phil had not seen a girl all summer, and on their trips to the beach near Ellensburg during spring term Darla had worn a modest, one-piece bathing suit, which had not particularly rung his bell. But now it was clear that she had a very voluptuous figure, which while certainly not perfect, was good enough to turn Phil's head in a hurry. By the time two or three dates had gone by before she headed for Alaska, Phil could think of nothing else but Darla in that bikini, and he was on the hook.

In retrospect, it's not difficult to figure out what happened. Darla was a nice girl whom Phil liked and respected, and she provided pleasant company, which he could take or leave, as evidenced by his not caring enough even to write to her in Hawaii. After a lonely summer of virtually no social contacts, exposure to an alluring girl with lots of skin showing was too much for poor Phil. He was instantly in love, or at least so it seemed. Darla went on to Alaska and Phil continued his activities much as he had been doing, except that now, he had that swimming suit on his mind. He was looking forward to seeing Darla again and actually wrote to her.

When September came, it was time for school to resume; Darla returned to Washington from Alaska, and the youngsters began their reconstituted relationship with a bit more fervor. By October, they were really getting serious, and their make-out sessions in the car were going a lot further, although they were still not having full-fledged sex. One night, as they were done sweating it out in the car, Darla asked, almost off-handedly, "So when are we getting married?"

Poor Phil was caught completely off guard, since although the thought had occurred to him briefly as a possibility for some year in the distant future, the prospect of right now, or of even getting engaged, had not even entered his mind for a second. He was twenty-one and she was nineteen, they were both woefully ignorant of the ways of life and love, and they were college kids, for crying out loud. Phil was getting a little help from his parents, but was working at janitorial jobs during the school year and at temporary industrial-type jobs during summers. Marriage was a bad idea from a strictly practical standpoint, but they both came from a socialization process that said that if you are getting physical, then you pretty much have to get married. They weren't going "all the way" but they were going quite a long way, and there was this sense between them that he now owed it to her to get married.

After some thought, Phil recognized that, although he liked, admired, and respected Darla, it was clear that he did not really love her that much. Phil knew that marriage and family life were definitely in the cards for him. The only birds-and-bees-type instructional interaction Phil ever had with his dad was, one day when Phil was about thirteen, Loren passed through the front yard where the boy was mowing the lawn. As Loren walked near his son, and as Phil paused from his grass-cutting to acknowledge his dad, Loren said, completely out of the blue, "Yup, the truth is, marriage is the only way to go for a good life, Yes-sir-ree."

He then moved on, and Phil resumed his mowing. The two of them never spoke about the exchange, or the subject, ever again, but it stuck with young Phil, both as a very odd thing to have happened, and as an expression of his father's wishes and intentions for him. Phil knew that his mother disliked firemen who were past thirty and unmarried, because men like that just "used" women.

So, it seemed that Darla's idea merged pretty well with what Phil knew to be his family's expectations. This fact, when coupled with Phil's complete conviction that he would never be someone who could play the field or expect success with women in general, led him to decide, "What the heck, this is as well as I am going to be able to do."

Phil thought of Darla as someone whose integrity and good values made her likely to be a good wife and mother, and he really thought she was a nice person. Phil had occasion to observe Darla in action in public, as a greeter and hostess for college social events. She was very gifted at this, and her lack of physical beauty seemed to melt away in the glow of the genuine charm, cordiality, and sincere interest in people, which burst forth from her in the most amazing way in that setting. She appeared to be truly special in that sense, and Phil was quite impressed with what she showed. The two of them never fought, argued, or squabbled, and it looked to Phil as though a peaceful life was in the cards for him with Darla. After a few days of considering her idea, Phil decided to go along with it. He would live to regret his decision.

They set the date for March of the following year, 1966, during spring break. The kids broke the news to their parents, who did not object, ask them to wait, or offer alternative suggestions. They just went along, much as Phil was doing. This thing was actually going to take place.

A few weeks after Phil and Darla came to the decision to marry, Darla announced that she had decided to join the Alladist religion. This disturbed Phil, because although he enjoyed the exposure to the new people and concepts he was encountering in the meetings he occasionally attended with Darla, Phil had developed no inclination to sign on. Darla's having made this decision without consulting him rubbed Phil the wrong way, and he told her so. After a week or so of contemplation, Phil informed Darla that if she went ahead with this, then the marriage was off. She reconsidered for a few days, and then informed him that she had changed her mind. She would not become an Alladist. Phil said, "Okay, the wedding is back on."

Christmas break came, and Darla went home to Alaska while Phil, being unable to afford to go anywhere if he wanted to pay for the next school term, stayed in Ellensburg and spent Christmas alone. When Darla came back to spend New Year's with Phil, her boarding house let her check in early, so she had a place to stay, and the young couple began the stretch run toward the day of their marriage. They found a non-denominational church in Seattle located near downtown, made the catering arrangements, sent out the invitations, and looked for a place to live in Ellensburg. About a week before the wedding, they came across a cute little two-room, upstairs apartment with a bathroom. The owners were a sweet, old, retired couple, and the rent, which would begin after the wedding, was $47 per month. The prospect of living there together before the wedding never even occurred to Phil and Darla. There was still no full-fledged sex. Darla insisted on this, and Phil went along even though his own inclinations tended otherwise. He believed it was the right thing to do, so was okay with it.

Darla's parents arrived from Alaska a couple of days before the wedding, and Darla and Phil met them at the Seattle-Tacoma Airport and drove them in Phil's car to the cousin's house, where they would be staying. This was an extremely awkward and strange experience for Phil. After initial introductions and getting their luggage into the car, the twenty-minute or so ride was, except for attempts by Phil at conversation, an exercise in utter silence. Phil's thought was that, since this was their first meeting with the person their daughter was going to marry, they might have been able to think of something to talk about. No such thing. Phil would initiate a subject, get minimal response from anyone, wait for someone else to start something, encounter tomb-like silence, and try again; same result. Phil's feeling at the time was, "Yikes, what is this?"

Phil's parents, along with his sister, arrived from Cheyenne the day before the wedding. They were a good deal more convivial on this occasion than Darla's folks had been, and they and Darla seemed to like and approve of one another. The day before a wedding is always going to have some tension, and this was no exception. For reasons that Phil, after many repeats of this same scenario, came to think of as a psychosomatic reaction to stress, Darla got sick. This was a practice that Phil was to learn would be standard procedure for her any time a stressful event approached. She was ill at her own wedding and on the honeymoon.

The wedding went off all right. Phil, along with several members on his mother's side of the family, has a chronic minor affliction that involves phlegm in the throat and difficulty speaking after periods of silence or when stressful circumstances present themselves. Keith Strong, Phil's old roommate who was best man, tells the story of his amusement as he stood next to Phil. Keith had to stifle his impulse to laugh as he heard Phil's attempts to clear his throat, with minimum sound, in anticipation of the time when he would have to speak. When Phil's big moment finally came, he squeaked and croaked somewhat, but managed to get the words out despite the very real presence of a couple of tons of goo in his throat, and apparently, nobody but Keith knew the difference. Sylvia, the Alladist roommate, was Darla's maid of honor.

After the reception, Darla and Phil hit the road for the Olympic Peninsula of Washington for their honeymoon. Darla was still sick, but it was pretty much a happy occasion, anyway.

The wedding night contained a lot of the activity Phil and Darla had been postponing, but at their level of experience and competence at such things, and also perhaps because they were not particularly compatible in that department, it could have been quite a bit better. On a scale of from one to ten, with ten being pure, ecstatic bliss, and one being horrible, it was probably a four or five, maybe six, for Phil. A couple of decades later, after their divorce, Darla took the trouble to inform Phil of how that night was a gigantic zero for her. "A complete nightmare," was her choice of words to describe her memory of the event. Phil had married the second girl he ever went out with more than twice, and they were now on their way to the rest of their lives.

4

THE NEWLYWEDS

The morning after Phil's and Darla's wedding night, while they were eating breakfast in the hotel restaurant, Phil was surprised to find himself experiencing a deep sadness, which did not arise from anything he was consciously thinking, but rather came from a silent part of his soul that was making itself known to him even though nothing particularly sad was on his mind. Phil was even more surprised to discover tears running down his face. Darla asked him what was wrong, and his answer to her was that he was worried for her and troubled because she was ill.

She accepted that explanation, but as Phil contemplated what was happening, he came to the understanding that his sadness was because he had just married someone whom he did not love with the passion and power that he thought he owed to his wife. Young Phil made the determination then and there that he would do everything within his ability to create that love for her, to honor the love she offered him, and to make the best effort he could to give her the life, the marriage, and the true love that she absolutely deserved. Once Phil made that heartfelt and sincere pledge to himself and, silently, to Darla, his tears stopped and the sadness lifted. The rest of the honeymoon must have gone all right, but Phil remembers nothing about it.

The newlyweds spent two days on the Olympic Peninsula and then returned to Ellensburg to start school after spring break. Their life as married students was under way, but not in quite the way Phil had hoped for. His thought had been that there should be a lot of sex so that he and Darla could learn how to do it better, develop some skill in that department, and make it more enjoyable and fun. Phil quickly found out that Darla did not share his view of the subject. Her responses to his suggestions that they get frisky became uniformly reluctant and unenthusiastic, and the experience itself reflected that attitude on her part. She also had a list of requirements that had to be met in order for her husband to earn his way into the promised land, and while a fair amount of give and take and compromise seemed reasonable, the hearts, flowers, and atmosphere setting before earning the right to get busy succeeded in taking a lot of the fun and enjoyment out of the whole business for Phil. As a result, there was a speedy reduction in the frequency of his suggestions that they fool around.

This was a disappointing development for Phil, but he was still optimistic that they had a good life together ahead of them. After all, they were both nice, well-meaning, sincere, decent kids who had the whole world out there waiting for them to conquer it together, and as love grew, so would the number of things they could enjoy doing as a team. Phil had the good fortune to be an optimist by nature, and that served him well during that time in allowing him to remain hopeful in the face of disappointment. Further rude awakenings lay in store for young Phil.

Phil's first experience with what would ultimately ruin any chance that marriage had to ever really make it came a few weeks after the wedding, as Mother's Day approached. Having been married such a short time, and not knowing much about women, Phil found himself slightly perplexed about exactly what he should do with respect to Darla and Mother's Day. She was not anyone's mother, but very likely would be, some day, so Phil wondered what would be the correct way to acknowledge the holiday for her, if at all. Believing that it was a simple question that could be reasonably addressed between persons of goodwill by a simple process of ask and answer, Phil decided to consult with Darla. My-oh-my, did he have a lot to learn.

In his innocent naïveté, Phil asked Darla to help him resolve the question concerning how he should handle the matter of Mother's Day. He explained what was on his mind and asked her what she would advise him to do. Naïveté notwithstanding, it was pretty dumb. It was completely forgivable, without malice or intention to harm and, given Phil's tender age and experience level, understandable, but really dumb. The boy was in for a real lesson.

If assessment about what Phil did were to have been based on Darla's reaction, one would have thought that he had punched her in the face with his fist or told her that he hated her and wanted to be with another woman. The shouting, the accusations, the door-slamming, the unbridled rage that came roaring out at poor Phil was incredible. He was completely dumbfounded. He had received no clue, at least none that he was competent to recognize, in any of his contact with Darla over the preceding year and a half, that she was capable of anything like this kind of behavior or that she had this kind of rage in her. She snarled at him that he was a heartless, insensitive beast who had no concern in him for her or for her feelings, and that she could not believe how he could be so horrible to her.

Phil found Darla's conduct to be unbelievable and awful. He tried to allay her rage with reasonable and low-key requests to be calm. He tried to reassure her that he meant well, that she needn't react like this to him, and that he certainly intended no harm. She would have none of it. The violent door-slamming was the final punctuation on the scene as she fled to the bedroom to get away from the monster—Phil.

Finding this out about Darla was the biggest shock of Phil's young life, to that point. He had spent all his years on this earth dealing with his temperamental father, but at least he knew what to expect from that quarter. To have this hit him from completely out of the blue was a tough one, particularly since part of Phil's basis for deciding to marry Darla was all the evidence he had that peace would always prevail between them because she was of as peaceful a temperament as he was. Phil can still recall with crystal clarity the devastation he felt on that occasion.

Darla's pouting began to ease, and over a period of a day or two, she seemed to return to her normal, nice self. Phil can't tell you what the final resolution of the Mother's Day question turned out to be, and it doesn't really matter. They must have gotten through the situation somehow. As petty and stupid as the issue was, the significance of it was that it gave Phil an introduction to the kind of stuff he was going to have to endure on a regular and recurring basis for the next almost twenty years.

To this day, Phil continues to consider Darla to be a decent, well-meaning, honest person who has many admirable traits and who, in general, relates to the world in a respectful and respectable way. She was not hateful like that to him nonstop during their life together, but it happened so often and so consistently that it became the primary factor around which Phil was forced to fashion his daily expectations from her and his reactions to her. This made any real partnership between them impossible and caused Phil to be on constant guard for the danger that was always present. Otherwise, Darla was a good friend to her many friends, which she made easily. She tried, and was mostly successful, to be a good mother to the children they had, whom she loved as much as Phil did, and she conducted herself with respect to society at large with integrity and sincerity, and in a dutiful manner. Except for her way of relating to Phil, and later, a second husband who came out of a short marriage to her pretty scarred up, she is a reasonably admirable person. The old saying that women grow up and marry men like their fathers and that men marry people like their mothers seems to have applied to Phil, except that he married the difficult side of his father instead of his mother, and Darla's temperamental outbursts were at a much higher energy level than those of Phil's father.

The amazing thing is that Phil had no conscious clue that Darla had this aspect to her personality. How can one so perfectly duplicate in the spouse so many of the undesirable features of the parent, in spite of the conscious intention to avoid connecting to someone like that? It's spooky.

During the next few weeks, until the school term ended, Darla showed a repeated tendency to pout and act put out and offended by almost anything Phil did, which was a surprise to him as well. She had concealed all this kind of behavior from him for all the time before the wedding. Phil came to the conclusion that he had married a child and that he had to finish her parents' job of raising her. Phil was certain that marrying a nineteen-year-old was a mistake, but still had hope that she would grow up and become a reasonable adult.

5

DISCOVERING ALASKA

Darla's parents offered to have the young couple come to Alaska during summer vacation, and the kids decided to accept the offer. Phil and Darla arrived in Fairbanks on a Pacific Northern Airlines Boeing jet in early June 1966, and Phil immediately fell in love with the wonder that is Alaska. He was enchanted by the place. In June, the daylight lasts virtually around the clock, and the farther north one goes from Fairbanks, the more broad daylight there is, no matter what the clock says. With so much daylight, the energy absolutely boils inside you, and there is no end of exploring, experiencing, and enjoying that can be done in that amazing place. Darla had expressed to Phil her dislike of Alaska because of the long, cold, dark winters, and he always suspected that one reason she married him was that he came from somewhere far from Alaska and presented a good chance for Darla not to have to live there. But "The Last Frontier" won Phil's heart instantly and he has loved it dearly ever since first arriving there. Darla's chance to go somewhere else to live with Phil was lost the minute he showed up.

The Oldburgs lived in a small house a half hour's drive southeast of Fairbanks in an area known as Moosehorn, where they had carved a home site out of free government land available in Alaska in the early days. Darla's father was a highly intelligent and capable man with an sixth grade education, who had risen to superintendent status in the construction trade because of his high level of ability and performance, and who spent his leisure time running a business as a hunting guide. He had secured for Phil a summer construction job with a contractor friend of his, so the young son-in-law had the highest-paying job by nearly double that he had ever had, waiting for him when he got there. Within two days of arriving in the neatest place he had ever seen, Phil took a train ride to the job site and was out in the middle of this fantastic wilderness earning the most money he had ever seen.

Mt. McKinley, also known as Denali, The Great One

The Parks Highway, named for a U.S. Army officer who led some exploration done in Alaska after it became a territory of the United States, was being built to provide a direct connection between Fairbanks and Anchorage, and this employer had a subcontract to work on a section of the road going in near Mount McKinley, also called Denali. With that lovely and majestic behemoth looking on, Phil worked as a truck driver and laborer and helped create an important part of the development of Alaska. Phil loved the idea, and the experience was wonderful for him. His boss had a Piper PA-18 Super Cub airplane, and he flew in it to get Phil one day when Phil had driven a truck for him to Anchorage. It was about a two hour flight back to the job site, and the scenery was fabulous. Phil was becoming interested in aviation, as he was learning to love Alaska. The Parks Highway job lasted only a few weeks, and Darla came on the train for a Sunday visit during one of the weekends. The kids had fun reuniting and exploring around Cantwell, the nearest town to the job site. Darla then went back to Moosehorn, and Phil worked until the subcontract was done. When Phil got back to Moosehorn, Darla's dad had another job lined up for him, this time with a small, general contractor who did repair and remodeling work in and around Fairbanks. The firm's regular laborer/truck driver was an Alaska native who fished commercially during the summer, so the contractor needed someone to fill in for him until he got back. Pop Oldburg had a lot of good connections, and he was getting some real value out of them for Phil.

In this job, Phil was able to learn his way around the Fairbanks local area, and he became very fond of Fairbanks. He had never before been in a city of 20,000 people that had more gravel streets than it had paved ones, and Phil felt like a pioneer. The truck driving was fun, and Phil was learning about how things went in the construction business. The bad part about the job was a nasty old guy who worked as a carpenter for this contractor. He had been the contact through whom Pop Oldburg connected with the employer to get the job for Phil. This carpenter, a skinny, wiry man in his fifties, was the ugliest person Phil had ever seen, and he had a disposition to match. He had a huge, scarred-up nose that looked like someone with palsy had cut it off with a hack saw and then sewed it back on in the dark with shoe laces. This guy enjoyed griping about everything under the sun and got a kick out of giving Phil a hard time by complaining about everything he did. The boss liked Phil's work so this guy did no permanent damage, but he took some of the fun out of the job for the young man. Phil got to the point of telling Pop Oldburg that he was about ready to tear the face off of Pop's ugly friend and shove it up somebody's ass. Pop found this amusing, but Phil managed to keep quiet at work and put up with this jerk for six weeks, until the fisherman came back and the job ended.

The summer was a happy and successful one for Phil despite the nasty coworker, and he knew that there was more of Alaska in his future. Darla's behavior toward Phil was better while they roomed at her parents' house, and he had almost forgotten what she had revealed to him during their first three months about how she could be. Unfortunately, the pouting and tantrums resumed when they were back on their own in Ellensburg.

In Alaska, Phil had his first opportunity to observe the dynamics of Darla's family, and he began to get a sense of how things were as she was growing up. Darla told Phil that by the time she was old enough to leave home, her life with Pop had convinced her that her father did not love her. Phil witnessed no demonstrations of caring or affection from Darla's father and thought the old man treated Mom Oldburg very badly. She had a much worse time of it than Phil's mother got from her husband. Darla said that her father never hugged any of them and he never told Darla that he loved her. Her birthday was during the hunting season, and he was never present on her birthday throughout her entire childhood. She took this to be an intentional message from him about which was more important, Darla or hunting.

Phil's experience with a father who was very loving and affectionate, but who used anger as a tool of control, was different from what Phil observed with this Alaskan man who ridiculed and demeaned his family and made no outward demonstration of caring for them, except that he made a good living and let them spend his money on nice things. Phil was disturbed by what he saw and found himself feeling sorry for the little girl who Darla had been, growing up in this household.

6

CHILDREN OF TRAGEDY

A year or so after Phil's marriage to Darla, the Oldburgs, apparently suffering from empty nest syndrome, took in two foster children who had spent the prior several years with a very loving and nurturing military family stationed in Alaska. That family had received orders to a new location elsewhere and had to relinquish custody of these children, who were wards of the state of Alaska and could not leave with the foster parents. The children were a brother and sister of mixed racial heritage, Alaskan Eskimo and Caucasian. The girl was eight years old and the boy was six. When they first arrived at the Oldburgs', the children were clearly accustomed to a lot of close personal attention, affection, and demonstrations of caring. They expected adults to help them get ready for bed and were used to assistance with brushing their teeth and washing their faces. They would go around and kiss and hug everyone good night, and they were used to being tucked in. Phil's take on them was that they were two of the sweetest and dearest little ones he had ever seen. Having been a child who got tucked in himself, Phil knew how important that could be. It was obvious that these youngsters had received a great deal of loving and positive attention in the home they came from. Phil never met that family, but at that time, he held those unknown people in high esteem because of the beautiful and heart-filling effect their care had on those precious children. His feelings remain the same today.

One of the saddest things Phil has ever, in his whole life, had the opportunity to watch was the transformation of those children from being affectionate, demonstrative, secure, healthy little love muffins into withdrawn, lonely, damaged, and in the case of the girl, angry people who will carry for the rest of their lives the scars resulting from the decision by the state to put them in that home. The treatment they got, particularly from Pop Oldburg, was harsh, controlling, mean-spirited, cold, and heartbreaking to see. Mom Oldburg was not so bad, but was cowed by Pop and took her cues from him. She may have had more loving instincts, but largely withheld them from those children, perhaps out of fear, or maybe at the direction of her husband. As years went by, Phil thought long and hard about reporting his concerns to the child-care authorities, and even consulted with some relatives of Mrs. Oldburg's who had come from out of state to visit and who approached Phil with their fears about what damage was being done to those children in that setting. They were as horrified as Phil was about what was going on there. They and Phil discussed the matter at some length, after which the relatives returned home, leaving Phil to continue considering what, if anything, he should or could do about the situation.

The Oldburgs were not beating the children, although corporal punishment sometimes took a somewhat harsher form than was appropriate. The kids were not chained to heat registers or confined in dog kennels, the way one sometimes reads about when especially notorious or egregious cases come to light. The children were dressed satisfactorily, were warm and dry, received nutritious food, attended school regularly and did their school work, and there were few, if any, glaring signs that their home life was lacking. There was unlikely to be evidence, apart from personal opinion, that would compel the authorities to remove the children from the Oldburgs. It was probably not the worst the state could do for those children, and there is always a need for foster homes.

Phil's other concern was about the potential impact his raising a fuss about this would have had on his own home life. To accuse his in-laws of malfeasance or cruelty would create an enormous rift between himself and them, and he already had enough problems at home without stirring up more. Darla had dedicated herself to fixing her unsatisfactory relationship with her father and had become adoring and almost obsequious in her treatment of him, although from what she had told Phil about the feelings she grew up with, and with what Phil now knew about how she was raised after he saw what went on with the foster children, Pop more nearly deserved to have his behind kicked. She had blinded herself to any possible criticism of the way her parents raised children, and feelers Phil put out to her about discussing the situation met with stern refusal to consider such discussion. To force the matter would have resulted in more insane and hateful accusations by Darla against Phil as an attacker, and he said no thanks.

Phil's decision was to do nothing, because he probably could not have helped the foster children, and the only thing he would have been likely to accomplish would have been to further mess up his own life. Phil suffered some with that decision, and if he had seen any way to feel sure he could have saved the kids, he would have done so, because he could see what was happening to them. But he has forgiven himself because what he did was the only reasonable thing he could have done under the circumstances. Phil had occasion to experience further contact with child protection authorities in years since this went on, and learned from it that without flowing blood, broken bones, and obvious evidence of violence or physical abuse to point to, getting something done in a situation like that one is virtually impossible. For this reason, Phil is convinced that he had no reasonable choice but to do what he did.

For Phil, this knowledge does not help with the sadness he feels for the children about the impact on their lives of all they had to put up with. The girl grew up to be a true man-hater, with enormous, almost overwhelming bitterness toward the Oldburgs. She has had to undergo a tremendous amount of counseling and therapy just to try to get herself out of the hate she feels, especially for Pop Oldburg. She showed a lot of courage and pluck as she grew older, because she chose to fight back when she became a teenager and would no longer lie down for the treatment she got there. She has managed to overcome some of the harm done to her, and Phil admires her strength of character, but her life is not one most people would wish to have.

Her brother, on the other hand, became the most passive person imaginable He never complained about or resisted, as a kid, any of the unkindness he endured from Oldburgs, no matter how demeaning or unjust it got. He was compliant, cooperative, obedient, and silent, and it almost seemed like he thought he deserved to be treated that way. As a young adult, he got trapped by pregnancy into marriage by an abusive and controlling nut case who created a life for him that made Phil's life with Darla look like a walk in the park, by comparison. He divorced her after twenty years, but, as far as is known, no one ever heard him complain about the incredibly awful married life he had allowed himself to be sucked into. He is so silent and uncommunicative that it is impossible to get a good sense of what he is thinking or feeling, but there is little doubt that the damage to him was as great as the damage done to his sister in that home, he just doesn't act out as overtly as she does. The story of those children is a great tragedy.

7

LIFE GOES FORWARD

This review of circumstances in the Oldburg household has been a rapid advance to a point several years ahead of where we were in the story, but an examination of that family dynamic is key to understanding what led to the difficulties that existed in Phil's relationship with Darla. Having witnessed what went on in that home made clear to Phil, beyond any question or doubt, what the source must have been of the rage that lay waiting inside of Darla until some hapless soul such as he should come along to give her an outlet for that rage. She was inflicting upon Phil the vengeful treatment that was earned by, and perhaps should have been reserved for, her father because of the way he raised her. Phil was accustomed to dealing with a temperamental and troublesome person in his father, and Phil's efforts at peace-making played right into Darla's hands as she learned, step by step, how enjoyable it could be to raise holy hell and inflict genuine punishment on him in her effort to get even with the world for what she had been forced to endure. By dumping her rage on a person who did not respond in kind, but who rather continued to try reason, good sense, and persuasion in dealing with her, she was answering an internal imperative that was greater than either of them. She would have nothing to do with Phil's efforts at reasonableness. Darla seemed to experience a real thrill associated with dishing out that punishment, and the longer it went on, the more she became addicted to it. By the time Phil achieved full realization about what was happening to his life, came to comprehend what had caused it, and recognized that it was not going to get better, he had two children. He was then faced with making a decision about whether to tough it out so that his kids could grow up with a loving, dedicated, and present father, or let them grow up as children of divorce. At the cost of any chance he might have for all-around happiness for himself, Phil chose for the benefit of his children. They became the source and objects of love in his life, and, for a quite a long while, he succeeded in making a satisfactory life for himself as the father of his children.

Dr. Laura Schlesinger, the well-known radio talk-show personality, has written about situations such as the one in which Phil found himself. In her book *The Proper Care and Feeding of Husbands*, she very accurately describes how many women make the mistake of believing that nagging, complaining, bitching, snarling, and acting hateful are what it takes to get men to do what the women want. Dr. Laura recognizes how easy it would be for women married to men like Phil to have happy and successful marriages. All the woman has to do is recognize that men are simple beings, that most of them just want to do right by their women, and that they want to provide and do everything they can to make them happy and content. The truth is that a good man will do almost anything for a good woman who makes him feel appreciated, respected, and important. A woman who does that will have a happy man and will, in turn, be happy with what she gets from him. Traditionalists like Phil agree with most of Dr. Laura's positions on duty to children, spouse, and family; patriotism; teen sexuality; shacking up; promiscuous behavior; doing the right thing; and so on. She gets pretty tough on some of her callers, and she does not pull any punches, but kudos are owed to the good doctor for her profound insight into the truth about men like Phil. If large numbers of women like Darla read Dr. Laura's books and did what the doctor recommends, there would be many more happy marriages, and the world would be better for it. That's a very smart lady.

To return to where we were in the story, after Darla and Phil returned to school in Ellensburg, Washington, after their first summer in Alaska together, the temperamental behavior, the pouting, the tantrums, and all of that resumed, and it gradually became clear to Phil that the peaceful life he had assumed he would have was not going to happen. Darla was a seriously afflicted victim of PMS, and there is now something called PMDD, or premenstrual dysphoric disorder, which is described as monster-making in its effect on the women who have it. Such a thing was not known about in 1966, but Darla must have had it, because "monster" is a good characterization of what she could become. But PMS or PMDD was not always the reason for Darla to tear into poor Phil, because her attacks were not always related to which part of her monthly cycle she was in. Sometimes, she would get horrible about some issue that came up between them during the opposite end of the month from her PMDD time.

The difference was that during her PMDD time, she would snarl, pout, and be awful for no apparent reason. During other times of the month, she would be her more usual nice self, but could immediately be set off if a matter for discussion arose that made her feel like Phil thought he had any reason to be critical of her. Phil learned very early that to indicate, even in the most benign way possible, that he had a problem about her or about anything she had done, was to invite another of her crazy attacks because she thought he was attacking her. The name she most often called Phil was "attacker," and he learned to hate the word. The truth is that Phil has never attacked anyone, about anything, in his whole life, and the insanity of constantly being called an attacker by the worst attacker imaginable is monumental.

Darla was in charge of the family checkbook when they first got married, and she was not very good at managing it. She had trouble keeping the balances up to date, and over the first couple of years, she bounced a few checks. In an effort to deal with this problem, Phil attempted to talk about it, always in the most gentle, diplomatic, kindly way possible, because he had learned how she typically reacted, and he hoped that being extra nice would make it better. It didn't. Darla would soon be shrieking at Phil and accusing him of being an attacking monster, and any chance to solve the problem was lost. Phil eventually took over managing the checkbook and the problem of bad checks ended. One time Darla lost the checkbook and her wallet, and whoever found them wrote a couple of checks on the Temple account. Phil provided prompt notice to the bank about the loss, and later, when he discovered the erroneous deductions from their account, the bank made good on the checks they had improperly honored. The signature was nothing like Darla's. When Phil attempted to discuss, once more in the most peaceful, noncritical, respectful way possible, what could be done to avoid future episodes of this sort, conditions soon collapsed into another of her tantrums. Over time it became increasingly rare for Phil to undertake any kind of problem solving or adult discussion about anything with Darla because he hated so much having to deal with this awful behavior.

Darla was a fairly good cook, and she made a respectable effort to feed the two of them nutritious and palatable food. Once, after they had been married for a year or so, she prepared a meal that did not turn out as well as most of her efforts, and as they ate it, she asked Phil how he liked it. Phil was an honest person as well as a peaceful one, so his response was an effort to be diplomatic without being untruthful. It came out vague and hesitant, which Darla took to be criticism and which set her off on one of her screeching assaults on Phil. She told him that he was a vicious attacker who did not deserve her loving efforts in the kitchen. It was one of her worst, and Phil was shaken considerably by the ferocity of it. Later, after she had calmed down, he remarked to her that this was a bad one and it looked like the honeymoon was really over, which had, in fact, been true for Phil almost since the beginning. This brought on an even more violent and hate-filled explosion than before. It was a bad, bad day.

One might ask why Phil stayed around to be subjected to this kind of unfair and undeserved treatment. For sure, Phil thought long and hard about it. There was no divorce in his family, so avoiding the stigma of being the first to bring on that shame was worth a lot of effort. He was no quitter. Phil recognized the many good qualities present in Darla, and he knew that he had married a child. Phil was hopeful that as Darla matured emotionally, she would outgrow the terrible behavior that was ruining the marriage. Phil still believed that she was a good person and that there was potential for them to succeed. Phil thought that Darla would eventually realize that he was a sincere, loving, lovable, and admirable man, and that she would stop having these awful outbursts. Dream on, pal. It never happened.

Darla and Phil proceeded with his final year and her third year of college, and Phil continued working part-time. Some of their time together was relatively peaceful. She was nice enough and sane enough part of the time for Phil not to be in complete despair about the possibility of there eventually being some hope for the marriage when she finally reached adulthood. But she was consistent enough and dangerous enough with her unreasonable and hateful behavior that no chance for making a real partnership with her ever developed. Phil just kept hanging in there and hoping.

Phil graduated from Central Washington University with a baccalaureate in economics and business administration. All his credits from Western State of Colorado and from Columbia Community College had transferred, but not all were applied to his degree or to his elective requirements, so, six years out of high school, it ended up taking five years of college for Phil to get his four-year degree. The Vietnam War was getting larger and the draft was taking more people, including those who had graduated from college, so Phil had been investigating, throughout his final months in school, alternatives to getting drafted. He took qualifying tests for both Air Force and Navy Officer Candidate programs and was accepted for both. Phil was too tall to be admitted to Air Force pilot training, and he had serious doubts about the wisdom and survivability of trying to learn to crash land airplanes on the flight decks of ships bouncing around in the ocean, but elected to go to Naval Aviation Officer Candidate School (NAOCS) at Naval Air Station (NAS), Pensacola, Florida.

Darla and Phil spent that summer in Cheyenne, and he obtained a warehousing job there in anticipation of leaving for Florida sometime in the fall. It was kind of a strange summer, with Phil working the midnight shift in the warehouse, and with Darla spending days doing whatever she did while he slept. Phil's parents were glad to have the young couple there, but it may be that they had begun to get a glimmer of the fact that Phil and Darla were not a match made in heaven. Darla was a nice and likable girl, however, and apart from some occasional pouting by her in their presence, Loren and Molly did not witness the worst of how it could be. Years later, Phil told his parents about how bad things were in his marriage, but he said nothing at the time. The truth is that no one but Phil ever really got to see how Darla was at her worst, and some still find it hard to believe that she could be as bad as she was. She had a couple of major blow-ups that summer, and Phil's fear continued to grow that this marriage might fail. They finished their summer in Cheyenne and headed back to Ellensburg, where the plan was for Darla to start her final year of college while Phil was in Officer Candidate School.

Darla was ill for the car trip to Washington, and when they arrived there, she enrolled in school and Phil enlisted in the Navy at the Sand Point Naval Air Station in Seattle. Phil joined on Darla's birthday and received orders to report for active duty on his birthday in January 1968. It had been expected that Phil would have to report sooner, so this development caused them to revise their plans. They decided to delay Darla's senior year and to drive north to spend the last four months of Phil's civilian status experiencing winter in Alaska.

They drove up the Alaska Highway in Phil's 1956 Pontiac, and in those days, that road presented quite a challenge. The drive from Ellensburg to Fairbanks was around twenty-five hundred miles, over twelve hundred of which was gravel road. Except for the first fifty miles out of Dawson Creek, British Columbia, which was mile zero of what used to be called the Alcan, and except for about ten miles on either side of Whitehorse, the capital of the Yukon Territory, on the entire twelve hundred-plus miles of the highway east of the Alaskan/Canadian border, the Temples and their old car were pounded by unpaved road. Darla was sick for the whole trip, but they made it anyway, and Darla got pregnant on the way to Alaska. Phil remembers exactly when and where that happened, in Fort Nelson, British Columbia, because that behavior was pretty rare for those two, given how much they did not enjoy each other in that department. By the time Phil left for Florida in January, they knew about little Hercules, which was the name Phil gave to the tiny, unknown person in there, who was due in late June 1968. Phil already loved that little one, and told him or her so every chance he had to say it through Mama's tummy. Darla and Phil were on their way to parenthood.

Phil got a job at Woolworth's in Fairbanks through the fall and the Christmas season and earned enough to keep them eating. Phil learned during that time that he was not too crazy about the retail trade and would opt to make his living another way if he could, when he finished his hitch in the Navy. Phil and Darla set up housekeeping in Moosehorn, near her parents' home. The young couple was in a little one-room cabin with an oil heater and an outhouse. Because the oil stove got so clogged with soot that it just burned fuel without warming the cabin, their hair froze as they slept and their winter in Alaska was turning out to be more of an adventure than Phil could have imagined. He was absolutely loving his chance to have an Alaskan winter experience. Darla spent her days, while Phil was at work, in her parents' house with her mother. When Phil left for Pensacola, Darla moved back in with her folks because the cabin was unsuitable for human habitation in the winter anyway, and a pregnant girl alone in there was out of the question. Her job was to grow their baby and wait until Phil finished NAOCS to come and join him in Florida. Once Phil had a commission, the Navy would pay for Darla to move there to be with him.

A couple of weeks before Phil was scheduled to leave for Pensacola, Darla and he borrowed a snowmobile and rode around the countryside near their little cabin trying out the new technology of fun that was sweeping the northland at the time. Snow machines were emerging as a major source of recreational enjoyment in Alaska because they gave people a means of having a lot of fun on a recurring basis over the many months of winter that are a fact of life in the far north. There is also the important practical feature of a fast and economical way of going to places most people could not easily get to before the advent of this type of equipment. This was the first time for both Phil and Darla on a snow machine. Phil was driving and Darla was riding behind him as a passenger. Phil's lack of skill and experience on the snow machine led to a mishap that was to have a serious effect on how things went for him at NAOCS.

They were making their way down a backwoods road, which was no more than a one-lane trail along the edge of a muskeg swamp. The trail had been a deeply rutted jeep route in warmer weather and was now a solidly frozen mass of ruts and ridges, which, even though covered with a foot or more of snow, still provided a very uneven and wildly variable surface on which to drive a snow machine. Eight or ten miles per hour was as fast as it seemed safe to go on this stuff, and at one point, the going got so wobbly and unstable that Phil thought they were going to roll over. To avoid having the machine roll on them, Phil made the instantaneous decision to execute a diving dismount from the machine; a big mistake, as it turned out. The machine righted itself as soon as he performed his leaping, diving roll, and it came to a stop, with Darla still riding on the back, several yards farther along the trail from where Phil had dismounted. Darla was fine, the snow machine was fine, but Phil was not fine. He had smashed his knee on a stone or on a frozen ridge of mud and was in so much pain that he was sure his knee was destroyed. In addition, his left thumb was hurting and he could not move it.

By the time they got back to the cabin, Phil's knee was still sore, but was far less painful that it had been and seemed to be working normally. Ultimately, it became clear that, though bruised, the knee was not seriously injured. His hand, however, was a different story. He was unable to move his thumb, and while not excruciatingly painful, it was plenty sore and was obviously very damaged. Phil was not on active duty, but was an enlisted member of the military, so he contacted the Air Force clinic at Eielson Air Force Base (AFB), near Moosehorn, and made an appointment to have a doctor look at his injury. The doctor examined his hand, X-rayed it, and pronounced it as a minor displacement injury, which would heal shortly with no lasting effect. He had failed, however, to X-ray the hand in an extended, stressed position; had he done so, it would have revealed a ruptured ligament, repairable by surgery, but a serious injury, nonetheless. Phil decided, since the hand was supposed to heal with no problems, not to make an issue of the thumb and to report for duty as scheduled.

The event that took place during the Temple's four months in Alaska, before Phil left for the Navy, which was of the greatest long-term effect on their lives was that Darla once again, without consulting Phil, made the decision to join the Alladist religion. Phil's sense at the time was that this had been Darla's intention from the beginning, and once the marriage was accomplished, there was not much he could do about it. When she determined that the time was right, Darla told Phil what she was going to do, and he was left to take it or leave it. Phil decided not to make an issue of it, because he was still glad to see people truly seeking God and trying to be decent and righteous, and he thought that most Alladists were doing that. Darla and Phil had not been attending any particular church, and the subject of God did not come up between them very much. Basically, Phil would have preferred that Darla not do this, and if they had not been married, he would have taken the same position he did before, of not allowing it. In retrospect, it would have been much better for all of them if he had done just that. Phil had the sense of having been played, but his wish was to avoid trouble, so he did not put up a fuss.

As it turned out, it was as bad a thing as could have happened in Phil's life, because the belief that Darla and the children have that Phil, a good, decent, loving, and honorable man, is some kind of defective reprobate is based, to a significant degree, on his non-belief in a religion they embrace in a fanatical way. The faith has its roots in Islam, from which fanatical evildoers are one of the worst problems in the world. Those roots are made obvious in the unreasonable and cruel actions that these Alladists justify by invoking their faith, even though what they do is evil and wrong. Darla's decision to join as she did is an important part of the reason Phil no longer has children. There will be more discussion of that later in this book.

8

YOU'RE IN THE NAVY NOW

Phil was supposed to report to Navy AOCS the evening of January 23, 1968, but in no case later than 6 AM on the twenty-fourth, his birthday. He left Fairbanks on an Alaska Airlines Boeing 727 just after midnight on the twenty-third. Repeated delays en route caused the anticipated twelve-hour trip to become a thirty-hour ordeal. By the time Phil reported to NAS Pensacola, He had not slept for about forty-six hours and was exhausted. He arrived about an hour after the deadline, for which he was severely reprimanded. He was threatened, by the Marine Corps and Navy personnel who were there to greet the newly arriving candidates, with being held back and subjected to two weeks of hell until the next class was to begin. They made an example of Phil as encouragement to others never to be late for the Navy. After sufficient screaming at Phil for his tardiness, it was decided to let him proceed with the rest of his class, all of whom had arrived the night before. Phil was hurriedly issued his equipment and briefed with more than his fair share of screaming and threatening, but was able to catch up with the rest of the class by mid-morning. The gear issued to all arriving officer candidates included two sets of olive-drab colored cotton coveralls, called poopie suits, and the candidates found themselves being referred to, with utter disdain, as "Poopie Suiters." The complete removal of dignity that resulted from wearing this ridiculous-looking bag and being called that ridiculous name was intentional, and it worked. By the time Phil finally hit the rack at 11 o'clock that night, he had been awake for well over sixty hours and was ready to collapse. That was the longest day of his life, and it was, hands down, the worst birthday he ever had. He was twenty-four, older by a year or two or three than almost all the sixty-three other members of NAOCS class 04-68.

The movie *An Officer and a Gentleman*, made in the early 1980s and starring Richard Gere, is about people going through the same Aviation Officer Candidate program with the U.S. Navy that Phil went through. The person who wrote the story clearly went through that training or had close contact with someone who did, because many of the details about what candidates experience are very accurate. The language used, with expressions unique to that setting, and the traditions and activities depicted in the film were very close to what actually goes on there. Of course, a candidate fist-fighting with a Marine Corps drill instructor is a preposterous concept, and the candidates were much too busy to have time to pursue serious romantic relationships. They could not even get off the base for the first six weeks, and even after that, there was no time to acquire girlfriends. Some of the candidates had their wives in Pensacola and could see them a little at first, and could spend more time with them later, and a few of the guys managed to connect with women from the WAVE barracks and fell in lust, but concerning the love story in that movie, there's no way. The setting was in a fictitious Washington State Naval training facility instead of Pensacola, but the authenticity was, with the exceptions noted, fairly well maintained. It was fun for Phil, as a veteran of the training program depicted, to critique the movie.

The first two weeks of NAOCS took place at "Indoc," short for Indoctrination Battalion. This was located in an old, pre-World War II derelict of a building, known to candidates as Splinterville, which was in truly terrible condition, and which was properly torn down not long after Phil went through. Marine Corps drill instructors were in charge there, rotated from the main body of the training regiment, two D.I.s at a time, for two-week tours. The place was actually operated, also two weeks at a time, by the most senior class of officer candidates, who were going through their "applied leadership" experience, immediately prior to commissioning. Among the "candidate officers," as they were called, who were assigned to Indoc, there were some who carried a grudge about what they had been subjected to during the last few months, and this was their chance to take out their need for revenge on the hapless souls arriving for the new class. One of those candidate officers took a particular interest in Phil and decided to make it his business to torment him into DOR, or Drop-On-Request, a concept dealt with at length in *An Officer and a Gentleman.*

Everyone in the program was a volunteer, so a means of determining how sincere a candidate is in his dedication to the Navy is to see how miserable he can be made to feel and still stay in the training. Anyone can voluntarily withdraw from the training at any time and be returned to civilian status, although during the 1960s, the draft was in full operation, and it was rumored that anyone who chose to DOR was reported to his draft board as classification 1-A and was subject to immediate induction as a draftee.

A crucial feature of military basic training is that the new arrivals are placed under extremely stressful and completely unfamiliar conditions such that their identities as civilians are broken down and eliminated. The people are then reconstructed as military personnel who will adapt to, and be compliant with, the military credo and model of life. This includes prioritizing completion of the mission above the welfare of individual members of the organization, absolute submission of self to the chain of command and to accomplishment of the assigned mission, and unquestioning obedience to orders issued by those of superior rank.

Americans are accustomed to the freedom they enjoy in this country, and as a result, there is a substantial amount of breaking down of civilians required before the reconstruction of military personnel can begin. With Phil's state of exhaustion already compounding the intentionally high stress of what happens at the time of showing up for training, the focusing by an especially enthusiastic tormentor of the worst he could do to his victim may have made the initial phase of Phil's breaking down process even a little more difficult than usual. Phil actually brought upon himself some of the hatred of this jerk by demonstrating contempt for the candidate officer as soon as he started in on Phil. Phil was not aware of exactly what the term "standing at attention" meant, and that is one of the behaviors taught during the first few minutes after arrival at "Indoc." "Attention" means that you stand motionless, heels together, toes angled slightly outward, back straight, eyes directly ahead, thumbs and fingers touching lightly, thumbs along the seam of the trousers, and you remain in exactly that position, without movement, no matter what else goes on, until you are ordered to do something different.

Phil was set upon by this bespectacled twerp, whose nose pointed directly at his sternum when the twerp looked straight ahead, and whose spittle sprayed Phil's neck as he tilted his head back to scream at the much taller Phil. Candidate Temple found himself looking down and staring into the little man's eyes with the same amount of ill regard as was being spewed at Phil, and this served only to infuriate Shorty. Phil saw this guy as a pathetic jerk, and the fellow could see this in Phil's attitude. Shorty the twerp reported Phil to the drill instructor and made the effort to have Phil charged with insubordination, even though Phil had scarcely said a word to the guy. The look was enough.

Phil was called on the carpet, and a hearing, presided over by the gunnery sergeant in charge, was held concerning whether or not Phil was to be removed from the program as defiant and insubordinate. The drill instructor was somewhat amused by the furious effort on the part of this creep to cause so much trouble, and the gunny was even a little bit compassionate toward Phil, in a hard-nosed and profane sort of way, about his unfortunate target status. The decision was made to allow Phil to return to the class, but Phil's sense that he did not belong there was growing by the minute.

Once Phil learned what was involved in standing at attention, his defiance was no longer apparent and he learned, along with everyone else, just to take the punishment. Phil's nemesis was gone in a few days, having reached his commissioning date, and no one else ever singled Phil out for abuse during the rest of his time in OCS. What went on in Indoc, however, was still plenty stressful, and Phil soon found himself experiencing, for the first time in his life, depression. The despair attendant to having no control over all the unbelievable and disagreeable things that are happening to you is, by design, an integral part of initial training in the military service. After the first few days have gone by, the individual is already beginning to learn how to perform in the manner required and is regaining some sense of at least a little bit of control over his own existence. As a result, the feelings of hopelessness begin to lessen.

In addition to the training, the new candidates underwent a lot of physical and psychological testing and analysis during the first few days in the program, and when one of the forms they filled out asked for a rating, from one to ten, of what they saw as their emotional condition at this point, Phil entered "one." If there had been an option to enter zero, he would have indicated zero. By the end of the two weeks at Indoc, he was probably up to two, and it continued to get better for him as time went on. By the time Phil got commissioned, he might have been up to five or six, but he never learned to be glad about being in the Navy.

After the two-week stint at Indoc, the candidates knew what they needed to know about what was expected and required of them to get through the program, and they were ready to move on to the training battalion. There were sixty-three candidates in the class, and they knew, to a man, that if it moved, you called it "sir," and if outdoors, you saluted it, and that you were the lowest form of life on the planet. The word "you" was never used when addressing a superior, because all spoken communication with higher ranking personnel was carried on in the third person. You never spoke to someone higher in the OCS chain of command without first saying, "Sir," then identifying yourself using your rank, last name, first name, and class designator, and then requesting permission to speak, then finishing up by repeating, "Sir."

There is no end to the fun that can be had by a drill instructor or a candidate officer in hassling a new candidate who is still not very good at successfully obeying these requirements to the letter, and who must endure, without complaint, all the ridiculous foolery that can be piled on him while he stands there at attention. Marine Corps Staff Sergeant Rufus T. Washington was the battalion drill instructor assigned to Class 04-68, and he is a man Phil will never forget.

A candidate's final grade and class standing were based on his performance in three areas: academics, physical training, and military efficiency. Fifty percent of the grade was based on academics. The other half of the grade was divided between physical training and military performance.. It was 35 percent to physical training and 15 percent to military proficiency. The trainees spent about seven hours a day in classrooms being exposed to subjects such as military justice, Naval history, Navy protocol, officer conduct, chain of command, career progression, navigation, seamanship, public speaking, speed reading, and any number of other topics about which a Naval officer needs to be knowledgeable or in which he should be proficient. There was a lot of reading to do as well as review of lecture notes, tasks at which Phil is very good, and he did very well in academics, graduating third in that category out of the class of sixty-three. If Phil had studied hard, he might have been able to do even better. Phil's diligence as a student still left something to be desired.

The physical training portion of the program included morning exercises, additional calisthenics at various times during the day, timed obstacle course and cross-country runs (one or the other performed every day), completion of a standardized list of fitness performance items called "JFKs" because they were instituted in the early 1960s while John

Kennedy was president, and finally, swimming and water survival. Phil was a married guy who had been working instead of playing sports for almost two years when he showed up at OCS, and was less fit than he had been as a single college kid who played basketball, softball, touch football, and so on. As a result, Phil didn't start off so well in the PT category. The first time through the obstacle course, he could not even get over the eight-foot wall, and his injured hand made it especially difficult to hold on under the elevated horizontal ladder to swing from rung to rung. Phil found his lack of fitness to be quite humiliating and vowed never to allow himself to become that unfit again. As a result, he has maintained his own personal exercise program ever since. With the vigorous level of PT that was imposed on trainees, within a few days Phil was able to get over the eight-foot wall and figured out how to compensate for his hand injury to hold on and swing along the horizontal ladder.

A few years ago, Phil had occasion to visit NAS Pensacola and found the obstacle course looked pretty much exactly as it had all those many years earlier when he was there, and he could still get over the eight-foot wall without difficulty. Phil's final PT grade put him in the top half of the group for that portion of class standing, although not far from the middle. Having begun as one of the half dozen or so candidates who were in notably poorer condition than most of the rest, Phil felt pretty good about improving as much as he did in that category. Phil had taken life saving and water safety instructor training in high school and college, so he was among the most advanced and accomplished swimmers in the class, which helped his PT grade.

Final marks in military efficiency were based on seven items: 1) daily inspections, dealing with such concerns as shoe shine, haircut, neatness, condition and presentation of uniform, quality of shave, and shine of brass; 2) general military bearing; 3) ability to take direction in and 4) to conduct close order drill of the assembled troops; 5) skill and knowledge in the Manual of Arms, both with an officer's saber and with a disabled M-1 carbine; 6) marks received from the candidate officer in charge during watch and sentry duty; and 7) living quarters inspection. Phil's unusual height meant that the uniform shirts issued to him were not long enough to fit him well. As a result of that, he had a hard time keeping his shirt tucked in. Constant tucking and re-tucking quickly spoils the press on a cotton shirt, and Phil soon realized that he was one of the most rumpled people in the battalion. Phil never got to be very good at spit-shining his shoes. Sometimes he did a good job of it, and sometimes he did not, and he was never able to figure out why his efforts turned out either one way or the other. Phil's inspection marks were not among the best, or even among the most average of those in his class, mostly because of his shoes and his rumpled uniform.

In addition to the trouble it created in physical training, Phil's injured hand caused him great difficulty in performing the Manual of Arms with the M-1. When the drill instructor stopped in front of each candidate during the rifle inspection, the candidate was required to come to the "order arms" position, with the rifle at a 45 degree angle across the front of the body. The next step was to snap open the rifle's receiver with the left thumb so that the inspecting NCO could look inside the firing mechanism to see if it had been properly cleaned and oiled. This inspection process was problematic for Phil because his useless thumb could not do what was required, so he had to bend his arm at an awkward angle and try to force the receiver open with the heel of his hand. At the speed of movement required for this maneuver, which was to proceed "smartly," sometimes Phil could pull this off, more often, he could not. Staff Sergeant Washington noticed the trouble Phil was having, and when Phil told him, using the required method of addressing a superior, about the hand problem, the Staff Sergeant said that either Phil had to go to sick bay to get excused or mended, or he had to stand rifle inspection like everybody else. Phil did not go to sick bay, and he continued to stand rifle inspection and to screw it up. Staff Sergeant Washington cut poor, old Phil some slack, God bless his ornery soul, and Phil got through the rifle inspections, even though he never got them right.

One feature of Phil's military efficiency grade that saved him from being at the absolute bottom of the class in that category was that he was extremely good at conducting close order drill. There is a certain rhythmical musicality to marching troops that he was able to tap into, and in the time allotted to learn how to do it, he became one of the very best in the class at that skill. Phil was assigned to Indoc Battalion for his applied leadership week, which is a billet having as one of its primary duties the marching from place to place of the newly arriving candidates after they learn the fundamentals of close order drill from the drill instructors. Phil was put in that billet because he could march the troops so well. Despite that portion of his military grade having been excellent, there is a high probability that Phil was not far from the bottom of the class in his overall military grade. Military efficiency is not a long suit for Phil Temple.

Phil's final class standing, based upon being third overall in academics, slightly better than the middle of the class in physical training, and fairly near the bottom of the class in his military grade, was tenth out of sixty-three. Phil felt pretty good about that. The guy who was first in academics was ninth overall, and his grades in both PT and military were worse than Phil's. The guy was a classic bookworm type who looked like Michael Pollard or Mickey Rooney. The candidate who scored second best in academics was comparable to Phil in PT and much better in military stuff.

What was going on with Phil, however, was that he had definitely decided that the Navy was not a good place for him, and that he did not want to learn to crash land airplanes on floating air strips. As a peacemaker and a gentle soul, Phil is unsuited for a life in the military, and that became clearer to him during every minute he was in OCS. Phil has great respect for those who are suited for such a life, and recognizes the need our country has for a strong military, but the armed forces don't need somebody like him and he doesn't want to be part of them. Phil decided not to DOR early because he was not going to let that system think it could break him. Phil completed the program and achieved standing in the very top of his class. Phil proved what he needed to prove, and he wanted out. Phil notified the Navy three days before commissioning that he was withdrawing from the program.

The surprise that Phil's decision created among the career Navy and Marine Corps people in charge around him was substantial. They could not understand why someone who had come this far and was on the verge of becoming a well-paid gentleman by act of Congress would want out. Phil was sent to the commandant of the Air Training Command in an effort to get him to change his mind. They did not want to lose a guy who could rank third in academics out of a class of sixty-three without even trying, and they did not want to write off the money they had already spent on Phil's training, so they wanted him to stay in the Navy. It was suggested that if Phil did not want to go into flight training, he should consider Naval Air Intelligence, which included eight months of training duty at the Armed Forces Air Intelligence Training Center at Warren Air Force Base in Cheyenne. When he found out that he could spend that much time in Cheyenne if he accepted the commission, they had Phil's attention. When he learned that even though he was an expectant father and the Selective Service System was not drafting such people, there was a high probability that, because of having already volunteered for active duty military service, and having had a lot of taxpayer money spent on his behalf, Phil would be drafted anyway. That did it. Phil really did not want to be there, but it seemed a lot better than lugging a rifle through enemy-infested rice paddies as a draftee, so he opted to return to the class and accept the commission.

After the commissioning ceremony, Staff Sergeant Washington, following tradition, issued the first salute received as an officer by each member of Class 04-68, and the new ensigns each paid him in United States Currency. That tradition provides drill instructors with a pretty good additional payday once every few months, when their latest class graduates. Phil thinks of Staff Sergeant Washington from time to time, and remembers him with a mixture of fondness, respect, and distaste. Phil had a lot of unpleasant experiences under his tutelage, but as anyone who has learned at the hands of a demanding and harsh taskmaster knows, once done with the ordeal, you recognize the good that was done you by the person who required you to perform and succeed. The staff sergeant had already completed a couple of tours in Vietnam when Phil knew him, and the war went on for another five years after Phil went through OCS. Phil hopes that Staff Sergeant Washington made it and hopes he had a happy life.

As soon as Phil received his commission, he was eligible to have his dependents travel to join him, so the next day Darla, by then seven months pregnant with Hercules, arrived in Pensacola. Phil had rented a furnished house in Warrington, the town adjacent to the Naval Air Station, and their time as a Navy family began.

9

BNAO SCHOOL, HAVING A BABY, AND ON TO CHEYENNE

The summer of 1968 was passed in the muggy heat of the Florida panhandle, with Phil as a student officer in the Basic Naval Aviation Officers' (BNAO) School on the Navy base. Now that Phil was an officer, being treated like a human being was a great improvement over the life of a scumbag candidate puke. BNAO School was the most fun Phil had during all the time he was in the Navy because the training had a lot of neat things to go through. The trainee officers went under water in the famous "Dilbert Dunker" machine, a device to provide training in a swimming pool on how to escape from an ejection seat when the aircraft was upside down in the water. That machine got quite a bit of play in *An Officer and a Gentleman* because it was such a memorable experience, but at the time Phil went through the training that experience did not actually go take place until after commissioning. The training was scarier in the movie than it was in real life, because it was easy to get the hang of and it was fun, but the underlying reason for the device was very serious indeed. While Phil was there, he witnessed no life-threatening mishaps with the Dunker of the sort depicted in the movie.

As BNAO trainees, Phil and his comrades also got to jump off towers, platforms, and boats to learn how to land and roll and also how to get themselves out of parachutes in the event of emergencies requiring egress

71

from crippled aircraft. They were required to practice deep-water survival by extricating themselves from parachutes at sea after jumping off a tower on the back of an LST and then deploying inflatable life rafts. They then got out their compactly stowed fishing gear and went fishing. Phil caught some fish, but nothing worth keeping.

The new officers got to fly in jet and propeller-driven aircraft to learn both high and low-altitude instrument navigation, as well as low-altitude visual navigation. Phil learned the fundamentals of flight, air navigation, aviation technology, and the air traffic control system during the five months he was in that program. It was all to assist him in the understanding of his relationship to naval aviation as he did the job he was going to do as an Air Intelligence officer. There were also several days of applied survival, escape, and evasion training at Eglin Air Force Base, not far from Pensacola. That involved camping out; making tents out of parachutes; and catching fish, squirrels, snakes, and whatever else could act as a meal. They were captured and made prisoners of war, and were required to escape from and evade the enemy to avoid recapture. The trainees practiced overland navigation and plant identification for food, and it was all a great adventure for Phil and his compatriots.

For the Temple family, however, the most important thing that happened that summer was the birth in June of their son. Little mystery-person Hercules emerged and was named Colton Gabriel Temple. Almost from the beginning of her pregnancy, Darla experienced intermittent bouts with a condition called pre-eclampsia, a serious complication in some pregnancies which, if uncorrected, can result in toxemia. A toxemic pregnancy can end in the death of the baby or the mother, or both, and so a woman showing the signs of pre-eclampsia requires continuous monitoring and must be handled with great care. The baby was due at the end of June, but when this problem cropped up again in early June, the decision was made by the staff at the Naval Hospital to induce labor and take the baby early.

From the time of the initial injection of the drug that would cause birth contractions to begin until Phil and Darla had a squalling baby boy, four hours went by. Four hours of labor for a mother's first birth is extremely short and involves major stress and major pain. Darla said it was the worst experience of her life, and she was sure that she never wanted to go through that again. At the very last, they got a saddle block into her, and her agony was relieved, but she took a while getting over her anger at Phil, the so-and-so who was responsible for all that suffering.

The Navy let the expectant father off from school to be present for the birth, although he was not allowed in the delivery room. Phil was not, however, granted additional time off to help at home in dealing with the new baby. Darla was therefore on her own, at least during working hours, and she did not like it much. She was pretty miffed at the Navy for making Phil go to work instead of getting time off to help her, and she pouted about it, but she realized that it was not his fault and opted not to punish him the way she was capable of doing. Phil was extremely helpful, however, when he was not at work, and they had a pretty good system in place to share the workload with the new baby. Starting off as new parents is stressful, and Phil's sense of it was that they did pretty well. Phil recalls that period as one of the happier ones for him in his marriage to Darla. He was having fun at work and was keeping very busy at home, and Darla was too preoccupied with the baby to make a lot of trouble for him, so it was a good time.

Colton was not a pretty baby, but to Phil and Darla he was adorable. His head was somewhat misshapen, probably due to the extreme pressures applied during his unusually rapid, difficult, induced delivery. It is also possible that the forceps used to extract him from his mother's body contributed to the way he looked. It may be that the cause was unrelated to the circumstances surrounding the delivery and instead were from some hereditary or genetic source, or the result of some anomaly in the pregnancy that caused him to develop this way. The doctors could not definitively explain why the condition existed, but told the Temples that they could reshape the baby's head by means of repeated molding and sculpting actions with their hands, which would take advantage of the soft skull of a newborn to bring about a less irregular conformation, and therefore a less noticeably odd shape to his head.

Neither Phil nor Darla had the guts to apply forcible mashing, kneading, and sculpting pressures to the skull of their precious little guy, so he remained as he was. He was to endure a lot of cruelty and teasing from other children because of his appearance as he grew older, but he ended up being a person with great strength of character who could endure difficult situations with equanimity and to whom superficial physical beauty had no importance, so it may be that his condition was a blessing to him in that sense.

The Temples' sweet baby had the obnoxious habit of vomiting up at least half of everything he ate, and he could project a stream of puke across a room with remarkable power. He soiled any number of well-meaning baby holders who were not aware of his proclivity for up-chucking, and Darla would become uproariously amused at some of Cole's vomit victims who demonstrated greater than average distress at getting drenched in puke. Phil felt sorry for the poor souls, but for Darla, the more horrified they were, the harder she laughed. Phil developed the policy of warning potential drenchees, but most could not conceptualize the notion of power-puking from such a small person and would opt to take him anyway, much to the regret of some of them. Colton eventually outgrew his propensity to super-vomit, but there were many months before that happened, during which he represented a very grave danger to people's clean clothes.

When Colton was about a month old, his parents took him to an air show featuring the Navy's famous Blue Angels flight demonstration team, who were based at NAS Pensacola, and the baby got sunburned as he lay in his stroller. Phil and Darla had not acted quickly enough to protect his little face from the broiling Florida sun, and he received a pretty serious burn. they felt very guilty about their neglect of him and worried about possible additional harmful effects, but he peeled, recovered, and seemed to suffer no permanent harm. They learned a lesson from that, and it did not happen again.

It was not until September, when the Temples headed for Wyoming with orders for Phil to report to the Armed Forces Air Intelligence Training Center at Warren Air Force Base in Cheyenne, that Darla's difficult ways reared up again. Phil's worries about how mercurial and dangerous she could be had begun to fade, and the otherwise very nice person he believed her to be seemed to be becoming the primary performer in her relationship with Phil. He had purchased a 1963 Chevy Nova station wagon for $600 on the day he was commissioned, and that was the vehicle in which the family headed out for Cheyenne, with three month-old Colton in a car bed in the back, the seat down, and with all of the stuff they had packed into the car stowed in a flat, level load.

The Temples left Pensacola late in the afternoon of the day Phil graduated from BNAO School, and their intention was to drive until late and then get a room. Their route was to take them from Pensacola to Mobile, Alabama, then to Meridian, Mississippi, north through Memphis, then west to Little Rock, Tulsa, and on to Cheyenne. What they had not anticipated was that, in those days, the sidewalks rolled up in the evening in rural Mississippi. They went through Meridian sometime after dark, and that turned out to be where they should have stopped. As they continued north, they could not find anything open, and they could neither buy gas nor get a room. The gas gauge was getting low and Phil recognized the possibility of running out of fuel before morning. He decided to stop at a gas station and wait for it to open. That way, at least they would not run the chance of being stranded who knows where when the last of the fuel was burned.

Their progress brought them to a town named Scooba, Mississippi, and there they found a gas station with a sign on the door saying that opening time was 7 AM, so they stopped. Phil parked next to a gas pump and crawled in the back of the station wagon, on top of the load, to sleep, with Colton safely in the car bed next to him. As he lay on his back, Phil had about two inches between his nose and the roof of the car, and he could not roll over. In later years, Phil has had the experience of an MRI, and it reminded him of sleeping in that loaded station wagon. Darla lay down in the front seat to sleep, and there they remained, uncomfortable, but at least with a plan to deal with the way things were going, so they were okay. It was around 2 AM.

At about five-thirty, while it was still dark, the family was awakened by voices coming from outside the car. Phil looked around, as much as he could while lying flat on his back as though in a coffin or an MRI machine, and he saw, in the dim light from the gas station, a large number of black faces, completely surrounding the car and peering in at the three of them. Darla sat up in the seat, and Phil scrambled down from his bier, which took quite a long time because he was really trapped like a rat in there. When Phil finally got out of the car, he found himself facing fifteen or twenty agricultural or mill workers; He guessed that they worked in the cotton production that went on around there, and they were quite surprised to see the Temples where they found them.

This gas station was apparently a shape-up point for work crews to gather and where a bus would pick them up and take them to wherever their jobs were. Finding this fully packed Chevy wagon with two young white people and a baby inside, parked right in the middle of the spot where they waited for the bus, was something of a novelty for these folks, and they were very curious about why the travelers were there. It was quickly apparent that the workers meant the little family no harm, and Phil was very pleased to note the concern and kindliness they directed toward him and his family.

The workers asked, "Are y'all awright? Y'all havin' a problem? Kin we hep y'all?" and so on. Phil explained the situation, indicated that he and his family were fine, and thanked them for their concern. Phil was quite touched by the genuine goodwill and friendly care that he witnessed from those people. He realized that the pounding heart and frantic scramble to defend his family, which had begun his contact with this group, were appropriate but unnecessary. The travelers and the workers visited a little more, exchanged some additional pleasantries, and pretty soon, the bus came.

As the workers boarded the bus to leave, Phil thanked them again for their kindness, and the Temples were once more alone. Both Darla and Phil were duly impressed by the goodness of heart that they perceived in their encounter with those people, and it was almost enough to overcome Darla's displeasure with Phil for putting the family in that precarious circumstance. Phil and Darla were wide awake now, with little likelihood of getting any more sleep, so they sat and watched as day began to dawn and little Colton slept peacefully on. Phil could not disagree that they had been vulnerable to whatever might have happened, but he chose to look at it as a positive experience, having had very agreeably reinforced his belief in the goodness of people and the greatness of this country, where you could be safe almost anywhere. This was more than forty years ago.

Phil did not think that it meant that foolhardy risk-taking was suddenly a good idea, but he felt that they could be thankful for such a nice outcome and remember the lesson about the need for caution for times when things might not be so nice. It was not as though Phil had deliberately put them at risk. Unexpected circumstances had been encountered . That is to say, nothing was open in Mississippi at night, and Phil dealt with it in the best way he could. Darla was pretty steamed at her husband, but she managed to keep a lid on it, and so after the gas station opened and they got their fuel, they continued toward Memphis.

They passed through Tupelo, Mississippi, the childhood home of Elvis Presley, a fact that was fun for them to contemplate. They crossed a bridge spanning the river through the town, which caused them to remember the song, popular at the time, which spoke of Tupelo and of youngsters throwing something off the Tallahatchie Bridge. By the time The Temples got to Memphis, they were so tired from lack of sleep that even though it was early to be stopping, they got a room in a nice motor inn and rested. Dr. Martin Luther King Jr. had been murdered in that town a few months earlier. That actually happened during the time Phil was busy marching new candidates around Splinterville in their poopie suits. It was an odd feeling for Phil and Darla to be where that terrible and historic event had so recently taken place. The next day, they left Memphis fairly well rested, crossed the mighty Mississippi River, an impressive sight to see, and headed west.

When a member of the naval service is traveling by privately owned vehicle on orders to another station, a mileage rate and per diem are paid to cover fuel, food, and lodging en route. It is then up to the traveler to make the cost of the trip fit into the dollar amount being paid by the government. If one is tough enough, it is possible to economize by driving long hours and days, by buying food at grocery stores and eating in the car, by sleeping in the car, and by doing whatever else one can think of to save money on the trip. The other side of that coin is that some people choose to live extra high on the hog, with fancy lodging, expensive meals, side trips, and so on. They pay for the additional good living out of their own pockets. Either way is fine with the Navy, because they pay what they pay, regardless of the choices the traveler makes. The only thing the service requires is that the member report for duty at the new location on time.

Phil, as someone with a pretty good understanding of how to get maximum value out of a buck, liked to do things in such a way as to end up with a few extra dollars at the end of the trip. Having just spent the night in a very nice hotel in Memphis, and making good time across Arkansas into Oklahoma, Phil thought they could just keep driving until they got to Cheyenne. Phil's parents were expecting them, and the travelers could sleep all they wanted at the folks' house, so it seemed an idea worth considering. The trip had been delayed a bit in Oklahoma because they visited Loren Temple's old hometown and looked around a bit there, so as Phil, Darla and Colton entered Kansas, still several hundred miles from Cheyenne, darkness was upon them. If they followed through with what Phil had in mind, they were going to make an extremely late arrival in Cheyenne, so he figured he had better tell Darla what he wanted to do, to see what she thought of the idea.

Anyone who knows Phil knows that he is not dogmatic or immovable about any issue. Just about the only thing Phil would ever insist upon, if he could, is that everyone be reasonable, considerate, and open to discussion about any subject of potential disagreement. Phil simply wishes for everyone to be willing to negotiate and even compromise, to find reasonable solutions satisfactory to all concerned, about whatever might come up. As mentioned before, this reasonable and peaceful attitude toward life played right into the hands of Darla, who got a real thrill out of occasionally tearing into Phil and raging right over the top of his efforts to be reasonable and civil. This was one of those times, and when Phil suggested, in the most reasonable and inoffensive way possible, that they forgo finding a room in Kansas and just drive on, she blew up.

If Phil had ordered her to put on a harness and start dragging the car the rest of the way to Cheyenne by herself, and then began horse-whipping her to get it done, her conduct would have been appropriate. As it was, the behavior was inexcusable and she was just raging because she could. It may be that she was still smoldering about the scare they received in Scooba, with the curious workers waking them in the middle of the night, and that she had just waited until this time to let loose her anger. As usual, when any big event or change came up, she was sick, and maybe she felt so awful that she just lost control. Whatever the reason, it was another occasion for Phil to regret ever having gotten connected to this person.

By this time, Phil was accustomed to the timing of Darla's illnesses and had decided that she was a hypochondriac who got sick every time anything stressful happened. He did not think she was faking, but neither did he think that she was organically ill. It was utterly predictable and utterly the same every time. It may have been that Phil was not as sympathetic to her as he could have been, but he was not critical, bitchy, or complaining, either. Phil continued to hope that she would outgrow this childish behavior, just as he hoped she would outgrow her tantrums. Phil lived on hope for a long time.

The Temples ended up staying overnight in Holly, Colorado, just west of the Colorado/Kansas border, which made it an easy partial day's drive to Cheyenne the next day. Their stopping for the night is exactly the way it would have turned out even if Darla's response had been civil and decent instead of spewing out all that anger. Amazingly, some people think that hateful and abusive treatment of others is the way to get what they want. It may work in the short run, but no matter how many skirmishes you may win by being mean and nasty, you will lose the big campaign in the long run. Darla never learned that.

The Temples made it to Cheyenne in mid-afternoon the next day, and Phil's parents were thrilled to get their first glimpse of their only grandchild, three-month-old Colton, whom Phil and Darla had begun to call "Cole." It was fun to see the unbridled joy to be found in new grandparents who were finally getting to see the baby. By this time, Cole had become a real cutie, although close inspection could still reveal the incongruity in the shape of his face and head. Nobody has perfect symmetry in that regard, and in this adorable baby, it had ceased to even be noticeable to Cole's parents. The grandparents did not seem to detect it at all.

Loren always had a weakness for babies. Another of Phil's strongest childhood memories of his dad was how thoroughly overcome Loren would get in his enchantment with the presence of a baby, any baby. Loren was utterly unabashed and unashamed in how much he made over them, laughed with them, played with them, goo-gooed them, and absolutely enjoyed the spell they cast over him. This was redoubled when the baby was his own grandson. It was great fun for Phil and Darla to watch.

10
LIVING IN CHEYENNE AGAIN

There was a little time to spare between the Temples' arrival in Cheyenne and the date Phil was required to report for duty at Warren AFB, and in that time he and Darla found a pleasant, economical, furnished apartment to rent in West Cheyenne, not far from a nice park. They moved in, and thus began eight months of service to the Navy that Phil considered a real gift to have been allowed to perform because he was in his hometown, and his parents could bond with their grandson.

Students from the Navy, Marine Corps, Army, and Air Force were all in attendance at the Armed Forces Air Intelligence Training Center at Warren. Officers attended classes from 6 AM until noon, and enlisted personnel attended from noon to 6 PM. Officers had no additional or collateral duties, so once school was out, Phil's time was his own. The subjects studied and the materials handled for the courses were classified, so nothing could leave the secure spaces, and Phil and his classmates had no homework. They received instruction in photographic science; aerial photography; photo interpretation; mapping and map reading; weaponeering; public speaking; military briefing; aviation weather and weather forecasting; special weapons; strategic and tactical warfare planning; performance specifications, characteristics and recognition of aircraft, ships and weapons systems; and intelligence gathering.

It was mostly pretty interesting, and Phil learned a lot about what goes on in the military that he had never even thought of before then. It was, for the most part, a favorable experience for Phil, and the duty was as much like civilian life as anybody could ever hope for and still be in the military, but it did little to make him like being in the Navy. There was a war going on, and Phil would have chosen 100 percent of the time to do what he was doing, as opposed to running off to Canada or otherwise dodging the draft, but there was certainly no military career in his future.

Phil got in contact with a number of his old friends who were still around Cheyenne and spent time introducing his new family to them and to his many relatives who lived in Cheyenne. This eight-month stretch was the longest period of time that Darla and Phil had stayed in one place since their wedding, and the patterns that would characterize their lives began to be more clearly established. Darla needed a lot of sleep, was ill a lot, and seemed to have little energy. It was as though she was depressed, even though Phil was doing his best to do what he thought would make a wife happy. Phil was a loyal and faithful husband, treated Darla well, and created no strife in the marriage. He often found himself wishing that he could have married someone who was as easy to get along with as he was, instead of what he had in Darla.

Darla's virtually congenital dislike of men, combined with her basic decency and intention to be a good person, created a sort of neurotic or schizophrenic way of living for the Temples. Much of the time, Darla was civil and respectable in her behavior, but she was often hostile, petulant, and impossible to communicate with in any meaningful way. Then, sometimes, she was a monster. Phil was never more than a moment away from the potential for his wife to accuse him of being the most base, horrible, and despicable person imaginable and to call him names that bore no relationship to the person he was. Phil came to the conclusion that it was safer just to lay low and not risk confrontation with Darla. This is where any real chance for that marriage to make it began to be lost. The first stages of giving up had been established in Phil.

Conditions were not unbearable or impossible much of the time, however, and the Temples had this wonderful baby to distract them from the deficiencies in their relationship, so they settled in to what is probably true of many marriages, a sort of unsatisfactory but endurable standoff. Phil was still young, optimistic, idealistic, and cheerful by nature, so life could have been worse. He continued to hold hope for the marriage.

Darla connected with the Alladist community in Cheyenne, and they became her primary source of human contact outside the home. They were, for the most part, decent, kindly people with only the best of intentions.

When they departed, they packed the car in a manner very much like the way they had done it when they left Pensacola, except that now, Cole could crawl around on the level load, which would now be illegal under child passenger restraint laws. From time to time, after they got going, Cole would crawl over to a spot behind his dad and play with Phil's ears and hair as Phil drove. It felt good, because Cole was not rough or aggressive with his play; in fact, he was quite gentle. Going down the road with the dear little one behind him, using Phil's hair, his ears, and even his face as toys, is a sweet memory of his children that Phil cherishes.

Phil's orders included two weeks in Pacific Fleet Orientation at NAS Alameda, California, before reporting to Moses Lake, so the Temples headed for California, where they both had relatives they planned to visit. Darla's mother had a brother who was an aerospace engineer in Southern California, who was married with two daughters a little younger than Darla. Darla told Phil that she did not like that family because of the way they treated her when she visited them as a child. That made Phil wonder what made her want to visit them now, but she did, so they did. These relatives turned out to be very nice people, and Phil found himself rather surprised about Darla's expression of dislike for them. Darla's uncle was a highly intelligent and scholarly engineer-type who, although a bit stiff and understated, was a kindly and good man. He had flown a large number of missions over Europe during World War II as a bombardier aboard B-24 bombers, which made him a hero in Phil's book. The uncle obtained his engineering degree on the GI Bill after the war and was a well-paid participant in the U.S. aerospace effort.

His wife, Darla's aunt, was a gregarious lady who was most pleasant, welcoming, and thoughtful, and who was a delightful hostess. Their elder daughter was very pretty and was a lot like her mother by way of being very outgoing and sociable, and those two women showed a special fondness for Darla. It was obvious that they did not know of her dislike for them. The younger daughter bore some kind of mild developmental disability and was very nice, as well, although quite shy. They all made a great effort to help Phil and Darla enjoy their stay with them, and by the time of the Temples' departure, Phil had become quite puzzled about Darla's expression of dislike for them. When he asked her about it, she said that she grew up regarding them as thinking themselves to be better than Darla and her family. She said she still felt that way, and her negative feelings persisted, even after their having had what Phil thought was a nice time. Phil had gotten no sense of anything like their feeling better than or superior to anyone, and he found them to be delightful folks. Phil found himself thinking that if Darla could continuously demonstrate the hostility she felt toward him by repeatedly accusing him of being such an awful person, there could easily be others in the world concerning whom she bore such delusions and to whom she could be as unfair as she was to Phil.

This uncle and aunt were the people mentioned in the earlier discussion of the foster children who came into the home of Darla's parents. When these relatives came to Alaska for a visit several years after this first meeting with them, they approached Phil with their concerns about the effect that life in the Oldburg home must be having on those children. The relatives had been around that foster situation long enough during their visit to witness what was happening to the children and were deeply troubled by what they saw. One thing about Pop Oldburg was that he bore no shame about the way he treated children and made no attempt to conceal what he did. He believed that kids were supposed to be treated that way.

It may have been that Darla's dislike for these kinfolk arose when Darla and her parents detected and resented disapproval from these people about the way Darla and her brother were raised. Also, the cousin was pretty and Darla was not, so Darla may have carried a grudge about that. In any case, it was clear that there were nice people in the world whom Darla chose to dislike, other than just Phil.

11

JOINING THE SQUADRON

Following their departure from the aunt and uncle's home, Darla, Cole, and Phil visited briefly with some cousins of Phil's in Southern California and then had an interesting couple of weeks in the San Francisco Bay Area while he attended fleet orientation training. Then it was on to Moses Lake, Washington, where Phil reported to his squadron for duty. The unit to which he was assigned was Attack Squadron 222, known as VA-222. Neil Armstrong walked on the moon a few weeks after Phil reported for duty.

VA-222 flew the Grumman A-6 Intruder, which at the time was the Navy's workhorse, subsonic, carrier-based, all-weather attack aircraft. The plane was not sleek or swift-looking, but rather had an appearance that reminded Phil of a big-eyed, smiling insect. The bomber had a two-man crew consisting of the pilot, who was a designated naval aviator, and the bombardier/navigator, or B/N, who was a designated naval flight officer and was a graduate of BNOA School, which Phil attended in Pensacola.

The A-6 Intruder had a computer/radar-controlled, all-weather navigation and bomb delivery system that was, for that era, quite sophisticated and that enabled the crew to find ground targets, moving or stationary, regardless of weather and visibility conditions. The aircraft was able to deliver bombs at computer command when the system perceived that the bombs would hit targets based on the speed, direction of flight, and altitude of the aircraft, and the speed and direction of travel, if any, of radar-detected targets on the ground. The system was a precursor to the modern, advanced ordnance-delivery systems we see on television nowadays, but was far less accurate and efficient. The year 1969, the year Phil arrived in the fleet, was after transistors and miniaturization of circuitry had begun their evolution, but the A-6 was designed before the science of electronics had reached that stage, and the computers on board still contained vacuum tubes, which were very susceptible to problems. Later models of the same aircraft included solid state circuitry, which eliminated many of the difficulties attendant to vacuum tubes.

There were around three hundred and fifty officers and men in the squadron, of which about fifty were officers. Three or four were maintenance officers, most of whom were prior enlisted men who had worked directly on aircraft prior to becoming officers, and who knew what was what about aircraft maintenance. There was one other Air Intelligence type like Phil, and the rest were pilots and B/Ns, half and half. Phil's jobs included running the squadron intelligence section and functioning as division officer for the half-dozen or so enlisted intelligence men and photo interpreters in the squadron. He was also classified materials control officer, director of planning and materials preparation for strategic attack planning, order of battle and weather briefer, and enemy systems recognition trainer.

Phil most enjoyed being in charge of his enlisted crew, who came to know that he cared about them, that he truly had their interest at heart, and that, when such defense was warranted, he would stick up for them to the squadron heavies and the squadron leading chief petty officer. For this reason, the men gave him their loyalty and made an effort to perform well for him and help him look good. Phil carried a positive feeling inside concerning the high-quality relationship he had with those who worked for him. When Phil read "Marine, the Life of Chesty Puller", the biography of Marine Corps General Lewis "Chesty" Puller, by Burke Davis, the descriptions of Puller's regard for his men and his determination to do right for them reminded Phil of his own sense of obligation to his men. Although Puller was a great warrior and Phil was definitely a square peg in a round hole in the military, he felt some kinship to the general for that reason. Phil's greatest satisfaction from his time in the Navy came from the sense that he was a good officer to his troops.

Concerning Phil's brother officers, he was fascinated to learn of the wide variety of personality types and philosophies of life to be found among people who had volunteered to fly into combat in some of the most heavily defended areas in the history of air warfare. As Phil got better acquainted around the squadron, he had occasion to interview some of the officers about their wartime experiences. There were quite a few of them, both pilots and B/Ns, who were veterans of Rolling Thunder, the code name given to the long air war over North Vietnam, and who had experienced every sort of anti-aircraft menace the Communists could throw at them. They were about to go back for more. There were a few who were headed back for their third combat cruise of the war. Some of these men expressed to Phil their feelings of love for combat, their passion for the thrill of successfully facing and emerging from mortal danger, and their yearning to return to the adrenalin rush of war. This was amazing to Phil, as one who had been through one fistfight in his life, hated it, and intended to have as few more experiences involving physical combat as possible.

One of the thoughts that crossed Phil's mind as he was exposed to this was that if everybody in the world was like he was, there would be no people like these, and there would be no need for such people, because nobody would make trouble for anyone else. Disputes and disagreements among honorable people, which everyone would be, would be worked out through reason, compromise, and diplomacy. Given the way the world really is, with bullies, abusers, dishonorable people, and evil to be found everywhere, we can thank God for such Americans who protect the rest of us. Phil is one who will fight for honor, justice, and goodness when the need is present, but to make a career of combat is for others.

There were some among the flight crews who were unwilling to share their thoughts and feelings about what they were doing and what they faced, so Phil was left to speculate about whatever was going on inside them. He felt more actual comradeship for these men than he did for the ones who were more vociferous about their love for war, but they were all fascinating to him. Many of the officers in these two groups, the overtly passionate warriors and the noncommittal warriors, were men who had career intentions in naval aviation and would spend their lives risking their lives. Perhaps 20 percent of the officers in the squadron were Naval Academy graduates. The rest were products of the AOCS program (through which Phil had come), were NROTC graduates from college, were prior enlisted who had received commissions due to superior performance or educational achievement, or were people without college degrees who had come through the Aviation Cadet Program, which had been recently discontinued. There were a number of officers who were just regular people, like Phil, who were serving their country in a unique way, but who had no plans to stay in the Navy.

Navy pilots have a reputation for being rowdy and capable of pretty bad behavior, as in the Tail Hook scandal of some years back, but to some extent this is truer of fighter plots than of attack pilots. Many of the officers, both pilots and B/Ns, who chose to be in the A-6 program tended to be more serious minded and more adult in their conduct. There were, of course, exceptions to this, but in general, the A-6 community had more grown-ups in it than the fighter community did. Some of the VA-222 guys were downright scholarly, and these were usually the ones who were more inclined to keep their feelings about combat to themselves.

One of the pilots in the squadron went on to become an astronaut and flew the Space Shuttle. A replacement pilot, who joined the squadron after they got back home, later became a well-known author whose stories of wartime experiences became top-selling books and Hollywood movies. "Flight of the Intruder" By Stephen Coonts was a hit both as a novel and a motion picture.

Because Phil and Darla were both determined that Darla would finish her college degree, they rented a house in Ellensburg so that Darla could be near the school while Phil was overseas. That meant a one-hundred-mile round trip daily for Phil back and forth from Moses Lake, but he did not mind that much, and the mixture of rolling hills, wide-open farm land, and long vistas of central Washington provided a pleasant trip for him each day. Coming home to Ellensburg was rather like it had been coming home to Cheyenne. The Temples had friends there from college with whom they spent a lot of their leisure time, and it was again, at least during Phil's off hours, almost like not being in the Navy, which was fine with him. Living so far away, they had very little contact with other squadron personnel and their families, so never developed much a sense of belonging to the unit.

The squadron was preparing for deployment in October, 1969, with pre-cruise operational readiness exercises at sea scheduled for September aboard USS *Kitty Hawk*, the aircraft carrier that would take them to the Western Pacific, and from which they would conduct combat operations. Getting ready for war made it a busy time at work, and the summer passed quickly. Phil's parents came for a visit in the late summer, and Phil took his dad, who had become an avid golfer, to the Navy Moses Lake Golf Course. He had taken up golf at age fifty and demonstrated a real talent for the game by breaking a hundred the first time he played. At this point in 1969, Loren was fifty-two, was playing three or four times a week on his off days from the firehouse, and was getting to be very good.

Phil had no such talent and did not really like the game, but he loved fresh air and greenery and enjoyed just getting out with Loren to visit. This was when Loren told Phil, with such sadness, about Molly's drinking. The folks were still nuts about little Cole, and the visit was quite pleasant, despite the news of Molly's alcoholism. Phil really did not fully understand the scope of the information he received and did not give it a great deal of thought after his parents left. Phil learned more about alcoholism in later years and came to recognize that there was more to worry about than he knew. Phil was happy for the visit from his dear parents, and it meant a lot to him, as he was about to go off to war.

Darla's behavior during that summer was her standard cyclical, mood-swing, roller coaster ride, and there was a growing sense of disappointment and loss in Phil's heart because it was not turning out to be possible for him to fully follow up on his secret, honeymoon pledge to God, himself, and Darla to nurture his love for her so that they could become the exemplary, loving, great couple he hoped and believed they could be. Phil had the capacity for love that gave every possibility of his becoming part of a great love story, but Darla's behavior and treatment of him was why that was not happening.

It was not possible for Phil to have a child with a woman, no matter how unpredictable and dangerous she might be, and not care about her. Raising a child with someone who loved that child just as much as he did provided Phil with some common ground for caring, and being sent off to war brought this up for him. He was very sad to leave his family, and his focus as he prepared to leave was on the fine and admirable qualities present in Darla that had led to his choosing her in the first place. There continued to be opportunities for Phil to witness the charming and impressive presence that Darla could project in group settings and social situations, and this led to a growing sadness in him that she never, ever showed any of that charm for him when they were alone. It was as though she really believed the vile and hateful things she regularly said to Phil about the kind of person she found him to be, and that she felt he did not deserve to be shown what was best about her.

It was during this time of transition that Phil experienced a powerful moment when the young father felt utterly swept away by the love he felt for his little son as he watched him sleep. Phil had lived through similar moments with his son on any number of other occasions since Cole's birth, but the reason this particular one stuck in Phil's mind so strongly is that it was the point at which he came to understand that the experience he was having with this child was also a first solid grasp of what God was all about. It was a very sweet and monumental instant in his life. The overpowering and all-encompassing love Phil felt for his child had been present ever since he first learned of the baby's existence inside his mother, and becoming a father was the most profound experience of love Phil had ever known, becoming even more complete after Cole's birth. Knowing that he would not hesitate to give his life for this little person, and the elemental understanding that all this was more than just chemical changes in the brain or pulses from the endocrine system, was the true opening of Phil's eyes to the existence of God. Subsequent moments like this, of which there were many, would serve as the most perfect moments of worship and communion with God that Phil would know for many years.

On the day Phil left for overseas, he and Darla left Cole with friends in Ellensburg and drove to Moses Lake, from where the Navy transport plane would take Phil and the other ground personnel from the squadron to Alameda, California, home port of the *Kitty Hawk*. Phil felt very down and wept with sadness as he left his family for the better part of a year. Darla was calm and unmoved, and shed not a tear.

During the predeployment exercises the month before, Phil had had his first look at the open sea from aboard a ship, and he found it to be thoroughly incredible. Now that he was leaving for the long haul, and as the ship steamed away from the California coast, Phil had an even bigger chance to be amazed by the vastness of the ocean. It was a stark and wondrous thing for him to behold. Seeing all those endless miles in all directions of nothing but water allowed Phil to sense in a new way how very small each of us is, and it was quite humbling. On the second day at sea, the airplanes from all the squadrons—fighters, single-seat bombers, two-seat A-6 bombers, photo-reconnaissance birds, command and control aircraft, and electronic warfare/in-flight refueling planes—all came aboard for the cruise to Hawaii. Then it was on to the South China Sea and the war.

An aircraft carrier is an extremely noisy place in which to try to live. Phil was one of the most junior officers in the squadron and, as such, had to share a four-man bunkroom on the level just beneath the flight deck. As he lay in his bunk, there was about two feet of air space between his nose and the steel plating that made up the ceiling, or in Navy parlance, the overhead, of his compartment. That steel plating was three inches thick, and the top of it was the flight deck. When airplanes landed aboard the ship, the tail hooks that extended from the underside of the planes would snag one of four large arresting cables, which stretched across the deck. The best approach and landing that a pilot could accomplish would end in catching the number three wire, and planes that caught the three wire would come to a stop right above Phil's face. In order to ensure survival of the aircraft, as soon as the plane touched the deck, the pilot was required to advance the aircraft's power setting to 100 percent. This way, the plane was still going at a high enough speed and developing enough thrust to again become airborne in the event that the tail hook did not catch any cable. So when the airplanes stopped less than three feet above Phil's reclining body, their jet engines were screaming at horrific decibel levels from the full power settings, and the noise was unbelievable. If the tail hook did not engage an arresting cable, then the aircraft would roll over Phil's compartment at high speed with the hook scraping on the deck and the engines screaming as the plane prepared to again become airborne. All this was extremely noisy. If the recovery aboard ship was successful, then the ship's crew would release the tension on the cable, and the aircraft would taxi out of the way so the next plane could "trap" aboard, and even just "taxi power" makes a lot of noise.

Aircraft carriers launch airplanes by use of a steam catapult system. This gigantic mechanical device generates enough power to take a bomb-laden airplane, weighing anywhere from twenty thousand to fifty thousand or more pounds, from standing still on the deck, to flight speed of 140 miles per hour in less than 1.5 seconds. One might imagine how much noise comes out of such an enormous and powerful machine. Phil's bunkroom was located right next to the propulsion portion of the steam catapult.

The first time Phil experienced the noise levels in his compartment came during pre-cruise exercises, and he thought he was in hell. He could not believe that anyone could live in a place like that. By the time a couple of weeks more of pre-deployment exercises in Hawaii had been completed, with many hours of ongoing flight operations before leaving for the Western Pacific, Phil was able to sleep through the noise and had to set alarm clocks to wake himself up for work. It is amazing what the human organism can become accustomed to.

The ship spent some time in Pearl Harbor, and prior to heading west, Phil got to explore Honolulu, Waikiki Beach, and the Arizona Memorial. He even found himself, quite by accident, walking down Honolulu's infamous Hotel Street, which was off-limits to naval personnel. He got whistled at by some big, burly guys in dresses, and got out of there as soon as he realized where he was. While passing through on Hotel Street,

Phil was able to observe quite a few Navy people who were ignoring the off-limits rule. He was feeling the sadness attendant to going off to war, but the rich, heavy air of the subtropics was a new sensation for Phil, and he determined that he would like to come back to Hawaii someday under happier circumstances. The *Arizona* Memorial at Pearl Harbor is something that no American should miss. Much like the Vietnam Memorial, being there is a powerful and deeply moving experience.

12

WAR

When the *Kitty Hawk* pulled out of Pearl, they were really on their way. Kitty Hawk stopped at Subic Bay Naval Station in the Philippines, and Phil got an even heavier dose of the air that fills one's nostrils in the tropics. In the temperate and subarctic regions, where Phil had been spending his time, air is just air, and you live on it without noticing it very much. As one nears the equator, the air becomes something of which it is possible to be much more aware. It seems to have greater weight than it does in the north. It could be that someone who has been in the tropics for a lifetime is amazed to find the hairs in his nose freezing in Alaska. Some of the nasal experience for Phil in the Philippines and, later, in Hong Kong, was due to the fact that raw sewage was dumped directly into the waterways where ships berthed and where people swam and boated. Coming, as he did, from a country where sanitation is just generally accepted as necessary, this was an eye opener for Phil, and a nose closer, all by itself.

Upon leaving Subic Bay, the *Kitty Hawk* headed for Yankee Station, the code name given to the portion of the South China Sea off the coast of Vietnam where U.S. carrier operations were conducted. There were two carriers operating at a time on Yankee Station, and the arriving ship relieved the one that had been on the line for thirty days. The ship that had been on station for fifteen days began operating midnight to noon, and the newly arriving ship started flying operations from noon to midnight.

At the time Kitty Hawk arrived on station, the United States was no longer bombing in North Vietnam and most of the Navy's air effort was directed at what was called the Ho Chi Minh Trail. That was the mountainous jungle area in Laos through which the Communist North Vietnamese were supplying the weapons and materiel needed by their army and the Vietcong in the south. The North Vietnamese had very heavy concentrations of anti-aircraft artillery deployed on the peaks and ridges overlooking the network of paths, trails, and roads which, together, comprised the Ho Chi Minh Trail, so even though it was a very remote, unpopulated area, flying bombing missions over it was extremely hazardous.

On the very first day of combat operations, two of VA-222's A-6s were shot down. It was a very bad first day on the line. The pilot of one of the planes lost was the executive officer (XO) of the squadron. This was the title given to the second in command. His B/N was a young Naval Academy graduate named Mike Dexter, who was almost as junior as Phil was and who was making his first combat cruise. The crew of the other plane were Mike Collier and Dick O'Quinn.

The XO was picked up and saved by the Air Force Jolly Green helicopter rescue unit operating out of Thailand. He was seriously injured during his ejection, parachute descent, and landing after leaving the crippled aircraft, and did not return to the squadron. He was sent to the States for recovery from his injuries and came back to the war zone the next year as commanding officer of another A-6 squadron. Collier, O'Quinn, and Dexter were not recovered; they were initially listed as missing in action (MIA); and their names now appear on the Vietnam War Memorial in Washington, D.C., as killed in action. Mike Dexter was a quiet, pleasant, studious, likable young man; he was newly married and was a great loss to his country. Mike Collier was a dignified, pleasant man whom Phil did not get to know very well, but who struck him as a quality person. Dick O'Quinn was a funny, friendly guy who had been an enlisted man prior to becoming an officer and B/N. His dedication to his country and to the Navy moved him to seek this career upgrade, and he was a good man.

The squadron lost two more planes to anti-aircraft fire during the next four line periods. The crew of one of those planes was not recovered, and their names also appear on the wall. Bruce Boyle and Nick Lake were fine men, good officers, and brave warriors, and America was the lesser for their loss. The squadron had a beach party in the Philippines a day or two before New Year's, 1970, just before returning to Yankee Station for the second line period. At that party, Nick Lake, a handsome, talented, personable Naval Academy graduate and B/N on his first cruise, stated, with alcohol-enhanced bravado, that there was no way the enemy would ever get him. Three days later, he was

MIA. Phil happened to notice an item in the newspaper in 1982 that Lake's remains had been returned to the United States by the North Vietnamese. It was a poignant moment of which to take note.

A day or so after the loss of Boyle and Lake, Phil was present to hear a voice recording of a debriefing of the young Air Force rescue airman, based in Thailand, who had descended from a Jolly Green helicopter on the jungle penetrator in his attempt to recover Bruce Boyle, Nick Lake's pilot. Boyle, also an Academy grad, was either unconscious or dead when the rescue man reached him and was unable to assist in the rescuer's effort to get him secured to the jungle penetrator. The helicopter and crew were receiving very heavy small arms fire as they tried to accomplish this rescue, and when the helicopter pilot found it necessary to depart the rescue point because of the enormous volume of gunfire, Boyle had not yet been sufficiently strapped to the penetrator and fell off as the chopper gained altitude. The rescuer last saw him lying motionless on the jungle floor. It was wrenching to hear the heart-broken emotion in the young man's voice as he told of his inability to successfully recover the downed aviator. Boyle and Lake were two talented and gifted standouts who really seemed like they might be invulnerable to what can happen to regular people. War is hell.

Phil visited the Smithsonian Institute in Washington, D.C., in 1996 and found a POW/MIA bracelet on display in the war memorial section with the name of Dick O'Quinn of VA-222 on it. It was an honor for Phil Temple to serve with all of those who were lost.

Grumman A-6 "Intruder".

The crew of one A-6 lost to enemy fire was recovered uninjured and went right back to flying missions after a couple of days off. It was good to find that shoot-downs could end well for the crews. The squadron lost one A-6 to a mechanical malfunction when the engines flamed out on final approach to the ship, and the B/N of that aircraft was injured on ejection and was sent to the States to convalesce. There were also half a dozen aircraft from the F-4 fighter and A-7 attack squadrons aboard the *Kitty Hawk* lost to operational accidents, with the deaths of five flight crew resulting. The only planes from the *Kitty Hawk* lost in combat during the deployment were A-6s from VA-222. All the rest of the plane losses were from operational accidents and not from combat.

The television show "M.A.S.H." had a character in the cast who reminded Phil of Stan Parks, VA-222's operations officer. Parks was Frank Burns of "M.A.S.H." all over again. Stan was a competent aviator and a brave warrior, but he was a nit-picking detail freak whose priorities were all out of whack. The enlisted people in the squadron liked to play anonymous practical jokes on him, and he never seemed to get the idea that establishing moral authority was better than pulling rank about minuscule nonsense. He was Phil's boss, which was another reason Phil never learned to like being in the Navy.

Phil liked and respected most of the officers in the squadron, but a tradition that seemed to prevail among many if not most of them, and indeed, in the Navy at large, was one that troubled him, and one with which he never became comfortable. That tradition was one in which the wedding rings went into the personal effects locker when the ship pulled out or the planes left home base, and men became single for the duration of the cruise. Some of the officers had agreements with their wives that there were no expectations of marital fidelity during deployment, and it was widely accepted that "WestPac Widows," meaning Navy wives whose husbands were at sea in the Western Pacific, where the Vietnam theater of war was located, were fair game for men on the prowl back home. Similarly, many, if not most, of Phil's brother officers behaved as though they were not married, and he had absolute knowledge, based on observations that particular officer revealed about his intentions, of only one other officer besides Phil in the squadron who was totally faithful to his marital vows during that deployment. That is not to say that there may not have been others, or even several others, who honored their vows, but Phil could not testify as to any more than himself and one other.

Phil's marriage may have been unsatisfactory, but he was still trying to make it work, and dishonoring that commitment was not something he was able to see a way clear to doing. During the Kitty Hawk's in-port period in Hong Kong, a collection was taken among the Air Wing officers to pay for air transportation and lodging of a plane load of "round-eyed" women, mostly teachers, nurses, government employees of various assignment, and any other American or European women who would volunteer to travel for free to Hong Kong to provide "companionship" to Navy officers looking for a good time. Phil did not contribute to the fund and did not seek to pair off with any of the women who arrived, and he spent most of his time in Hong Kong alone. Phil's natural and instinctual mode of behavior includes no screwing around.

The Uniform Code of Military Justice clearly states that adultery by commissioned officers of the United States armed forces is prohibited and is a punishable offense, but such offenses are widely committed and almost never prosecuted. The only officer Phil has ever heard of who was prosecuted for adultery was a woman who was sleeping with an enlisted man. The most flagrant violator of the no-adultery rule in VA-222 was an officer who had women other than his wife following him around to meet him in all the ports where the ship called. He was also a winner of the Navy Cross for gallantry and superb performance in combat. Later in life, he achieved the rank of admiral and was a carrier group commander. It would seem that, for some people, when you are living on the edge in war and could be dead any minute, there is a different set of standards. The rule against adultery was scoffed at and is generally disregarded, except by Phil and a few others. Darla probably never gave any thought to that fact about Phil or realized the truth about him when she was judging him to be such a bad person. His greatest fault was that he was a man.

Darla caused Phil a lot of distress when she decided that she wanted to move to the Philippines while he was on deployment. Her idea was to drop out of college and move with Cole to Olongapo City, near the Subic Bay Naval Station, thereby attaining access to Phil during the two or three weeks the ship would be in the Philippines on this cruise. She would also be within traveling distance of Japan and Hong Kong when the ship pulled into port in those places. Having seen Olongapo City, with raw sewage floating in the river, with pickpockets, hustlers, whores, and lowlife characters of all sorts running around loose everywhere one looked, Phil had no wish to have to worry about the welfare of his family while he was at sea. The Navy had recently declared Olongapo temporarily off-limits to Naval personnel during a political election because marauding gangs were tearing around the city threatening voters, beating people up, and even killing a few.

Phil put his foot down about Darla moving to the Far East in a very noisy, scratchy, technically low-quality and difficult-to-accomplish phone call from Subic Bay. He said that there was no way that was going to happen. Darla was very angry at him about this, and although Phil often acceded to her wishes just to avoid her vicious anger, this one was too big. She had no idea how crazy this scheme was, and why she wanted to do it is a mystery. Phil trusted her implicitly, with respect to the matter of marital fidelity, and he assumed that she trusted him equally, but it may be that she did not, and she wanted to be nearby to keep an eye on him. She may not have believed it possible for Phil to conduct himself honorably unless she was around to provide enforcement.

Phil believed that it is easier for trustworthy people to trust others because the trustworthy ones know what is in the hearts of those who can be relied upon to keep their promises. Conversely, people who do not keep their word think that others are equally dishonest. These people therefore trust no one. Probably the best thing about Phil's marriage to Darla was that he never feared that she would step outside the marriage. The time came when he did not care what she did, but for a good number of years it was very meaningful to him to be married to someone he was sure would not dishonor her vow of fidelity.

The squadron wives organization scheduled a group excursion to meet the ship on its first call at Sasebo, Japan. Darla looked into taking that trip, but instead decided to travel on her own to Japan. She flew from Washington to Alaska and left Cole with her parents, then flew on to Japan to meet the ship. Phil and Darla had three or four days together in Japan, and Phil's recollection is that they had a nice time. They visited Hiroshima, which was a sobering experience for both of them. The city was very new and clean, having been obliterated twenty-five years earlier by the atomic bomb, then rebuilt. The people were very polite, but Phil began to be irritated by the scenes that would develop as he and Darla walked down the street anywhere in Japan. Phil's unusual height would attract the attention of the Japanese children and a shouting, laughing crowd of them would gather around him to marvel about the visiting giant. This was amusing at first, but it occurred repeatedly, and there seemed to be no regard, either among the children or their parents, who were sometimes present to witness this, for the inconvenience or the rudeness of creating a mob scene over someone's appearance. It eventually became a real nuisance, and by the time Phil left Japan, he was beginning to feel pretty hostile about how little the people seemed to care about whether or not anyone liked having them make a fuss about him. After Darla left for home, Phil bought some sound equipment, some musical instruments, and two bicycles to take back to the States with him. The ratio of the yen to the dollar was so favorable in those days that the stuff was super cheap. Phil has mostly favorable memories of Japan but no wish to ever return there.

One F-4 from the *Kitty Hawk* was lost during operations while Kitty Hawk was in the Sea of Japan, near Korea, and the pilot was killed as the aircraft failed to attain flying speed during the catapult launch. The video of the event showed the plane wobbling around as it passed the front of the ship, then the canopy being explosively jettisoned as the crew initiated ejection. The Radar Intercept Officer, or RIO, who rode behind the pilot, was seen being rocketed out of the aircraft on his ejection seat as the plane, rotating to the left, reached about 45 degrees of tilt. His parachute deployed and he survived, as the plane guard helicopter picked him up almost immediately. Those helicopters are always airborne and nearby during flight operations for just this eventuality. By the time the pilot emerged from the aircraft, it had continued its roll to a point where the pilot was propelled directly down into the water, and he was killed. He was not recovered and his body was discovered a few weeks later, washed up on the beach in South Korea. At the close of those operations, the ship returned to Sasebo for another in-port period in Japan, during which time Phil traveled to Nagasaki and Fukuoka to explore. The *Kitty Hawk* then headed back to the war.

The *Kitty Hawk's* final line period for this cruise was in the spring of 1970, at the time when President Nixon ordered renewed bombing of North Vietnam, and operations were conducted into Cambodia, as well. This was when the infamous Kent State University shooting was committed by National Guard troops against students who were demonstrating their objection to that escalation of the war. The bombing of the Ho Chi Minh Trail had become more or less routine for air wing flight personnel, despite the loss of so many A-6s. The renewal of flights into the North, where surface-to-air missiles, or SAMs, had shot down enormous numbers of American planes in prior years, had the result of creating a whole new sense of tension and apprehension among the flight crews as well as the rest of those aboard the *Kitty Hawk*.

There was a lot more detailed flight planning, order of battle review, and debriefing when bombing in the North than there had been while bombing in Laos, mostly because of the enhanced threat of SAMs, and things were even busier during the last line period than they had been up until then. They got through the period without losing any more planes, and the renewed attacks on the North ended before Kitty Hawk left Yankee Station. When the last thirty days on the line ended, the ship headed for home. That was a pretty exciting moment for Phil and for everyone else after having spent so many months living with the routine of the ship.

During that time, Phil gained what he thought of as a bit of understanding about how people in prison survive incarceration. To be where you don't want to be, to be unable to go anywhere else, and to be doing what you don't want to do could be crazy-making, but you don't go crazy. Your mind and body just transition into a sort of suspended animation, where one day blends into another and time passes without creating a lot of anxiety in you, and suddenly, it's over. You do your job, you interact with other people, you deal with the bad stuff that comes up, but all in all, it's not so awful. The human organism can adapt to a great deal. Phil did not like the Navy and was not really cut out for that kind of life, but he considers it a privilege to live in America where the people are free, and he does not begrudge his country any of the disagreeable time he spent in the service.

The voyage back to the States took two weeks, and when the ship was a day or so out of San Francisco Bay, the airplanes all flew off the ship back to their home bases, the A-6s and EA3s to NAS Moses Lake, the F-4s to NAS Miramar (near San Diego), the A-7s to NAS Lemoore (in the San Fernando Valley of California), and the RA-5s back to Georgia. As the ship entered San Francisco Bay, ship's company and the remaining Air Wing personnel amassed on the flight deck in full dress uniform and acknowledged the large numbers of people on the Golden Gate Bridge who had gathered there to welcome Kitty Hawk home. The ship and crew were hailed by fleets of sailboats and other pleasure craft that had come out just to greet them. It was June in California, and the weather was gorgeous. Fireboats and tugs from the various ports around the bay lined up and performed salutes with great discharges from their firefighting water cannons pointed straight at the sky. It was a wonderful and impressive display, and Phil could not help getting choked up about it.

The ship settled into its berth at NAS Alameda, and the squadron's ground personnel boarded the old Navy Reserve C-54 aircraft, the military version of the DC-6, for the flight back to Moses Lake. While they were en route, one of the engines caught fire; the crew extinguished the blaze with the built-in fire suppression unit, and the rest of the trip was made on three engines. When they landed at Moses Lake, Darla was there to greet the plane, having left Cole with friends in Ellensburg, and she cried as she kissed Phil hello. It was supposed to be a joyful occasion, and some people cry for joy, but this did not seem to Phil to be what was happening. Darla had not shed a tear when he left, and for her to be sad now, upon his return, seemed creepy to him. Crying was something she virtually never did, and it struck him as very strange. Perhaps it was an indication of her feelings about the "great attacker," which was what she routinely called her husband, being back in her life. They went back to Ellensburg, and Phil was reunited with Cole.

Phil's son seemed to remember him, because the child was not standoffish, as Phil had been in his father's story of his return from World War II. At the age of almost two, Phil had never seen his dad. Cole was now within a few days of his second birthday, but he had spent the first year-plus of his life with Phil. Cole was a real toddler now and was getting around very well. He had just started walking when Phil left. Cole was a cuddly child who just ate up all the hugging, squeezing, carrying around, and smooching you could put on him, so the father and son were reconnected immediately. Phil learned that after he left for overseas, Cole would have nothing to do with the men who were family friends or who were Darla's Alladist friends. After Phil returned, Cole was once again willing to be friendly to men.

Family life was resumed for the Temples, and the first important event to take place was Darla's graduation from college. She had completed the requirements for a degree in elementary education and was now documented as an educated person. Phil's Aunt Carey and Uncle Phillip came from Kalama, close to two hundred miles from Ellensburg, for the ceremony, and although they had lived in Ellensburg some years earlier while Uncle Phillip taught at the college, and therefore had other reasons to visit there, Phil took it as an expression of their regard for him and the relationship that had been had established while he lived with them. Uncle Phillip and Aunt Carey had been unable to attend Phil and Darla's wedding because both the folks had health concerns at the time, so this was their chance to make up for that. They were good and kindly people, and Phil truly appreciated the love they showed by this gesture.

Darla underwent her practice teaching with a sixth grade class while Phil was overseas and later admitted to him that she had felt an attraction to the man who was her supervising teacher. Phil certainly noticed other women, but had no intention of seeking their companionship, so, knowing that honorable and committed people, which he believed Darla to be, do not act on these attractions, was not troubled by this. He thought it was healthy that she could act appropriately when this sort of issue came up.

Phil was approached one day by a woman who was a neighbor from three or four doors down the street from the house they had rented in Ellensburg. With a mixture of pity for him, outrage at what she had witnessed, and pride at being an upstanding person, she told Phil of all the weird-looking people she saw coming to his house at all hours of the day and night to spend time with his wife while he had been gone. Phil had never met this woman and had no sense that the neighbors were even aware of the Temples' presence there, but a young Navy couple with a baby, moving into an established neighborhood, and then the husband disappearing for months while a war is on, apparently gained the attention of the neighbors. Phil was acquainted with some of the Alladists in Ellensburg, most of whom were connected in some way to the college, and many of them had adopted the long hair and thrift store clothing look of the sixties and early seventies. The visitors to the house were there for religious purposes that were honorable and were not a threat to Phil. Alladists occasionally have midnight gatherings for worship at members' homes, and Phil was sure that this was what the neighbor had seen happening. The lady clearly thought that bad stuff was going on in Darla's house with all those marginal-looking people coming around, but Phil believed that she was mistaken. Without disagreeing with her, he thanked the lady for her good intentions. Later, Darla and Phil had a good laugh about what the neighbors had thought was going on.

Darla and Phil decided that it was no longer useful for him to commute the long distance to Moses Lake every day, so he found and leased a house in Moses Lake, the lovely, little town adjacent to the Naval Air Station, and after trips to Alaska and Cheyenne to visit their parents, they moved there, and Phil's one-hundred-mile round-trip commutes were over.

Because of the respect Phil felt for what the aviators he was associated with were doing, he found himself feeling some regret about his earlier decision to relinquish the chance to undergo Navy flight training, so he joined the Navy flying club on the base and took flying lessons to see if he really liked flying as much as he would need to in order to be a pilot. Phil determined to get one hundred hours of flight time in his pilot's log book, which he thought would be enough time for him to get to know his true feelings about pursuing further goals in flight. He obtained his private pilot's license in minimum time and continued flying long enough to firmly establish that he did not like flying airplanes. He did not quite make it to one hundred hours, but did not need to.

That propeller spinning out there always seemed tentative and iffy to Phil, and he found himself constantly looking for places to land without power when the engine quit on him. That never happened, but he grew weary of the constant tension of expecting engine failure. He liked airplanes and found it fascinating and enjoyable to be around them and to regularly witness flight operations, but he never liked getting out there and taking them up. He flew Cessna 172 Skyhawks because the Cessna 150s, which made up most of the flying club fleet, were too small and cramped for the six foot, six inch Phil. His knees actually interfered with the full range of movement of the controls, and he did not think it safe to be flying under those conditions. The 172s cost more to fly, but there was enough room in them for Phil's size not to create a safety issue.

Phil had several pretty serious thrills, to use the negative sense of that word, while he was flying around central Washington. Most of those thrills had to do with bad weather and with trying to mix his Cessna with the Navy jet traffic around the Naval Air Station. The people working in the control tower at the Navy base made the effort to be accommodating to flying club aircraft, but when there were jets in the traffic pattern, fitting a slow-moving "bug smasher" airplane into the flow took some ingenuity on the part of the controller, and some pretty good performance by the flying club pilot to get it down. Phil would have to create his own holding pattern outside the jet traffic flow, and when the controllers had a momentary opening, they would give the option of a short approach over mid-field, such that Phil really had no final approach to speak of. If the flying club pilot did not take the short approach, he would just have to wait out there until the jets were done.

With a normal landing, there is enough of a straight final approach to get the aircraft stabilized in descent, lined up with the runway, and to continuously evaluate the status of the process. With those short approaches, Phil would be instructed to fly between the center of the field and the tower, and would have to be slowing, turning, descending, and planning the positioning of the airplane all at the same time, so that rolling out on final and touching down on the departure end of the off-duty runway occurred virtually simultaneously. Being able to do that as a new, low-time pilot gave Phil the sense that he probably had enough talent to do the job, but he hated the experience.

The biggest thrills had to do with the weather. Phil went out a few times when it was raining, but with visibility good enough to allow noninstrument flight. He disliked flying in the rainy weather. He went out a couple of times when there was no rain, but the ceiling and visibility were marginal for visual flight rules. He found himself surrounded by clouds and fog with almost no pilot-in-command experience and no training in instrument operations, and it scared the heck out of him. He knew stories of untrained pilots getting into the clouds, becoming disoriented, and crashing. He reached the point where he would not fly unless the weather report said, "Sky clear, visibility unlimited."

High winds and turbulence were some more conditions Phil had to deal with that he did not like. At altitude, those things are not a problem. Because Phil understood principles of flight and knew what made the plane stay airborne, he was aware that if a strong wind is present such that the plane is being blown off course, the pilot simply adjusts the heading of the aircraft to compensate for the wind and he can get where he is are going. Phil found that turbulence, if it was not too strong, was sort of fun at altitude, what with getting bounced around, jostled, and jiggled as he proceeded along. Why he was not fearful that the airplane would come apart in turbulence, even though he was always expecting the engine to quit never became clear to Phil. He never experienced severe turbulence. If he had, he might have hated that too.

Strong cross winds on final approach made it necessary to cross-control the airplane so that it is almost flying sideways as it continues heading toward the runway, and that seemed like increased risk and peril as the approach got closer and closer to the ground. Phil did not like it. Turbulence on final approach, where the airplane is getting kicked around and the pilot's view of the runway keeps changing as the bumps push the nose up, then down, then sideways, and he doesn't know which way the next one will knock him, was another lousy one for Phil. Most plane crashes happen either during or shortly after takeoff or just before or during landing. If all there was to flying was being at altitude and enjoying the wonderful view, it would be great. As it really is, Phil found that there are too many dangers to worry about for him to like it.

Even before Phil reached his objective of one hundred hours as pilot in command, it was clear to him that he was never going to learn to like dealing with all the stuff he had to deal with while flying an airplane, so he stopped forcing himself to keep going out there and enduring what he really did not want to do. He flew a few times after he got out of the Navy, but the result was the same. Being a pilot was not for him, and the decision he made in OCS was a good one.

Although Phil did not like flying, he was still fascinated by airplanes and aviation, and when he happened to see a recruiting film from the Federal Aviation Administration (FAA) entitled *How to Succeed without Really Flying*, He decided to take the FAA Controller aptitude test to see how he would do. He achieved very close to the highest score possible and filed the result for possible use when he was out of the Navy and looking for a job.

Phil was really enjoying being a dad. Little Cole was as sweet and adorable a toddler as ever toddled, and his dad carried a happy dream about having half a dozen just like him. Phil would have loved to have a houseful. Darla remembered giving birth as the worst thing she had ever been through, so it took some doing for Phil to persuade her to go through another pregnancy. She was as enchanted with little Cole as Phil was, so when he promised her that they would make sure that any doctor involved would absolutely know of and agree to her wishes for all the painkilling drugs, saddle blocks, and suffering prevention techniques known to man from the earliest possible moment in the delivery of her second child, she agreed to try for another baby. Their fertility quotient was clearly very high, because immediately upon making the decision to have another baby, they had one on the way, which they regarded as good news. As is clear from this decision, Phil was still making the adjustments necessary to living in a difficult marriage with a difficult person and was still committed to making a lifetime partnership with her. She had still not grown up, but there seemed to him to still be hope.

The most fortunate development of Phil's naval career came up a few months after the family moved to Moses Lake. VA-222 was scheduled for deployment in 1971 aboard the USS *Enterprise*, the Navy's first nuclear-powered aircraft carrier, so Phil thought he had another WestPac cruise ahead of him. But then the Navy put out the word that they intended to reduce the size of their officer corps and were seeking input from officers interested in obtaining early release from active duty. Phil jumped on that one with all the enthusiasm anyone could imagine, and after a couple of months of waiting, he got the wonderful news that his application for early release had been granted, and his date of discharge was to be in March of 1971. The Temples had just learned of the existence of little Phineas, the name Phil gave to the little unknown person growing inside Darla, and the slight downside to all this happening was that Phil would be out of work upon his release, so the pregnancy and birth could end up being uninsured unless he got a job with benefits pretty fast. Being a sharp cookie and a hard worker, Phil was confident that he could find work, so he did not worry.

Phil's last three weeks in the Navy were pretty enjoyable, and he even got to experience a tiny bit of the athletic glory that had eluded him while he was a school kid. Like most military installations, Navy Moses Lake had intramural sports. Phil enjoyed getting to play an interior line position on the VA-222 flag football team during the fall. Weighing around 230 pounds, he was able to push some people around and do the team some good. VA-222 was one of the best teams on the base, and although Phil was not a ball handler or a fast runner, he got the satisfaction of making a real contribution to a successful season. Then came basketball season, and as the tallest person in the squadron, Phil was invited to play. As has already been disclosed, Phil was, despite his height, only a mediocre basketball player. He was a good shooter and could get the ball in the basket with a good degree of skill, but he was slow, not aggressive by nature, so the battle for position under the basket did not come naturally to him, and he was a poor jumper. Even at his height, Phil could just barely stuff the ball with one hand, and spectacular slam dunks were out of the question for him.

It just so happened that there were several people in the squadron who had played college basketball. There was a third class aviation electrician's mate named Carlos Hart, who had played at a junior college in Oklahoma, a second class aviation machinist's mate named Bill Hines, who had played a year of college ball at an NCAA Division III school, a pilot named Ben Boggess, who had played at Morningside College, and Jack Brothers, Phil's counterpart in the AI section, who had played for Old Dominion College. There was a B/N named Brent Lorne, who had not played college ball but who was a good point guard and who, together with the others, made up a really good five-man intramural league team. Phil was probably the best of the substitutes, which is an indication that the team did not have great depth on the bench. VA-222 easily won the base championship, with Phil and the four or five other subs getting to play some. Phil was the backup for Hart, but was not a serious part of the reason the squadron team became champs. It was a surprise to Phil to learn that, as winners of the base league title, the team was eligible to go the naval district championship tournament, which was to be held on the other side of Puget Sound from Seattle where the Bremerton Navy Yard was located. At that time, the USS *Constellation*, a Forrestal class carrier that was a virtual twin to the *Kitty Hawk*, was in dry dock at Bremerton, and as a result, was a component of the same naval district as NAS Moses Lake. With a complement of 3,000 men in the ship's company (this was before they allowed women to go to sea in U.S. Navy ships), *Constellation* had a very large group from which to construct a team, and their team was really good.

The only game Phil remembered in that tournament was the championship game between USS *Constellation* and VA-222, which had 350 officers and men from which to build a team. He probably doesn't remember any of the other games because he most likely did not play in any of them. Somehow, with the strong starting five that VA-222 had, they got to the championship game, and it was a jim-dandy. Regulation play ended with the score tied, and with Hart, the team's best player, in foul trouble with four, and in danger of fouling out. The five-minute overtime period began with Hart in the game, but Phil was sent in to substitute for him after the first few seconds so that Hart could rest and avoid fouling out. Phil played for two or three minutes without doing anything terrible and actually handled the ball safely and grabbed a few rebounds. The score remained close. Hart came back in with a couple of minutes left in the overtime, and when the five minutes were up, the score was still tied. The second five-minute overtime began, and after a minute or so, Hart was called for his fifth foul and was out of the game. Phil had to go in for him and was not the only person in the Navy Bremerton gym at that moment who had the sense that VA-222's chances to win the tournament had just gone down by a very large factor.

The other guys on the team deserve credit for including Phil in the game, because one technique for dealing with a player who is not a regular is to just let him run around and take up space while the regulars keep the ball and the action among themselves. As play continued, Phil moved to set a pick on the high post and received the ball on a pass from the point guard. The man defending against Phil made a try for the ball and fouled him by reaching in over his shoulder. Phil went to the free throw line with a one-and-one, and sank them both. He had always been a good shooter. That put VA-222 ahead by two points. The teams exchanged missed shots and rebounds, and then, with less than one minute left in the game, and VA-222 still ahead by two points, *Constellation* put on a full-court press. As VA-222 worked the ball down the court against the press, Phil moved to the top of the key at the VA-222 end of the floor, and the man guarding him sagged off a bit to keep the pressure on the ball. Finding himself slightly open, Phil turned and broke for the basket. Bill Hines saw Phil get open and hit him with a pass as he moved toward the goal. As Phil went for the lay-up, the man guarding him threw a block into his back with all his weight in a desperate attempt to cause Phil to miss. He did not miss, and in addition, went to the free-throw line and sank the shot. VA-222 was now five points ahead, and the last few seconds of the game expired without any further scoring. Phil had made the last five points and had won the game for the team. They were naval district champions, and Phil was a hero.

There were three other officers besides Phil who were leaving VA-222 at the same time, and there was a good-bye party given at which they were honored for their service to the squadron. Darla, Cole, Phineas (Darla's little passenger), and Phil had vacated the house they had rented in Moses Lake and were spending their last night in the Navy with their friends in Ellensburg. Darla, having never become part of the Navy family, did not drive down to Moses Lake with Phil to go to the party, and Phil, also never having really belonged, put in a quick, thirty-minute appearance to be thanked for his service. He was applauded for being a basketball hero, the first and last time in his life for that ever to happen, and the skipper said that he was so proud of Phil out there performing so magnificently that it choked him up. Phil expressed his appreciation, waved to one and all, and left to drive back to Ellensburg.

The next morning, Phil made his last drive from Ellensburg and went through his check-out procedure, and as he walked to his car for the last time in the Navy, he was so overcome with joy that he jumped up and clicked his heels together, a procedure not normally easy for him as a true lead-foot, and not the usual behavior expected from a Naval officer in dress blue uniform. It was the happiest day of Phil's life, so far. He had the world at his feet, and he could not wait to get going on the exciting things that lay ahead.

13

CIVILIAN LIFE

Immediately upon Phil's officially becoming a civilian, Darla, Cole, little Phineas (growing inside), and Phil hit the road for Cheyenne. They drove through Pullman, Washington, where Phil's Aunt Carey and Uncle Phillip had moved from Kalama after Uncle Phillip retired. Their son-in-law was on the faculty at Washington State University, and they wanted to be near their daughter and grandchildren. The Temples had a nice visit with those dear folks, and it was the last time Phil saw his Uncle Phillip. He died the following year of a heart attack.

They drove through Yellowstone Park and saw the Teton Mountains along the way and arrived in Cheyenne ready to set up temporary housekeeping in Phil's parents' basement apartment, which was unoccupied at the time. A competitive test for new firefighters was scheduled by the Denver, Colorado Fire Department for April of 1971, and Phil wanted to go to Denver to take it. Phil's admiration for his father in Loren's career as a fireman and the incredible pride Phil felt as the son of a firefighter led Phil to aspire to become one of those whom he admired so much. Phil's old friend Lucca Bastelli, with whom Phil had grown up in North Cheyenne, and with whom he was still in regular contact, had finished college around the same time Phil did and was employed as a teacher by the Aurora, Colorado, School District, near Denver. Lucca had become disenchanted with teaching and was also scheduled to take the test for the Denver Fire Department. Lucca was how Phil had heard about the test, and he and Phil arranged to meet at the test location and to get together after the exam was over.

When the Saturday morning for Phil's two hour drive to Denver for the test arrived, Phil was ready to go, but when he stepped outside his parents' Cheyenne home, his '63 Chevy Nova wagon was gone. The car he had bought in Pensacola and still owned had been stolen. The ignition switch was broken, and Phil thought of his parents' neighborhood as a safe one, so he had not locked the car. Someone must have happened by, found the door unlocked, discovered that the ignition worked without a key, and took the car. The Fire Department test in Denver was not going to be postponed for Phil because of this, so he called the police to report the theft, then borrowed his folks' car and headed south to Denver to the test. It was good for Phil to see his old friend Lucca, and when they got together for lunch after completing the exam, they both felt that they had done pretty well on the test. Phil told Lucca of his distress at having his car stolen, and after a good visit, the two old friends wished one another well and went on their ways.

Phil drove the two hours back to Cheyenne, and when he arrived at home he was pleased to find his old Chevy sitting at the curb. Loren had decided to explore the neighborhood, just in case the car might not have gone too far, to look for it. He found it about three blocks away from the house, just sitting at the curb, undamaged and intact. It was an eight-year-old car, of very boring description, with nothing of interest inside, and it had just presented a target of opportunity for some kid looking for a little fun. There was no economic objective in the theft, and Phil felt pretty lucky that things turned out the way they did. He thanked his dad for the prescience he had shown in calculating what happened and finding the car, and they all celebrated Phil's sense that he had done well on the test, the results of which would be published in a few weeks.

After some more enjoyable visiting with the parents and a few opportunities for them to witness the pouting and moodiness that Darla regularly exhibited, Phil and his family were back on the road again, this time headed for Seattle, where they would deliver the Chevy to the docks for shipment to Alaska, Phil's home of record with the Navy, and then catch a plane for Fairbanks. The Navy pays, at the time of release from active duty, for return travel and shipment of household goods to the member's home of record, and in the case of Alaska, ships one car. They made it to Seattle without incident, dropped the car off, and flew to Fairbanks, where Phil was once again able to set foot on what had become his favorite place in the world, Alaska, Land of the Midnight Sun. Phil's intention now was to await the results of his Denver Fire Department test, and to move to Denver to take the job if things went well. In the meantime, he would look for work in Alaska, just in case the DFD job did not pan out.

It was at some point during this time that Darla settled the issue of where the family would end up by telling Phil that she was unwilling to live in a situation where he was at work for twenty-four hours at a time as a firefighter, leaving her alone with the children for ten nights a month. Phil was a little surprised that she was choosing to ensure that they did not go back to the Lower 48, because he believed that one reason she married him was that he might take her away from Alaska, which she disliked because of the long, cold, dark winters. Being a "glass half full and not half empty" kind of person, Phil was fine with this because staying in Alaska, the most wonderful place in the world, seemed to him to be an excellent option.

Phil learned, a few weeks later, that he had achieved the highest score of the more than six hundred applicants who took the Denver Fire Department test, but the decision had been made, and Denver would not get the chance to hire the number one guy on the list. Phil's friend Lucca also scored very near the top of the list of applicants and subsequently spent more than thirty years as a Denver fireman.

One very valuable life decision Phil was able to make as a direct result of his Navy service was not to become a police officer. Phil is a dutiful and service-oriented person, and as he contemplated possible ways to spend his working life, he began to seriously consider becoming a police officer. He wanted to serve his fellow man and help to make the world a better place, and being a policeman seemed one good way to do that. Having been to Olongapo City in the Philippines several times when the *Kitty Hawk* was in port at Subic Bay, Phil had a number of opportunities to witness people behaving at their worst. Except for observing a couple of instances of pick pocketing, he did not see any actual crimes committed, but sailors in port and the people who are there to get the sailors' money from them routinely conduct themselves in ways that it made him sad to witness. Phil found himself learning what an aching heart felt like when he had occasion to see how low people can go in the things they do when they want to have drunken fun and there are no rules.

Upon reflecting about the effect on himself of watching this stuff, Phil realized that cops get to see people at their worst all the time, and he could spend his whole life with this heartache if he chose to pursue that line of work. Spending a career that way could wreck a person's life. Somebody who is a lot tougher than Phil knew himself to be would have to take his place in the profession of policeman. It was a good thing for Phil to have realized before it was too late.

Phil applied for work as a news writer for *The Fairbanks News-Miner*, but the publisher told Phil that he would have to get some experience in journalism before being hired. Phil talked to the owner of *The Knik Arm Courier*, who told him that he could work for the paper for free, to give the editor a chance to evaluate Phil's ability, but that Phil would not be hired for pay. Phil was offered a job driving a cement mixer for a ready mix company, but he needed more than $3 per hour and needed medical benefits, so turned it down. Phil thought he had a pretty good shot at a sales position with Motorola Communications in Fairbanks, which would have paid well, had good benefits, and looked like a career-type job, but they made him no offer. He could have gone to Woolworth's and demanded the job he had before he went in the service, but did not care for retail store work, so did not do that.

After a couple of weeks of looking for work, Phil finally connected with a veterans' representative with the Alaska Department of Labor Job Service, and when Phil told the man that he was interested in air traffic control, that he had taken the aptitude test for controller and had received a very high grade, the representative got all excited. It just so happened that the Federal Aviation Administration was interviewing that week to fill several controller trainee positions. The man got Phil an interview appointment with the FAA Regional Office in Fairbanks, and before long, Phil was hired as a flight service station specialist trainee. As such, he faced several months of training at the FAA Academy in Oklahoma City, followed by assignment to one of the twenty or so flight service stations, mostly located in very remote, rural locations around Alaska. Phil was ecstatic. He was going to get to live with his family in the boondocks of Alaska, where he could breathe the clean air of this far north paradise and provide a service that could save lives and make life safer for many private and professional pilots in Alaska. It seemed to Phil that God was smiling on him and his family.

Darla was only lukewarm about living in who-knows-what remote location in Alaska, but she did not complain out loud. Phil wondered if maybe she felt some guilt about dictating to him about the firefighting job, so refrained from doing it again to avoid seeing herself as a control freak. Phil was so happy about getting this terrific opportunity that he did not question her about her silence.

14

A NEW JOB, A NEW BABY
AND A NEW HOUSE

Phil went on duty with the FAA in July of 1971 and was scheduled to report for training in Oklahoma City after a couple of weeks of orientation in Alaska. During that period, he was able to observe flight service operations at several locations around Alaska and actually got to fly on a logistics trip to Anchorage and Naknek with Jack Jeffords, the famed, old-time, pioneer Alaskan aviator who was then the chief pilot for the FAA's Alaska Region. At the King Salmon/Naknek airport, they off-loaded some cars and refrigerators from the C-123 cargo plane that Jack flew to haul supplies for the agency all around the state. When they left Naknek, Jack took Phil on a flight-seeing trip around Lake Iliamna and Mount Iliamna. Jack pointed out a crash site where a Wien Airlines F-27 had crashed a few years earlier on an island near the edge of the lake, and another site where an Air Force C-54 had hit the mountain many years earlier. It was a sobering look at some of the sad parts of Alaska's aviation history, but it was also quite a thrill for Phil to meet and hear some stories from one of the legends of flying in the north. Jack Jeffords retired not long after Phil hired in with the FAA and died a few years later. Phil remembers him with friendship for the kindness he showed him as a rookie with the agency.

Just before Phil was to depart for Oklahoma City, the Air Traffic division called him into the head office to discuss a possible change of plans.

They had apparently examined his test results and his personal history and determined that Phil was a pretty smart fellow, so they offered him a chance to train to work as a radar air traffic controller instead of a flight service specialist. It meant a higher pay grade much sooner and a much more difficult and stressful job, so Phil experienced some hesitation about giving up the chance to work in remote Alaska, but with Darla's support, for she was not that hot about the idea of moving to the bush, Phil agreed to the change. The new baby had been going to be born in Oklahoma, but the time spent in Oklahoma was now going to be much shorter than it would have been, with most of the training for radar controller taking place on the job. The baby was now going to arrive after they got back to Fairbanks. Phil was assigned to the Radar Approach Control Facility, or RAPCON, at Eielson Air Force Base, near Fairbanks, and would learn to be a radar approach controller. He was now more excited than ever about his new career.

The Temple family spent eight weeks in Oklahoma City in July and August, which was as hot and muggy as Pensacola had been, but Phil liked Oklahoma better because he liked his circumstances better. He was embarking on an important and responsible career, and was proud and happy to have this good fortune come his way. Loren and Molly came down to Oklahoma City from Cheyenne to visit, and Phil's old friend Keith Strong and his wife Marcy, whom he had met while he was living with Phil back in college, stopped by as they vacationed from their jobs as schoolteachers in Washington State. The time flew by, Phil completed the classroom training preparing him for the on-the-job training (OJT) he was to do at the RAPCON, and soon the Temples were back in Alaska.

One evening, Phil and Darla were visiting at the Oldburg's house and little Cole was sitting sideways on Phil's knee as he sat on the couch. Phil was not holding his son firmly, and the boy made an unexpected lurching movement that caught his dad off guard. Cole's feet swung under Phil's leg and the boy pitched forward, striking his face on the corner of a coffee table located in front of the couch. Cole sustained under his eye a fearful bashing wound that bled profusely as he cried heart-wrenchingly in his pain and surprise.

The same doctor who was providing Darla's prenatal care and who would later deliver the baby was called, and he met Phil and Darla at his office. The doctor said Cole's injury was serious and that it would require some stitches. The job fell to Phil to hold Cole while the doctor stabbed the needle containing the anesthetic into the child's face and while the wound got sewed up with a big, curved needle. Phil immobilized Cole by holding the child's hands and arms against his little sides as Phil knelt at the foot of the examining table where Cole was lying. By putting some of his weight on Cole's legs and torso so that he could not struggle, Phil held little Cole motionless while the doctor did his work. The terrified shrieks that emanated from Phil's precious little son, as the little guy saw and felt the doctor shoving those implements into his face, pierced Phil's soul. The horror and fear that the helpless child expressed as he screamed, sobbed, begged, and shrieked burned into Phil's heart as nothing else in the world had ever done, and Phil would have given anything to take his child's place and spare the poor little guy the experience. When it was over, it wasn't long until Cole seemed to have forgotten what he just went through. It took Phil much longer to get over what had happened to his son, and he will never forget the agony of listening to his little one screaming like that.

About the time that Phil was just getting going full-steam in his OJT, Darla reached, without any of the complications of her first pregnancy, the end of her nine months of carrying little Phineas. One evening in October, she began showing signs of labor, and the doctor was called. The family physician they were seeing had been very clearly briefed about Darla's extreme fear of childbirth after what she had gone through with Cole, and the doctor had repeatedly assured her that nothing like what she feared so much would happen. The way things worked out, however, was much different from what had been assured.

Phil and Darla got to the hospital sometime after midnight, and the staff reported to the doctor at home that the birth was still some hours away, so he stayed at home. By 5 or 6 AM, Darla's labor had progressed to the point that the doctor decided he needed to come in to the hospital. No serious drugs had yet been administered, and Darla was becoming increasingly angry and fearful that the promises made to her might not be kept. When the doctor arrived, things were advancing quickly, without problems or complications, and before much of anything else could be done, Phil and Darla had themselves a baby, born without any anesthesia.

Sylvia Mavis Temple, named Sylvia after Darla's beloved college roommate, was, at least from Phil's perspective, the most perfect baby anyone on earth had ever seen. Phil had wanted to name the baby something else, but it was very important to Darla to bestow the name of her dear friend, so Phil relented. After seeing what a perfect baby they had created, whatever the child ended up being called made little difference. Perfection is perfection, no matter the name.

By this time, little Cole had become such a sweet and adorable toddler that the unfortunate way he looked when he was born had been pretty much forgotten. But when comparing this baby to the recollection of how Cole had looked, the contrast was quite amazing. Darla was nobody's beauty, and Phil had spent his life believing that he was funny looking and unattractive, so for them to have this incredibly beautiful baby, especially after the way the first one looked, was hard to believe. But there she was, and it was true. Sylvia weighed almost nine and one half pounds and was lively and healthy. She bore that look of fierce innocence seen only in newborns, which seems to speak from the eyes the wisdom of the ages, miraculously revealed through the utterly blank slate of this tiny person's mind and soul, upon which the writing of a new life story has just begun. Laying eyes on her for the first time was a priceless moment that lives on in Phil's heart forever.

Darla was so angry at the doctor for having failed to keep his promise to spare her any suffering during this birth that it almost seemed to Phil that she had not noticed what a spectacularly lovely baby she had created. Even years later, Darla was still angry about what the doctor had allowed to happen. That was one serious grudge. The doctor's explanation was that the labor and birth went so well and so easily, totally free of any complications, that there was no real need for additional anesthesia. By the time Darla reminded him of his promise to her, it was too late. That excuse did nothing to soften Darla's feelings, and she probably still hates that doctor to this day. The wonder of this new miracle person eventually won out, and it was not long before Darla's rage at the doctor ceased to be her primary concern. Both Phil and Darla were happily stunned by the incredible beauty of this child.

At the time of Sylvia's birth, Phil was in his second month of his new job as an approach control trainee at the Eielson RAPCON. He was already beginning to feel the stress of the OJT he was undergoing in that complicated profession, and his stress level elevated a bit more when Darla became quite insistent that he take time off work to stay at home and help her with the new baby and the three-year-old. Phil and Darla had rented an apartment in the Moosehorn area, a half hour south of Fairbanks, and were within a mile of the Oldburgs' house. Darla's mother had expressed her willingness to help with the children as Darla recuperated from the delivery and while Phil was at work, and he thought that it would be reasonable to accept her offer while he was in the midst of beginning his new career. Phil had the sense that asking for extended time off in his first few weeks as a new trainee would put him in a bad light and start him off at a disadvantage in the training process. He therefore declined to ask for the time off.

If Darla's mother had not been nearby and willing to help, Phil would have tried to do what Darla wanted. Having no desire to incur a grudge against himself from Darla, and she had shown a remarkable ability to carry a grudge, Phil faced a tough decision in this instance, but decide he did, and the anger directed at him by Darla for this, while not as fierce as her fury at the doctor for his screw-up, was nonetheless very deeply held by Darla, and she never forgot it. They got the baby home, Phil kept going to work, Mom Oldburg was a great help, and things settled out all right. Beautiful Sylvia had started her life as their little golden girl.

Within a couple of months after Sylvia's birth, Phil was fully involved in the hard work of learning his new job. Darla had recuperated from the pregnancy and birth, and she had found out about and looked into a federal government program that would enable the family to become first-time home buyers. The program was called FHA 235 and was designed to give young folks like these a way to get into their own homes with no money down and with a government subsidy to help with the payments. Eligibility for continuation of the subsidy was reviewed annually and the assistance was changed or eliminated depending upon what changes had taken place in the buyer's income.

Phil had hired in at the pay-grade of GS-7, with the prospect of being at the GS-9 level in six months and GS-11 six months after that. GS-7 pay was low enough for the Temples to qualify for the program, and they had done nothing to harm their credit rating, so they got the loan. Darla had checked into this program in secret, and even had a surprise appointment to look at a house, which they ended up buying. Phil was somewhat perturbed that she had done all this without telling him, but the result ended up being favorable to the family, so he did not make trouble. The man had enough on his mind at work.

The house they bought was a new, 1,000-square-foot, rectangular, three-bedroom bungalow in the Spruance area south of Fairbanks. The house was very unspectacular, but pretty exciting from the standpoint of being their first home, so they were happy to get it. The deal was sealed before Christmas, and they moved in during January of 1972. Colton was three and a half and Sylvia was three months old. It was a very good time for the little family. Phil quickly determined that this would be his last house in Alaska without a garage. This was in the days before Alaska began becoming a warmer and warmer place, and temperatures of fifty or sixty or seventy degrees below zero still occurred occasionally in Fairbanks, and twenty or thirty or forty below happened regularly. Phil was spending more time than he wanted to out in the cold and snow working on that nine-year-old Chevy, getting it to run in the depth of winter. Phil was a fair back-yard mechanic in the days before emission controls and computerized cars, so they were able to stay on the road. Phil bought a four-wheel-drive 1964 International Scout later that winter, so then he had to lie around in the snow keeping two old-timers running.

By the time The Temples moved into their new house, Phil had completed the fundamentals of the on-the-job training and was well-started in working the radar and separating airplanes from each other. The work was exciting, fun, challenging, and a little scary, and Phil found himself looking forward to going to work each day for more of it. When actually working live traffic, the trainee is plugged into the control position and gives directions by radio to the aircraft on the radar. At the same time, a checked-out controller is plugged into an override jack on the same control position so that he or she can supersede the radio transmission of the trainee if the need to quickly correct a mistake becomes necessary. After a session on the radar, a debriefing takes place with discussion of mistakes and successes, advice and instruction are given, and a training report is completed. Initially, a trainee works light traffic, just to become familiar with how things go, and then, as comfort levels, proficiency, and skill levels advance, busier and more complex traffic situations are undertaken. This is how it has been done for as long as radar air traffic control has been used, and it is an effective system, but it has its drawbacks.

As time progresses, a trainee advances from working just light traffic to more difficult and complex traffic situations, where he is challenged and exposed to all that is involved in doing the really tough job he signed on for. As time went on and the challenges became greater, the debriefings became, for Phil, repetitive exercises in negative feedback. The trainee has to sit there and listen to recap after recap of all his screw-ups. If he is getting some portion of it right, that is minimally noted and left behind. The debriefing then moves to the areas where improvement is needed, so it starts to feel like harping, persecution, and punishment. This is where Phil came to believe that his upbringing, when he had one chance to get it right before his father began yelling and cursing, was harming him as an adult. Phil thought that he was reacting more unhappily to this negative approach to training than was appropriate or necessary, but couldn't help it, and felt that his dad was to blame for that.

Air traffic control is a complex and deeply analytical skill that requires many hours of practice. After hundreds and thousands of times of doing what it takes to safely and efficiently manage the movement and separation of aircraft with a minimum of delay or trouble, the trainee eventually masters the skill and is then checked out and goes it on his own. For someone who has the internal imperative to get everything right on the first try, this constant criticism and disapproval is hard to take. As the months went on, Phil's skill grew and his ability to do the job was improving and increasing, but he was finding himself feeling more and more dread because of the constant negativity.

For the second time in his life, Phil found himself dealing with depression. The experience was similar to what had happened to him back in Indoc at Navy OCS, in that he was under the power of people who tore into him eagerly and with gusto every working day, and he could say or do nothing about it. It was tough. By the time Phil had been in training for half a year, he was fighting to keep his head above water emotionally. Depression is a powerful force that imparts a gray and sickening feeling to the whole world, and it's impossible to fight it off. Everything is harder, more discouraging, less manageable, no fun, and hopeless. It is an awful way to live.

It was becoming apparent to Phil that a race was in progress between, on the one hand, his learning the job and becoming proficient enough to get checked out, and on the other, his sinking into this awful depression and disappearing in his own misery. One or the other of these possibilities would prevail, and in a state of depression, it's impossible to be optimistic about which it would be. The attitude among controllers is "Sink or swim," or "If you can't take the heat, get out of the kitchen," or "I went through it and made it, now it's your turn." Very little, or nothing, in the way of sympathy or understanding is available, and one suffers alone.

Phil developed an attitude of determination to tough it out and keep trying, keep learning, and not to let them beat him down. The only thing that saved him was a continuing awareness that he was learning and getting better, despite all the negativity. After seven or eight months of training, of which about three were spent in the gray hell of depression, Phil requested that someone different be assigned as his trainer. The foundation of skill in the job had been laid, and when Phil began to work with someone who believed in positive reinforcement, things really took a terrific turn for the better. Phil could feel himself really mastering the skills needed to do the job. It was a great time. Phil received final check-out at Fairbanks Approach Control just shy of one year following his first day there. He was one happy dude, and the depression was gone.

Phil worked at Fairbanks Approach Control as a checked-out controller for several more years, almost all of which were the most satisfying, exciting, fun, and wonderful years of his working life. It took another year after his initial certification for him to gain the experience, confidence, and skill sufficient for him to really be good at the job. There is a saying that getting checked out did not mean that you were good, it just meant that you had been deemed safe enough to really start learning how to do it. After about another year, when Phil had become really good at it, he came to absolutely love the job and to love to go to work. It was a special time in his life, it was a privilege for Phil to have a job he loved so much, and it is still fun for him to reflect on and remember those sweet days.

Fairbanks Approach Control is a place where a controller gets substantial exposure to all kinds of air traffic, although it is far from being the busiest radar facility in the system. Fairbanks is known as the Air Crossroads of the World, and there are large numbers of international air carriers that operate all kinds of commercial jets through there. Fairbanks is now one of the busiest air freight locations in the world, although UPS and FedEx were just getting started when Phil was there. A major Air Force base operates high-performance jet fighters, air search and rescue squadrons, air transport and logistics flights, helicopters, and miscellaneous military flights at Fairbanks. There is a large Army base and an Alaska Air National Guard base there, as well, which contribute significant numbers of flights to the traffic load. A very busy general aviation airport and a busy seaplane base are at Fairbanks, all of which make for a varied and interesting mix with which controllers must contend. At any given hour, a radar controller at Fairbanks can be as busy as any controller at any high-density facility in the country, and the skill and competence level required can be as great as anywhere.

Phil discovered the wonderful sense of accomplishment and strength that came when he was "in the groove" on a control position, and what a great experience that is. It is that way because the controller's mind is clicking like a fine machine, he smoothly assesses and handles every new situation that comes up, and it seems that there is nothing they can throw at him that he can't solve. Because of his efforts and ability, the arriving blips on the scope evolve from an explosion of planes coming from everywhere to a beautiful line of properly separated and sequenced targets, safely carrying thousands of people and mega-tons of freight to their destinations, and it's a great feeling. Separating those arrivals from the explosive bustle of commercial rush hour launches and military scrambles similarly requires alertness, wide attention spans, decisiveness, speed of action, depth of knowledge of the rules governing what the controller is doing, and the courage to face all that and take care of business. It was a great job; Phil really loved it.

15

DECISION TIME

An event of the very greatest consequence in Phil's marriage to Darla took place during this space of time encompassing all the new changes such as the birth of their new baby, their acquisition of a new home, and Phil's beginning his new career. By the time Sylvia had reached six or seven months of age, it had become clear that Darla was retaining much of the weight she had gained during the pregnancy. After the birth of Colton, even though she was compulsive about eating cookies and other sweets, Darla had slowly returned to a weight not much above where she had been before, and the subject had not come up. This time, she stayed heavy, and while it was not an issue of earth-shaking importance to Phil, it did matter. He had been married to this person for six years by this time, and he knew from bitter experience that bringing up sensitive subjects for discussion with her was perilous, to say the least. Phil hesitated about the undertaking because, although it was not a topic they had discussed before, it seemed to him that it could be risky territory. Phil's optimistic and hopeful nature caused hope to spring eternal, and after considerable thought about what might or might not happen, he decided to give it a try. It was unwise and he should have known better, but try he did.

Taking great pains, as usual, to speak to her in reasonable, polite, understated, considerate language and tone of voice, young Phil took the plunge. He had gotten no more than a sentence or two out of his mouth, asking what her thoughts might be concerning the weight not yet lost, when she exploded with the most vicious, hate-filled, crazy, and savage tirade he had ever witnessed from her. It was incredible and life changing. She screamed and shrieked at him that he was the most vile, loathsome, valueless, shallow, disgusting, horrible beast who ever fouled the planet, and she could not believe what a hateful, evil, unforgivable, and sickening monster she had gotten herself tied up with. She went on for a couple of minutes despite Phil's protestations that this was the craziest and the worst she had ever been. This was the first time she used the word *divorce* in her abuse of him. It would not be the last. This episode is one of the ugliest memories of Phil's entire life, and the memory of it remains very painful for him. He cleared out and went somewhere to contemplate his situation, and as he left, the realization came to him, at long, long last, that there was no hope for this marriage. There was no limit to the insults this person was capable of delivering, and it was clear the time had come for some major decision-making on the part of Phil Temple.

He knew, finally and beyond doubt, that his honeymoon oath to himself and to God, made with a pure heart and genuine commitment, was impossible for him to fulfill in the face of the rage and hatred that existed in the heart of poor Darla. Her utter inability to recognize the good in her peaceful and gentle man and her complete enjoyment of the tantrums she hurled at him were just too much for anyone to be required to endure. Another might be able to keep on taking the punishment without giving up and still try to make it work, but Phil had reached the end of his rope, and could not do it anymore. He believed that he was worthy of God's forgiveness because he had made it this far and had made a valiant try. It did not matter that he was the most peaceful, kindly disposed, least troublesome person he knew of. He was living with someone with whom all the good intentions, hopeful spirit, peaceful demeanor, and nonconfrontational style anyone could muster on this earth were to no avail. Nobody, not even he, could make a go of it with this person, so on that day, at that moment, in that place, Phil gave up. The question then became, "What about the children?"

It did not take Phil long to realize that his devotion to and love for his children were greater than his need to completely escape from this impossible marriage. He was convinced that God put him on the earth to do good and to fulfill his duties. There is no greater duty than that of doing the best you can do for the children you have created. Leaving them to grow up in a fatherless home was therefore not something Phil could consider doing. He made the determination to stay and to simply keep out of Darla's way as much as possible, thereby minimizing her opportunities to go crazy on him. Phil's mission, and a sacred one it was, was to provide his children with a loving, competent, and present father, and to raise them with all the love and strength he could deliver. With Sylvia barely half a year old, Phil established the intention to stay in the home until she graduated from high school seventeen years hence, and on that day, he would be gone.

Phil's perplexity was how to continue dealing with Darla. As time went on, there continued to be other occasions when, despite his efforts to steer clear, she went off on him instead of having a sane, respectful conversation. His attitude and his mantra became, "Rave on, you crazy, hate-monster bitch. The day is coming when you will have spoken to me like that for the last time. When these children are raised, I will be gone and you can choke on all the poison you have spewed at me for all these years. Damn your hateful soul." Phil never said anything like that out loud, although he was sorely tempted. He knew if he did, that would mean divorce, which she brought up more and more, and he was determined to stay with his kids.

On one occasion, Phil said to Darla that she had gotten increasingly comfortable throwing the threat of divorce at him, but that she had better look out, because on the day she heard that word coming out of his mouth, that was the day it was no longer talk, but would happen.

Phil finally and completely dropped out of the relationship emotionally and focused on enjoying his life as much as possible despite being trapped with this person who was incapable of a mature connection with a man. Once Phil completed controller training, it evolved that he had a great job that he was good at and which he loved. He had the two most precious and wonderful little children a man could hope for, and that was where he focused all the love he had stored up inside, but was prevented from experiencing with their mother. Phil knew that the best thing a parent can do for his children is to truly love their other parent, but that had become out of the question. All he could do was to love them with all his heart and treat their mom with civility and respect, which was more than she was willing to give him. Phil loved his kids all the more and hoped that it would be sufficient.

Life was fun and interesting in a great many ways, and despite Phil's awful marriage, he pursued life enthusiastically. He returned to sports as an enjoyable diversion and looked forward to softball and basketball games with his friends and coworkers. He even got selected as most valuable player on the FAA Controller softball team one year, having, over time, become a better all-around player. He became a fitness buff and spent time after work at the health club, as well as exercising at home. He became a household projects guy, hiring a contractor to jack the little bungalow up in the air and installing walls on the foundation, then setting the building back down, now as a two-story house. The contractor was then done, and Phil spent more than two years doing the rest, working toward finishing that project. He had a pretty good program in effect for fulfilling his commitment to raising his children and having a happy life in spite of Darla. Phil was lonely some of the time, but he kept busy, loved the children with all the power in him, and he was fine. A strong sense of mission can make difficult circumstances a lot better.

16

BUILDING A NEW WAY TO LIVE

One day, not long after Phil made the determination about giving up on Darla, he came home from work and found that she had a meeting going on with a number of the Alladists of Fairbanks. Phil had become acquainted with some of the Alladists in the Moosehorn area while the family lived out there, but now that they had moved into Spruance, most of these people were new to Phil. One of the attendees was a tall, willowy woman with dark hair and big, blue eyes, and Phil found himself very impressed with her appearance. She was over six feet tall and projected a merry and wholesome aura, and at the same time, she was very sensuous, and Phil was quite taken with her. He had always appreciated women, but was never a ladies' man, a womanizer, or someone inclined to cat around. In the life he was living, it is not surprising that he should have found himself noticing an attractive woman.

Her name was Silver Hampton, and she was to become, some years later, an important figure in Phil's life. Silver and Darla became close friends, and Silver became a good friend of Phil's, as well. Darla and Phil got to know Silver's husband, who was a strange and quirky sort of guy who was likable enough if he wasn't allowed to get too close. This was because he had a way of tricking people into sharing personal things with him, after which he would turn the confidential information back on them with mildly malicious humor and make unkind fun of them. Phil saw him do this with others, and he managed to do it to Phil a time or two, but Phil kept him at arm's length after that and learned to deal with him in a way that kept things safe. Meanwhile, the man's wife was a good friend to both Darla and Phil. They both found Silver to be an intelligent, thoughtful, pleasant-natured person of good character, whom Phil observed was also very sexy, in a clean-cut, wholesome sort of way. Before long, Silver and Darla were each other's best friends. Silver and her husband had two children about the age of the Temples', and the two families were to see a lot of each other over the next several years.

Life was moving on, and those years were mostly happy ones for Phil, despite Darla. He adored his children and took a lot of pleasure in just being with them. He loved his job and had lots of interesting things going on in his off-work time. Phil was active in the Professional Air Traffic Controllers Organization, known as PATCO, and spent a year as president of the local chapter. He lived in the most exciting and wonderful place in the world, Alaska, and his focus on his mission for the children made the unbearable marriage bearable.

Phil stayed out of Darla's way as much as he could while still spending a lot of time at home, and he was fairly successful in keeping it peaceful around there much of the time. Darla still had her episodes of severe PMDD and her other times of being hateful to Phil, but she did not get ugly with him very often when the children were present and could witness it, and they grew up in what appeared to them to be a pretty peaceful environment. Phil takes most of the credit for that, although until the children were grown, Phil never had any reason to believe that Darla had anything but their best interest at heart. That is why Phil believes that Darla had the intention of restricting her hatefulness toward him to times when the children did not see it.

If Darla had been as peaceful a person as Phil was, there would never have been any trouble around there at all, and Phil is the reason it was kept to a minimum. His wish was to address problems and get things solved, but he disliked fighting, and any reasonable person who does not want strife never has to have it from him, although he became fairly well-known in a few circles as someone who does not take crap. That was because he got so much of it in his marriage he became even more intolerant of crap from other people than he otherwise would have been.

Darla resumed the pattern of being extremely tired much of the time, having to spend a lot of time in bed, being sick a lot, and generally showing signs that she was depressed and did not like a lot of things about her life. She worked at being a good mother to the children, although she was more inclined to hit them, punish them, and be hard on them than Phil was. She busily pursued her participation in the Alladist religion, and those two things provided her with some measure of fulfillment. But so much sick time, tired time, and having-to-rest time were clear indicators to Phil of her unhappiness and of her finding the marriage unsatisfying. She never realized that her own conduct was the reason her husband discontinued trying to share an emotional life with her. Phil never mistreated her, never showed her disrespect, never spent time criticizing her, never (until much, much later) cheated on her, never spent money foolishly, and never did anything else to harm her or the children. Phil was almost completely, except for the part about giving up on trying to love his wife, what most people would think of as the ideal husband, and one whom he thought any sane woman would feel lucky to have. He spent time in those days wishing he could have had a wife who recognized who he was and who appreciated him. Darla never did.

Phil had a good role model in his dad, as far as devoted and dutiful husbands and fathers go, and Phil went him one better by leaving out the temperamental and angry control stuff. Phil recognized Darla's dissatisfaction, but he was having a fairly happy life without and in spite of her, and figured that she could do the same if she wanted to. Whatever role Phil might have been able to play in adding to her emotional satisfaction, she had driven away, and he decided that she deserved whatever punishment she was inflicting on herself. It came to pass that Phil stopped caring whether she was happy or not, and stopped caring what she did as long as it was not damaging to him or the children. As a result, Phil was able to realize a measure of freedom, even though he was, by his own choice, stuck. He wished that he could count on her to be civil, but could not.

Not once in all the years those two lived in the same house as husband and wife did Darla ever apologize for the awful things she said to Phil, nor did she ever take any of them back. This makes it seem that she believed the horrible stuff of which she accused him. The strange part is that anyone would choose to continue living with someone she thought of in that way made even stranger by the fact that none of it was even remotely close to being true.

Concerning the differences in style between Darla and Phil in their dealings with the children, Phil did not need to be hard on them or punish them very much at all, and this held true from the time they were very small until they were grown. There was an understanding between their dad and them that there were certain kinds of behavior that he found unacceptable, and they did not violate that understanding. Exactly what it was about Phil that caused this to be true is not entirely clear, except that Phil had a very clear notion in his own mind of how properly raised children should behave, and he was able, without undue harshness and with very little corporal punishment, to convey that sense to them and to get their compliance with the standard. They were not afraid of their father, but they knew better than to cross him.

Except for the pure joy Phil got out of just loving and cherishing his children through the years, the most satisfying thing for him about being their dad was how nice, sweet, good, and well-behaved they were. They made Phil proud because they were such good kids, both when they were with him and when they were not. They went out and met the world politely, respectfully, and with courage, and showed themselves to be nice people from a home where they were loved and guided by both parents.

The two of them gave their mother a notably harder time at different stages growing up than they gave Phil—they did not give him a hard time at all—and the conflicts they had with their mother, mostly after she and Phil split up, were not anything that would ever have gone on with Phil. There was one period of time when Phil was guilty of uncharacteristic and some unnecessary harshness with Cole. That will be addressed later in this story, but for the most part, Phil's children's lives growing up with him as their dad were very good ones.

17

PLAYER

One day Phil came home from work about 3:30 PM to find Glen Mackie, the president of the local Spiritual Assembly of the Alladist faith at Phil's house with a guitar, a bottle of non-alcoholic wine, and a book of love songs for guitar players. It's amusing to see how naïve Phil was about things like that. He later learned that this guy had been going around seducing and having sex with young wives and other young women who were members of that religion in Fairbanks, and that he was responsible for at least one divorce among the membership because of his predatory ways.

On the day Phil found Mackie at Phil's house, Mackie had miscalculated about the oddball hours that Phil worked, for it had not been expected that Phil would show up while Mackie was there. Old Glen rebounded pretty quickly by offering to take Darla and Phil out to a nice steak dinner, which they accepted, and it never crossed Phil's mind until much later that Mackie was there to screw Darla. Phil thought that someone elected to a high position in the local branch of the religion, and who was recognized by the faithful as a deeply spiritual and pure-hearted man, was above suspicion in such matters. Mackie was separated from his wife at the time, and Phil heard that she described him as "a low-life son-of-a-bitch and a terrible human being." This was puzzling to Phil, because how could someone be that and also be elected as a holy leader? Even after witnessing what Phil had seen while he was in the Navy, he still wasn't catching on that scoundrels and vow-breakers can be found anywhere. This spiritual leader was very good-looking and a superior athlete, and had a sparkling sense of humor. He was probably used to getting all the chicks he wanted, and adopting a religion that his wife chose just gave him a new source of ways to get laid.

A few months after Phil found this guy with Darla, Phil stopped by the home of their friends Silver and her husband to pick up a post-hole digger Phil had arranged to borrow from them. As Phil got out of his truck, he noticed the same guy's car parked at the curb. Glen and Silver were the only ones there, and it took them several minutes to answer the door while Phil went around back to the tool shed and looked for the digger. When Phil came back to the front, the two of them emerged from the house. Silver looked pretty disheveled and was in sort of a panic of embarrassment from being caught like this. Old Glen just smirked. As a person who almost never had sex, Phil was not able to clearly conceptualize what had been going on in there when he knocked on the door, but in later years, he was better able to figure out what was happening. An occasion came when Phil asked Silver about the episode, and she firmly denied that anything major took place, but there are reasonable doubts about that. This was the time when the light finally dawned on Phil what Glen had been doing at Phil's house.

Darla confessed to Phil that she found this man attractive, but Phil's response was the same as it had been when she told him about the supervising teacher she liked. Phil saw plenty of attractive people but made no play for any of them, and he figured it was the same for Darla. From this experience, Phil gained a little bit of wisdom about sexual players and where they might be found.

18

LSAT

The time came when Phil found himself getting a little restless about what kind of challenges he was going to undertake in his life and to think about looking for ways to do greater things. Phil's favorite courses in college had been Constitutional law, and he received some of his best grades there. Phil learned that his mind worked well at comprehending and retaining points of law and legal precedents, and Con law was one of the few courses that interested him so much that he would actually stay up late studying just because it fascinated him.

There was a controller at work who had been accepted to a law school in the Puget Sound area and who had obtained a transfer to an FAA approach control facility near where he was going to go to school. Because of Phil's college experience, law school had always been in the back of his mind as a possibility, and this example of a married man who figured out a way to attend school while continuing to make a good living for his family made this seem like a possible course of action for Phil, so he signed up and took the Law School Aptitude Test, or LSAT.

The test was given on a Saturday morning on the University of Alaska Fairbanks campus, and Phil showed up for it, ready to go. Phil had not studied for it, but had always been good at tests and didn't think he needed to. The testing began, and it seemed pretty much like others Phil had conquered before. He has something of a talent for language, and there was a section in the LSAT devoted to just that, language aptitude. They set up a make-believe language with its own vocabulary and grammatical rules, and then asked questions to test the candidate's grasp of linguistic structure, rules, and application. Phil understood the objective of the exercise right away and proceeded to zip through that part of the test until he had a stomach-flopping realization. He had been too cocky in his estimate of how well he could do in the exercise and had made a mistake in his application of the grammar established for the make-believe language, and the error compounded itself the further through the process he went. Ordinarily, it would have been a simple matter to just backtrack to the point where Phil first misapplied the recurring rule, make the corrections, and continue with the test. The problem was that each section of the test was time limited, and there was not sufficient time remaining for him to correct all the compounded errors and finish the section. When the time was up, he had not been able to fully correct the errors and make it to the end of the section.

Had it not been for that little misadventure, Phil's grade would have been higher than the mark he received. As it was, Phil scored in the ninety-second percentile of all persons taking the test nationwide, and he was both pleased and disappointed, knowing that he could have done even better. This reaction reminded Phil of his father's habit of reliving some of his best golf games by saying, "If I had only used a six iron instead of a seven on that hole," or "Just one putt better on two holes and I would have ... etc." For Phil it was, "I could have had a really fabulous score except for that one screw-up."

Despite Phil's regrets about his goof-up on the test, he guessed that a score as good as that would probably give him a pretty good shot at getting accepted by a law school somewhere. He investigated several schools and had some encouraging correspondence from several. Phil began looking into FAA facilities located near where those law schools were and was part way along a track leading to the complicated life of a combination law student/air controller. He was also doing some deeply reflective thinking about all this, and ultimately, came to recognize that his primary mission in life, that of raising his two children as a very present and involved father, would suffer greatly were he to undertake such a busy life-style. Phil's dreams of having many children had gone away when it became obvious that there was no way the marriage to Darla could ever be successful, but the two children Phil did have deserved the best he could do for them, and going to law school while working would not be in their best interest, so Phil dropped the idea. Someone involved in such an ambitious course of action would have to be in a marriage that was a partnership, and Phil's situation with Darla was not even close. Phil's search for greater challenges now boiled down to finding something in air traffic work.

19

PILGRIMAGE

In the spring of 1976, Darla disclosed to Phil that she had been stashing pocket change for a long time and had saved enough money to pay for a religious pilgrimage to Iraq and Israel. The Alladist faith required believers to make a religious journey to the home country of the faith and to Israel, where the founding prophet lived for an extended period. This is similar to the Muslim requirement that believers perform a pilgrimage, known as the Hadj, to the cradle of the faith in Saudi Arabia. Darla was determined to comply with the Alladist requirement and broke the news to Phil as she was in the process of making the travel arrangements. She also suggested to him that he travel overseas and meet her in Europe after she was done with her pilgrimage to the holy places.

In retrospect, it seems that her tactics were pretty clever, because her secretly squirreling money away for herself to travel would have been harder for Phil to swallow than her saving money for them both to travel. Phil was disturbed to find that she had done this, but she figured right. He decided that since he had not noticed the missing money, because he paid the bills and ran the checkbook, then she must not have been doing it to a degree that was harmful to the family's finances. Phil did not begrudge religious believers the chance to travel pursuant to their beliefs, and he did not mind the chance to do some traveling himself. As a certified FAA controller, Phil had access to no-cost travel within the United States in what was called the "Familiarization Program." Controllers could arrange to ride in the cockpits of U.S. airliners to observe the interaction between flight crews and controllers from the point of view of the pilots. It was a good training tool that promoted understanding and cooperation between participants in the air traffic system, and it also made it possible for controllers to go places at no cost. This made the cost of Darla's plan lower, and she had stashed enough cash to do her pilgrimage as well as to include something in the deal for Phil so he would be less likely to object.

In light of all the accusations Darla repeatedly hurled at Phil about being an attacker and an unfeeling beast, it is interesting that she knew him to be calm enough, peaceful enough, and gullible enough to fall for her deception. She knew that he was just a big teddy bear, and all the hate she threw at him was just how she was.

The trip took place in May of 1976. Darla, her friend Silver, and two other Alaskan Alladists departed for Iraq and Israel, and a week or ten days later, Phil left the kids with their grandparents at Moosehorn and flew out as an observer on a Northwest Airlines jet for Chicago on his way to Brussels, Belgium, via New York City. On his way, Phil had his first experience with a woman coming on to him so strongly that even he could not miss it.

The woman was a Northwest flight attendant who was based in Chicago and who expressed curiosity about Phil, a non-uniformed civilian riding with the flight crew in the cockpit. She told Phil she was lonely because her husband was away and said that she would be all by herself in Chicago. She asked where Phil was headed and what his plans were. She made it so clear that she had free time in Chicago and was looking for a way to fill it that even the inexperienced Phil could get what she was driving at. After the landing, the woman spent some time straightening Phil's tie and twisting his tie pin while she looked up at him sort of sidewise, letting him see how pretty she was. Phil had no clue as to how to deal with something like this, and had to catch a connecting plane to New York, so he rather abruptly left her standing by the cockpit door as he hurried off the plane. Phil had very little background that included being made to feel that a woman found him attractive, so this episode stuck in his mind.

Phil caught his connection to New York and spent a night in a hotel there, where he had another unusual adventure. In the middle of the night, someone who had a key to Phil's room came walking in, waking him from a dead sleep. The intruder looked very surprised when Phil came roaring up out of bed, shouting and threatening. The stranger took off running down the hall and Phil continued shouting at him until he disappeared.

The management offered no explanation about how this could happen, so after they promised to see to it that nothing similar happened that night, Phil went back to sleep and arose in the morning and continued his trip.

Phil arrived in Brussels as a paying passenger on a Pan Am Boeing 747 and spent three days in that charming city exploring, sight-seeing, sampling the food, and getting the feel of the place. He liked Brussels and his experience there reminded him a bit of his Navy days in Hong Kong, Japan, and the Philippines, when he did a lot of solitary exploring. After three days there, Phil took a two-day, one-night trip to Menorca, Spain, a beautiful island in the Mediterranean Sea where Darla had learned of an attractive villa that was for sale at a very low price. Why they would have been thinking of buying a villa in Spain is an odd question, but it was Darla's idea. At least it gave Phil something interesting to do while waiting for Darla to come back from her pilgrimage.

Phil rented a tiny Fiat automobile and drove it around the island until he found the villa. It was a very pretty building, but it appeared to have been severely neglected and would have been a major project for anyone to undertake. Phil had gained some knowledge and experience with basic construction in his jobs and in his house expansion in Fairbanks, and was able to see that it would have been foolish for them to get involved in such an enterprise. He was glad the place was an impossibility. Darla could not argue about this one.

Phil got back to Brussels the day before Darla, Silver, and the others were due in from Tel Aviv, so he had one more evening on his own in Brussels. He went to a movie and had dinner out. That was the extent of his last night alone in a European capital. There were plenty of prostitutes around, but just as he had done in Asia, he passed on the opportunity. As lonely as Phil's life was, that was still not something he would do.

When the El Al Boeing 707 containing the four Alaska pilgrims landed at Brussels, it was escorted by armed soldiers in armored vehicles to a location far from the main terminal in an isolated corner of the airfield. The passengers disembarked into a bus and were escorted by some of the same soldiers to the terminal, while the remainder of the military unit stood guard around the airplane. In light of all the terrorist activities going on in the world at the time, Phil was glad to see this kind of care taken. El Al, the Israeli state airline, was certainly a prime target.

The women entered the terminal from the bus with the other passengers; they appeared excited and enervated, as one might expect after their having spent two weeks visiting what they thought of as the world's most holy places, then being the center of this kind of military attention. They got through customs and the group went to the hotel. Darla was exhausted and just wanted to rest. As she slept, Phil visited with the other women and learned that Darla had been an absolute dynamo of activity, energy, and enthusiasm during the whole trip to Iraq and Israel. They said that she had seemed to be on fire with the spirit of the faith, and they were amazed to see how much pep, zest, and energy she possessed. As she lay collapsed in the hotel room, Phil's thought was that just seeing him in the airport was enough to take all the fire out of her in about two seconds.

The five Alaskans did some more sight-seeing around Brussels the next day, had a picnic in a beautiful park near a sort of in-the-city farm, and had a nice time. They visited with a pleasant and kindly Iraqi Alladist family who took them to another park where all had fun rowing boats around the lake. They turned in early that evening in preparation for an early start the next day. When morning came, they went to the airport and said good-bye to the other two women as they started back to Alaska, and then Darla, Silver, and Phil boarded a Sabena Airlines plane to Amsterdam. Phil was surprised to find Silver going with him and Darla on the trip because he had not been involved in the planning and had thought it would be just the two of them. Given the way things were, The Temples probably enjoyed the trip more with Silver along.

In Amsterdam, they visited Anne Frank House and some art museums (of which there were many), and had a chance to see prostitutes standing in shop windows encouraging passersby to come in and give them a try. Phil, Darla and Silver had not had the intention to get into the red light district, but somehow they were there, and as they walked along one of the streets, a pair of young men observed that the three of them were one man short of two couples and offered, in good English, to provide one of the women with Phil some professional company. Which woman would take the offer would be up to the customers. The potential clients agreed that this was offensive, and Phil told the men to leave them alone. Oddly enough, the young men persisted in their effort to make some sort of a sale, and Phil had to threaten to beat their asses to get them to break off from this disagreeable assault on the evening's enjoyment.

Phil's difficult life with Darla was one in which, if he wanted to be around to raise his children, Phil had to endure the crap that Darla put out on a continuing basis, but he had no such restrictions on taking crap from other people. Phil developed something of a pattern of shutting down drunks, scammers, and assorted other obnoxious people in public places, first with requests, then demands, then with threats, and there could be a few chapters on the kinds of adventures he has had on airplanes, in restaurants, in parking lots, in shopping malls, and at work, closing out bad behavior by nasty people. He is big enough that no one has ever tried to fight him, although a few of those problem folks were bigger than Phil. Maybe it is because there have always been witnesses and because Phil has always held the virtuous position that he has never had to carry out a threat to cram somebody's head up his ass or stomp him. Phil's sense of manhood was probably damaged by not shutting Darla down as she deserved, but then he would have been arranging visits with his children as an absentee father, so he didn't do it. By performing the public service of correcting ugly public behavior, Phil was reestablishing what he was losing at home.

In Amsterdam, the three travelers stayed in a boarding house where the stairs were so steep and narrow that it was hazardous just to use them. Land is at such a premium in the small country of Holland, where they have reclaimed a lot of land from the sea by building dikes to make the country bigger, that they build the houses tall and narrow to take up less space. In Holland, Phil saw more men at or near his height of six feet, six inches, and more women at or near Silver's height of six feet, one inch, than he has ever seen anywhere else.

The night they stayed in Amsterdam, all of them had very tired feet from walking, and Silver exercised her knowledge of reflexology by giving Darla and Phil each foot massages. It was very soothing and relaxing, and Phil was even gladder that they had brought Silver along. The next day, they flew via KLM Royal Dutch Airlines to Paris, where they cruised the Seine River and went up in the Eiffel Tower. Darla and Silver went to the Louvre museum while Phil went to the Cathedral of Notre Dame. They ate dinner at a fancy restaurant on the Champs Elysees, and there Phil had the first experience in his life of paying the equivalent of $100 for a meal. They spent time under the Arch de Triomphe and enjoyed the ambiance of Paris, although what is said about snotty Parisians is true. All three had a fun time, but Phil actually remembered more about Silver's being there than he did about being there with Darla.

A day or two later, they boarded Air France to London and checked into a nice hotel within walking distance of Piccadilly Circus. Phil went by himself to the British Museum, which is another place where one would have to spend many days, or even weeks, to take it all in. The British plunder of the world gained them a huge number of fascinating items of interest to display in their museum. While Phil was viewing many of those wonders, Darla and Silver went to the burial site near London of one of the leading figures of the Alladist religion, who died suddenly and unexpectedly in the 1950s while visiting England. Another of the Alladist rules is that a person who has died must be buried no more than one hour's travel from the place of death. For that reason, the man's final resting place is in Britain, even though he had not lived there and was not of English descent.

That evening, Darla was again utterly exhausted and wanted to stay in the hotel and sleep, so around midnight Silver and Phil decided to take a walk to nearby Piccadilly Circus. They bought some food in a restaurant there and had some time to just visit together. Silver told Phil of an Iraqi man who, along with the four Alaskan women and a large group of other Alladists from everywhere, had been on the pilgrimage. This man and Darla seemed to have developed a very strong connection, such that others on the trip noticed the chemistry between them. This man, along with others in the group, had been astonished at what a ball of fire Darla had proven to be in her zeal to make the most of her religious travels, and he made a strong effort to bond with her. Silver had no sense that there was anything intentionally romantic going on between Darla and her Iraqi friend, but something was definitely happening there.

Something was also happening between Silver and Phil, but just as with Darla and her friend, they were proper and well-behaved and nothing was said about it. Darla as a ball of fire was a thing of the past now that she was back with Phil and too tired and depressed to be so energetic any more. The three traveled back to Alaska, and Phil went back to work.

20

CALIFORNIA

As time went on in Phil's air control job, he had gotten better at it and began to receive recognition for the high quality of his work. This experience was somewhat analogous to Phil to his younger days when he learned how fast he could throw a baseball. When Phil was pushing airplanes hot and heavy at work, it was amazing to him how clearly the traffic picture continued to run in his head, how cleanly and effectively the answers came to him in resolving potential problems, and how swift and decisive he was in the judgments he had to make in keeping the traffic flowing smoothly. It was almost as if some greater power were running his mind as Phil worked the traffic. It reminded Phil of the awe he felt when it seemed that something beyond his ken was making that baseball fly so fast, it almost sizzled when he threw it. Phil found it to be a beautiful thing and a gift to be able to make his living with that feeling.

FAA control facilities fill their openings for controllers through a bidding system. A particular facility that needs controllers advertises the openings in publications and messages that are seen in other FAA locations. Controllers who want to work somewhere else can submit applications to the sites seeking applicants. Air traffic control is a profession that is notorious for how punishing it is to those who do it for a living. Within the ranks of active controllers there is knowledge about which places are the toughest, the most difficult, the most punishing, the busiest, and the best ones to stay away from because they are man eaters (or woman eaters) and the worst places to work.

Chicago's O'Hare Approach Control had the reputation during the 1970s of being the toughest of the tough and the worst of the worst. It may still hold that distinction, . Other U.S. terminal facilities with reputations that discouraged a lot of people from applying for transfer to them were New York, Los Angeles, and Bay Approach, which was located at the Oakland, California, airport and which managed air traffic for the entire San Francisco Bay Area. Once a controller is selected for transfer to another facility, when he or she shows up there, he or she reverts to trainee status, albeit at a much higher pay grade than a new hire. The person remains a trainee subject to the same training system in effect throughout the agency. This is described in the earlier discussion of the experience Phil had learning the job at Fairbanks.

Phil had gotten so full of the pure joy of being extremely good at his job, and had been experiencing the serious itch of wanting to do greater things. He decided to bid on openings at Chicago and Bay Approach and was selected by both. The scuttlebutt was that those places are so tough and are known to be so desperate for controllers because most people know better than to want to go to them, that they will take anybody who bids, and the washout rates at both are extreme. Phil was riding so high on the good feelings that accrued to him in this job that he chose to ignore the conventional wisdom that was available from all quarters, and he had forgotten about the suffering he did while in training the first time. Phil figured that as good as he had gotten at this job, there was no stopping him. He accepted the offer from Bay Approach, and the Temple family prepared to move to sunny California.

A controller at Fairbanks Approach played an important role in Phil's selection for the California job, and Phil was grateful to the man for the support given. The guy was an Alaskan who had initially hired into the FAA some years earlier, and had spent just about all of his career at San Francisco Bay Approach Control until he came to Alaska. He had been at Bay Approach for about ten years and had been very successful there. He was a very good controller in one of the most rugged places in the system to work. He came to a point in his life where he had taken the punishment for long enough, and the agency's policy was to allow anyone who had taken that kind of pounding for that long to transfer anywhere he wanted to go in the system when he had finally had too much. This controller had chosen Alaska, where he grew up, and he had been at Fairbanks Approach for a year or two when Phil came to the point of wanting to move on. This controller had had sufficient opportunity to observe Phil's work and made the judgment that Phil was good enough to make the grade at Bay Approach, so he recommended Phil for selection. He was very careful to caution Phil vigorously that it was no picnic down there, but Phil was eager for the challenge and took the job.

When the Temples departed for California, Cole was eight years old and Sylvia was almost five. Darla did not like car trips and the FAA would ship only one car to the new job at agency expense, so it was decided that Cole and Phil would drive down the Alaska Highway. Darla and Sylvia flew to Seattle to meet Cole and Phil after the drive down from Alaska, during which Cole expressed to Phil his fears of being caught out in the wilderness with no one to rescue them. This was nine years after Phil's first trip on the Alaska Highway with Darla, during which Cole got his start in life, and it was still a very long haul. There remained over a thousand miles of gravel road to negotiate through the Yukon Territory and British Columbia, although there had been a couple of hundred miles of pavement added since Phil's first trip. Even now in 2010, after twenty-five one-way trips since 1967 over that road which is all paved now, Phil recalls that journey with Cole as the toughest one of them all.

This trip took place in August, they hit a lot of rain along the way, and the road was in very poor condition. Phil had the only flat tire he has ever had on the Alaska Highway on that trip, and he had to change the tire in pouring rain and ankle-deep mud. That was when Cole was the most afraid. Phil got the spare tire on the car and had to replace the ruined tire at one of the most remote places on the whole trip, at Muncho Lake, B.C., for about double the price he would have had to pay in Fairbanks. Cole was very relieved to find that they had survived. This was when he was still of the age where dads can be looked on as heroes. Phil was happy to be able to ease the boy's worries by taking care of business under very difficult circumstances.

They did some boating along the way and watched on Canadian television as Gerald Ford was nominated by the Republicans to be his party's candidate for president against Governor Jimmy Carter of Georgia. By that time, they had reached the paved-road part of Canada, and Cole's fears of the wilderness had abated. Tough trip or not, Phil enjoyed that journey very much. Cole was still a sweet and agreeable traveling companion.

Darla and Sylvia arrived in Seattle by air on the same day Cole and Phil got there in their station wagon. The family collected their Toyota pickup from the Tacoma docks, where it had been unloaded after its ocean trip down from Alaska. Phil and Pop Oldburg had made a tow bar out of pipe and angle iron and left it in the pickup for use in towing it when it arrived in Washington. The day after the Temples' arrival in Seattle, they visited their friends the Strong family and then headed for California.

They took their time, visiting Phil's old friend Fritz Marsden and his family in Oregon as well as some relatives of both Phil and Darla. They had an enjoyable passage through Oregon, and when they arrived in the San Francisco Bay Area, they found their way to Alameda, just across the slough from the Oakland Airport, where the Oakland/San Francisco Bay Terminal Radar Approach Control (TRACON) was located. Alameda was where the Kitty Hawk had been home ported and where Phil underwent fleet orientation training before reporting to VA-222. The Temples settled into the motel that would be their home for the next four months, Phil reported for duty at the TRACON, and they started looking for a house to buy.

The radar system in use at the TRACON was more advanced than that to which Phil was accustomed in Fairbanks, so he got some orientation on that. He checked out in the support data positions and then began training on control positions. There were ten separate radar sectors covering the San Francisco Bay Area and all its airports. San Francisco, Oakland, and San Jose International Airports were the primary air carrier facilities, with NAS Alameda and NAS Moffat providing military traffic, and there were a bunch of general aviation airports all over the area.

Phil began working radar on the two departure areas for San Fran and Oakland. The eastern half of this pair of regional divisions was reputed to be the busiest radar sector in the world. . The airplanes really pumped out of there. Separation of aircraft is easier to secure and maintain in departure sectors because the planes begin with no speed and are climbing and accelerating as one follows another outbound. It got pretty tricky sometimes when fast movers were coming out of Oakland or Alameda, because they climb right up underneath and into the departure path of the planes leaving San Fran. But even then the targets, as radar returns of the airplanes are called, are gaining speed and altitude, and it just requires attentiveness and possibly a little directional control or altitude restriction to keep them separated until they are either lined up or headed in different directions and are handed off to the Air Route Traffic Control Center. That is the control facility that keeps the planes separated and passes them on to other FAA centers as they proceed, at altitude, to their destinations across the country. The big deal on the North Bay departure radar was the sheer volume of traffic.

Phil was doing well in his progress on SFO/OAK departures sector and checked out in a reasonable amount of time; He was happy to be doing fine in this new environment. He noticed that his level of tiredness, which had been pretty extreme even in Fairbanks after a hot and heavy day shift, was even more extreme just because of the virtually nonstop traffic. There were some days when he actually had to balance himself with a hand on the wall to keep from wobbling as he walked out of the TRACON, but he was managing the job and was feeling that the career move was proving to be a good one for him.

Phil and Darla hunted all over the East Bay area for a house to buy. They searched in all the towns from Livermore to Alameda, and from Vallejo to Milpitas, and found some acceptable possibilities in Dublin, San Ramon, Concord, and Pleasanton. They finally chose an agreeable, three-bedroom, two-bath Spanish-style house that they could afford in Vallejo, the place where Phil's parents first met. This place had an in-ground pool, which was pretty exciting, and they decided to buy it. This was in 1976, when the cost of housing in Alaska was still higher than it was in California. They were therefore able to get a nicer house in Vallejo than they had sold in Fairbanks, and the nicer house was not much more money. A house across the street from the one the Temples had in Vallejo, quite similar to theirs in size and style, sold in 2006 for $750,000. That is almost triple what the Fairbanks house would have sold for in the same year, although the value of both has declined following the national economic debacle of 2008/2009. So, comparative property values between Alaska and California have changed dramatically, almost unbelievably since the seventies.

The children had started the school year in Alameda, and Phil and Darla proceeded to enroll them in the school system in Vallejo, Sylvia in kindergarten and Cole in third grade. Phil liked the new neighborhood and liked California, but he was still marking time in the marriage, and the job began to take a serious toll on him.

After checking out on the busiest radar sector in the world, Phil was happy and optimistic, but was now really finding out how incredibly punishing the job could be. He checked out on the general aviation sectors in the East Bay and the feeder positions, which transitioned high-speed commercial and military traffic, received from Oakland Center, into the final approach courses at San Fran, San Jose, and Oakland, but those turned out to be real meat-grinders and became more punishing and destructive to Phil than he was able to endure.

The most enjoyable, and as well the most challenging, part of the job for Phil in Alaska was when a big rush of military recoveries occurred at the same time as a stream of civilian commercial jets, and he felt like he was jumping through his own butt taking care of business, but it was fun and exciting. Phil thought that the hardest part of work at Bay Approach would be more of the same. He found out different.

What made the most difference between Phil's success in the minor leagues of Alaska and his ultimate inability to take the punishment in the big leagues at Bay Approach was that there was nowhere to go with problems or mistakes. In Alaska, the approach control facility had fewer sectors and jurisdiction over all the airspace below twenty-one thousand feet for sixty miles around the city, with no airports of any consequence outside the immediate vicinity of the city. What that meant to a controller who was so busy that he had airplanes coming out of his eyeballs was that no matter how bad it got, there was enough airspace to take care of any eventuality by simply turning planes to where there was empty space. As long as the aircraft were kept inside the one large sector and were assigned altitudes high enough to keep them from hitting the mountains, any situation could be resolved and then the controller could get back to the planes he had turned and reestablish them back in the flow. Just having the knowledge that such an option could always save him gave the controller the confidence at heart to be able to deal with anything that might happen. As a result, the need to make emergency use of all the extra airspace almost never arose, and a controller could take care of business.

At Bay Approach, the arrival sectors were confined and surrounded by other sectors into which encroachment could not be done unless prior coordination was achieved with the controller of the sector you needed to violate. If both controllers involved were "going down the pipe" or "down the tube" or "losing the picture," which were some of the terms applied to the condition of being overwhelmed by the volume and complexity of a traffic situation, the two could not accomplish the precise, careful, and effective coordination that was required. When that happened, safety was compromised and separation was not assured. This happened so many times, not just to Phil but to every controller in the place, that it was scary. The difference between working in Alaska when it was super busy and Bay

Approach, which was always super busy, was like the difference between performing on the high trapeze with a net and performing up there with no net. There was no place to go with a separation problem that was not resolving, and the controller just had to eat it. Phil never figured out how to eat airplanes full of people.

Phil never actually had a situation come up in which things got the worst they could possibly be, but he saw innumerable times when they came close. There were so many times in the normal operation of that place when assured separation was lost and there was nothing that could be done about it that Phil began to carry the feeling around that there were always going to be times when things would become impossible and there was no answer to the problem. A developing sense of danger and doom became a constant part of his existence. His work was satisfactory as far as anyone could see, but as time went on, Phil became increasingly convinced that there was not a way to do the job in that setting that was safe enough to suit him.

This was a state of affairs to which Phil could find no satisfactory solution, no way out, no hope, and that opened the door for his old enemy, depression, to settle in on him once again. Two times before when depression had taken hold of him, either the situation passed and he recovered, or toughed it out because he could see a solution, eventually overcame the problem, and as a result, beat the depression. In this circumstance, Phil had concluded that the job could not be done safely, at least not safely enough to suit him. Having to face that impossibility made the punishing character of the job even more punishing. On top of that, the available solution of just quitting would have meant impoverishment and ruin, and that just made the depression worse. After two years of working in California, Phil reached a point where he was experiencing utterly incapacitating panic attacks while working traffic. He had become unsafe to do the job. Phil could no longer do the work. He came to the point of being repeatedly overcome with spells of anxiety and disabling terror attacks even when working the simplest traffic situations, and represented a genuine threat to air safety in that condition.

What finally happened, which directly led to Phil's decision to get help with the agony he was going through at work, did not occur at work. It happened at home and involved young Cole, who in the last few months of Phil's time in the FAA had begun to suffer the effects of what was happening to his dad. As Phil became more and more depressed and increasingly concerned about what would happen to the family if he could not continue in the job, there were times when Phil was directing anger and frustration at Cole in ways that were unfair and frightening to the boy. There was a time at the dinner table when Cole made a joke that Phil found inappropriate and Phil slapped Cole's face, something he had never done before, and never did again after that. Cole was becoming a source of irritation to Phil in much the way Phil had been a source of irritation to Loren and a target for anger when Phil was a child. Phil was aware that this was taking place between himself and Cole, and it troubled Phil, because he had determined years earlier that he did not want to cause his son to be fearful of him the way Phil was of his dad. Phil was firm in his intention to spare Cole this fate, but in his depleted condition he was having trouble following that intention. Phil continued to steer clear of Darla as he had done for years, and things were more or less the same between the two of them. She already disliked Phil enough just because he was male and alive.

One day, while Phil and Cole were in the back yard, the boy did something that displeased his dad and Phil reacted. . Whatever Cole did, it put Phil in a towering rage. Phil took an iron grip on Cole's arm as an incredible fury over the boy's behavior engulfed the dad, and Phil was almost overcome with the powerful compulsion to do something violent and terrible to his son.   As the image of what was taking place at that moment blossomed like a photograph in Phil's mind, Phil was horrified and appalled by what he was doing and cried out, "My God, what is happening to me? This child has done nothing to deserve this. Dear God, please help me!"

Phil released poor Cole and ran in the house, grabbed the phone book and the phone, and desperately called the psychiatric department of the family's HMO in Walnut Creek. He begged them for help and they got him in promptly. Phil took sick leave from work and very shortly began undergoing evaluation with a therapist. Phil was a wreck, but found some solace in the knowledge that he was doing the right thing for his son. The psychiatrist notified the FAA that it was necessary for Phil to discontinue working air traffic. The agency had Phil evaluated by their own mental health medical staff, who determined that he was suffering from extreme clinical depression and severe anxiety disorder. Phil was medically disqualified from his job, and his career in air traffic control was over. He experienced recurring dreams about some of the frightening stuff he saw in that job for a very long time after he left, and remained vulnerable to panic attacks in highly stressful situations for years.

21

MORE CHANGE

After eight years in ATC, part of Phil's personal identity had become that of an air controller, with all the authority, power, and courage that the job requires. To find that he could no longer be what he had been proved incredibly painful and hard to deal with. This was the most difficult period of Phil's life, and after all those years of being true to his marriage vows to a woman who despised men, and him in particular, Phil finally stepped outside his marriage. A woman at work who was a controller trainee had begun flirting with him, and the resolve that he had always maintained not to be a player slipped. Phil was miserable, depressed, and lonely, and responded to the woman.

Darla had developed the practice of taking the children to visit her parents in New Mexico, where they had moved after Pop Oldburg was forced by reasons of health to retire. Darla began taking the kids for a few days at a time and driving away to be with her folks, leaving Phil to work and spend time alone. Even though Phil liked and cared about Darla's mother, he intensely disliked being around the Oldburgs because of the way the old man treated his wife and the foster kids, and Phil avoided spending any more time in that house than he had to. The foster children were now nearly grown and had decided to move to New Mexico with the folks. Darla was clearly looking for ways to get away from the marriage that so completely failed to meet her expectations of happiness, and Phil did not care what she did as long as she left him some peace. The best chance for Phil to have peace was when Darla was gone.

The woman at work was blonde, attractive, clearly on the make, and neglected by her husband. She told Phil that he was a beautiful man, something he had not heard from a woman before, and so, on one occasion while Darla and the kids were in New Mexico, Phil and the blond got together. It was Phil's first time ever as a violator of his vows, and it was not a good feeling for him. Phil was carrying enough anger and resentment at Darla for her destruction of the marriage that he felt that she deserved whatever disloyalty came at her, and that took him a good portion of the way toward overcoming his misgivings about behaving this way. It was, "Take that, you hateful bitch." It felt good for Phil to have an attractive woman be nice to him and want to be with him, so he got through the experience with minimal emotional damage. After a couple of meetings, the woman was transferred to Oakland Center, and Phil never saw her again. The probability is that the woman's husband didn't change his ways and she probably didn't change hers, so it's unlikely that they made it as a couple.

Phil had now broken the ice on stepping out, so it was going to remain an option for him in his awful marriage, but it was never something that he thought was right or a good thing to do. Phil didn't have to lie about anything on this one, because Darla could not have cared less what he was doing, and anything like what really happened probably never crossed her mind. Phil was so uncomfortable with it all that it would never be a frequent occurrence, but on rare occasions for the next few years, this sort of thing was finally in his repertoire and did take place.

As Phil's FAA career was showing signs of trouble, he and Darla began discussing the idea of Darla's seeking an advanced academic degree. Phil's motivation for this thinking was that having determined that he would leave Darla as soon as the younger child was out of high school; he wanted Darla to be able to earn a decent living after he was gone. She most likely had the same idea and had no trouble getting a loan from her parents to enter a master's degree program in marriage and family counseling at a private university in Lafayette, California, not far from Vallejo. By the time Phil left the FAA, Darla had completed most of the requirements for her degree, and she actually received it after Phil had been enrolled at a community college for a few months. It's ironic that the person who had destroyed that marriage with her fits of hatefulness was now a credentialed repairer of other people's marriages.

A few months before Phil left the FAA, there was an occasion when he was able to hitch a trip to Alaska on a Reeve Aleutian Airways Lockheed Electra, which had been receiving some major maintenance work at the Oakland Airport. Phil had observed the plane, which he knew from his days in Alaska, as it was being worked on, and he contacted the crew to ask if he could catch a ride to Alaska with them when the work was done. They said that they would be happy to have him come along, and when Phil arrived in Alaska, he got together with some old friends from the Eielson RAPCON. Phil also contacted his old friend Silver, learned that, quite by coincidence, her husband and kids were away, and the two of them spent an evening together.

They dined out, went for a long walk, and had a nice time. They reminisced about their time in Europe three years earlier and spoke about the years they had known each other. One thing led to another and eventually, Phil got a little carried away. He disclosed to Silver that he was in love with her, and that he had been so for quite a long time. She said that she felt the same way about him, and the stage was set for them to consummate their love. Silver was Phil's for the taking. Uppermost in his heart, however, was his duty to his children, and to start an illicit sexual affair with someone who had been Darla's best friend was more than he could see his way clear to doing. There was certainly no love left for Darla, he didn't even like her, but dealing that kind of punishment to her, even though she deserved it, was too much for Phil, so he declined the chance to make love to the person he loved. Phil and Silver parted with barely a touch. Phil experienced enormous physical frustration, but believed that he had done the right thing. He departed Alaska and headed back to California and his children feeling more lonely than ever, but virtuous, having chosen for his children over himself.

A surprising thing began to happen to Phil as he pursued his career in the air traffic business and as he advanced in age into his thirties. He began to receive complimentary remarks about his appearance from a variety of people, and several times it was suggested to him that he should be a model or a movie star. With the exception noted above of the blond coworker, virtually all of the people who made such observations about Phil's appearance were not women on the make, but rather acquaintances or strangers of both sexes who were just making conversation. Phil was flattered by these comments, but did not take them seriously because, as a child, he had been teased about the way he looked and had grown up thinking he was unattractive and funny looking. Now, as he started to become accustomed to these kinds of compliments, Phil came to his own conclusion that the primary change in himself, which might have led to people starting to perceive him as good-looking, was that as he became successful in his job, his sense of self-confidence grew. It is often said that one of the most attractive features a person can display is just that, self-confidence. The job of air traffic control, for one to succeed at it, requires a sense that one has the intelligence, the decisiveness, the quickness of mind, the courage, and the personal power to properly and safely manage radar screens full of airplanes and the many lives of those aboard them, without hesitation and without fear. Phil went around for several years loving that job and loving how well he could do it, and figured that people could see that and liked what they saw. He had always been unusually tall and had always had a full head of hair, and nobody seemed to notice, so the job must have been the difference.

Finding himself no longer able to do the job he loved was a devastating experience, but Phil never lost the sense of pride that he had been good at what he did. He now needed to find a way to make a living. Having received all those suggestions that he be in the movies or be a model took on some significance now that Phil was out of work, so he began to investigate the possibilities of earning some money by looking good. He contacted several agencies, had some photos taken, and managed to get some work as a photographer's model for clothing ads, as a runway model for a couple of fashion shows, as an extra in a motion picture being shot in San Francisco, and as a participant in a couple of television ads. The experience was enough to be a bit of fun, to give Phil some insight into what went on behind the scenes in "show business," and to make clear to him that he was not really interested in being a part of that world. To compete effectively in the world of beauty and talent, one has to have a strong sense of being beautiful, or talented, or both. Phil had no real sense of either. He believed that he was smart and capable, but being around so many people who were in love with how they looked; who were determined to get all the "face time," camera time, screen time, and exposure that they could get; and who would do anything to get the exposure, was obnoxious to Phil and he wanted nothing to do with that whole scene.

People should be valued for the content of their character and for what is good and honorable about them, not for how good-looking they are or how well they can play a part. The way the extras were treated and the way some of them treated each other on that movie set was so hateful and disgusting to Phil that when he was told that he would be needed for two more days of shooting, he declined to come back. Phil required that respectful treatment and decent behavior be present for him to remain. They were not, so he quit.

Phil was not star quality enough at doing that stuff to get more than just the few jobs mentioned, and he needed either to be discovered and start making money right away, or to move on to something else where he could make a living. One agent offered to refer him to a maker of pornographic movies, but he declined. Phil thought of his children and what the effect on them might be of having a porno actor for a father. He would not have wanted to be the son of a porno figure and would not do that to his children. So much for the career in show business.

22

SPAIN

Phil had always had a knack for language and a good ear for accents and pronunciation. He figured out that some people said *nuclear* ("new-klee-er") and that some said *nucular* ("new-kyoo-ler"), and which one was correct ("new-klee-er"), when he was eight years old, and he was good at mimicking foreign accents of English. He reasoned that this could be an area of good potential for him and so decided to enroll in school and learn some foreign languages, which seemed like it could be an advantage should he enter the arena of international commerce. Phil already had a degree in business and economics, so this seemed a sensible route to take. He enrolled in a community college in Pleasant Hill, near Vallejo, signed up for GI Bill benefits, for which he was eligible because of his military service, and began classes. California offered free college education to everyone, so the GI Bill money could all go to supporting the family. Darla got a job driving a delivery vehicle for a pharmacy near where they lived and, later on, found part-time work in a family counseling clinic. Phil became Mr. Mom as well as Joe College, taking care of the children while Darla worked.

He enrolled in Spanish, French, and German classes, began learning them all at the same time, and started looking for ways to get maximum exposure to the languages he was learning. The idea occurred to Phil that the best way to learn a language is to experience immersion in it. The more the language is heard and spoken, the faster and better the learning of it will go. The nearer the exposure becomes to being continuous, the better the student will do. From this, Phil's thinking advanced to the idea of relocating to where he could have a real immersion experience and, thus, more quickly and thoroughly learn the languages. One hears about people who take language classes in school for years and still can't really do very well in the language. Phil wanted a practical, usable mastery of all three languages. A plan started taking shape in his mind that involved taking the family to Europe where Phil could maximize, in turn, his contact with Spanish-speaking, then French-speaking, and finally, German-speaking people while he studied these languages. He proffered the idea to Darla, who was not especially enthusiastic, but could see some merit to the idea, so she agreed.

Phil enjoyed being the primary caregiver for his children for a period of more than half a year prior to their departure for Europe, and has happy memories of that time with them. The depression lifted when Phil got away from that job and he was working hard to be a safe and loving father to Cole, who seemed to be glad that his old dad was back. Phil also enjoyed being a student again. Unlike during his college days in the sixties, he studied hard, got good grades, and obtained a good grounding in all three languages. He acquired enough knowledge to provide a solid base for learning them for real.

The family's income had dropped dramatically, but the house in Alaska had sold for a lot more than its' initial cost, which gave the Temples a big down payment on the California house, giving them a very low house payment. This was especially good given the now reduced income level. The lowered family income stream turned out to be a source of great fear and discontent for Darla, who had grown up emotionally ignored and neglected by her father. His high earnings made for plenty of disposable income around that household, and that was apparently what she substituted for the loving father missing from her life. When the good income went away in her life, she deeply resented the loss and blamed Phil for the abiding fear that consumed her.

While Phil was pursuing his college studies in California, Darla decided to take a trip to Alaska with the children. Her parents were spending summers in the northland following their relocation to New Mexico, and they bought tickets for Darla and the kids to visit them there. After she got to Alaska, Darla got together with Silver and compelled a confession out of her that Phil and Silver had declared their love for each other. Darla had suspected that something was going on and had put on a full court press to get the details. Poor Silver caved in under the pressure and admitted that something emotional had taken place. Darla also probably believed that something sexual had happened.

Whatever it was that she believed, Phil received a phone call from Darla from Alaska during which she shrieked at him that she knew everything and that he had "raped her soul." Perceiving the threat to his hopes of staying to raise his children despite the miserable marriage, Phil acknowledged that something had happened, nothing sexual, but did not fight her as she raved her hate at him. Phil refrained from mentioning that she had been raping his soul with her horrible mouth for the last thirteen years and did not ask how she liked it.

Phil and Darla agreed to discuss things further upon her return to California, and when she got back they went through a tense week or so of separation, and then decided to try again and see how it went. They agreed to reconcile, but Phil's plan to leave after the children were grown did not change. What actually changed as a matter of reality was the overt character of Darla's hatred for her husband. She nursed and fostered a loathing for him that far surpassed the dislike and contempt for him that had characterized the marriage up until that time. This new level of vitriol clearly showed itself from time to time over the next several years until Phil felt forced to leave earlier than planned.

Darla went along with Phil on the decision to travel overseas and decided that her method of justifying her participation in this endeavor was to undertake a mission to make Europeans aware of the Alladist religion. She sought advice from the Alladist world headquarters about where to go to execute her pioneer mission, and they suggested Cadiz, Spain. Cadiz was located in one of the poorest parts of Spain and would be easier to afford with the family's severely limited resources, so they decided to go there. They made arrangements for travel, rented out their house for substantially more than the amount of the house payment, and in September of 1979, when Colton was eleven years old and Sylvia was approaching her eighth birthday, they flew from Oakland to Los Angeles and then on to Madrid. The Temple family's big adventure was under way.

As the flight descended on the approach into Madrid, the capitol of Spain, great volumes of trash everywhere were the first thing that could be discerned from the air as a feature of the landscape around the city. It seemed that the Spaniards could use some landfill technology and a regular trash collection program. The Temples took a train from Madrid to Cadiz, met some Alladists who owned a rental apartment that was both priced at market value and affordable to them, and were set. Phil enrolled in Spanish-language classes at the University of Cadiz and engaged a private tutor for an amazingly low price. He also found a young Spaniard who was a college student and who wanted to work on his English. The young man was happy to find an English speaker with whom he could practice. A deal was made to speak Spanish one day and English the next, six days a week, thereby giving both of the students the practice they needed. The young Spaniard was a little lazy and they ended up in Spanish most of the time, which was fine with Phil. Phil was at a bit of a disadvantage with his family there because they spoke English around the house, but he learned well anyway. In the five months the Temples were there Phil became sufficiently skilled in reading, writing, speaking, and understanding Spanish to stand him in good stead in the use of that language for the rest of his life.

Arrangements had been made with the school district in California to home-school the children, and Darla submitted lessons for them while overseas. Phil and Darla also encouraged the kids to get out in the neighborhood and seek contact with other children. Colton showed great adaptability and good social skill by charging out there and meeting the new world around them with courage that amazed his dad. Sylvia, on the other hand, proved to be very intimidated by the experience. She clung to her mother's skirts and tried very hard to avoid getting out and interacting with the Spanish children in the neighborhood. This was different from the maturity she had showed at home and the reason for it was a mystery. Cole ended up getting quite good at speaking Spanish, while Sylvia learned almost none at all.

Phil developed the practice of walking to his university classes and to the home of his Spanish tutor, and learned his way around Cadiz. He liked to take different routes to walk to his destinations just to experience different parts of the city and to get the feel of this interesting place. The bullfighting season was during another part of the year, so the bull ring was closed all the while they were in Cadiz, and there was no chance for them to see a bullfight. That was all right with Phil because he never liked blood and guts much.

One day as Phil was walking to class, he passed by a sidewalk bar where some men were drinking outside and passing the time of day. He acknowledged them as he walked along, and as he moved beyond them, Phil suddenly heard a shout and then found himself with a passenger. One of the men had jumped on his back and had his arms wrapped around Phil's neck. Phil grabbed the man's arms, twisted out of his grasp, and without the assailant's feet ever touching the ground, Phil got his hands on the man's throat, stuck him to the side of the building, and held him there while looking at the group of friends to see what threat might still exist. There were four of them and they warily came over and took their friend in hand as Phil let the fool down from the wall where he was holding him. The friends made peaceful gestures to Phil and led the attacker away as Phil resumed his walk. It was a very strange thing to have happened. The guy made no real effort to hurt Phil, and, for Phil, it was almost like handling a passive child once control of him was attained. The man made no attempt to fight Phil or to escape from his grasp, and Phil had at least seventy pounds on him, so there was no contest. This was just a drunk acting out for his friends. It was Phil's first experience like that since his fight in college. It was pretty weird.

Darla decided that the way she would fulfill her Alladist mission would be to set up an informational table in the central plaza of Cadiz and pass out Spanish-language brochures about the faith to passersby. That lasted less than one day. The national police discovered her right away and directed her to leave. She was very discouraged to find that what she had in mind was illegal and would not be possible. She was not able to figure out another way of being a pioneer missionary, and the loss of her sense of mission was very hard for her. It damaged her ability to enjoy her Spanish experience. Phil's wish had been that Darla could be supportive of him in his efforts to expand his skills as he prepared for a new career. Phil hoped that she could enjoy being the home teacher to the children as they learned something about the rest of the world. The sad truth of the situation is that Phil and Darla were simply not partners enough in life for Darla to gain any sense of a joint effort for them.

Phil studied and practiced hard and got pretty good in Spanish. Cole adopted an assertive approach and made the most of his time in Spain. In addition to getting pretty good at the language, he learned soccer, called *futbol*, and had fun at that. Cole went on a camping trip to the country with Phil's language practice friend, who was a leader of a scouting-type group, and had some great fun. While on that trip, Cole had the memorable experience of watching some farmers slaughter hogs. Phil was very proud of how well Cole did as a social being during their travels in Europe. He showed his dad a lot of true grit.

Darla and Sylvia did not enjoy the Spanish experience much and were happy when, after five months, the family moved on to France. Phil's Spanish tutor had formerly lived on the French Riviera in a place called Antibes (pronounced "Onn-Teeb"), which was located on the Mediterranean coast between Nice and Cannes. She recommended Antibes as peaceful and beautiful and referred Phil to some friends of hers who might be able to give the family some assistance in relocating there. The Temples took a train from Cadiz to Barcelona, then on to Marseilles, France, thence to Antibes.

23

FRANCE

The Cote d'Azur, or the Coast of Blue, as the Riviera is called in France, is stunningly beautiful. The blue waters of the Mediterranean and the green hills of southern France come together in a place dotted with picturesque villas, stately mansions, winding roads, and ordinary French homes, such that once seen, its loveliness cannot be forgotten. Phil enrolled in a language-training academy in Cannes, a forty-minute train ride west of Antibes, and also found a person who would be willing to spend time with him on a regular basis so that he could practice his French. She was a young, quadriplegic polio victim living near where the Temples rented an apartment. She was bedridden and unable to move, and could breathe only with the aid of a positive pressure oxygen delivery system. She was able to speak just like anyone else and was glad for Phil's company as he came around most days to just sit and talk.

This young woman had been stricken with polio as a small child in the 1950s, just before the Salk vaccine became available. She had not been able to move for over twenty-five years, but could converse up a storm, and Phil gained greatly in his ability to speak French because of his opportunity to befriend her. Occasionally, her breathing apparatus would jam and a member of her family, one of whom was always nearby, would calmly fix the problem while she struggled for breath. It was very distressing to Phil to watch as she lay there with her tongue distended and her eyes bulging, not breathing, but once the alarm mechanism brought help and once they got the machine going again, she was fine. They all seemed to be used to it.

Phil studied hard, just as he had done in Spain, practiced diligently, and learned quickly. Because there are so many words of French derivation found in the English language, all native English speakers already know a great many French words, so it wasn't long before Phil was reading novels in French as well as speaking it.

Loren and Molly came to visit Phil, Darla and the kids not long after their arrival in Antibes, and they all had a nice visit, including trips to Nice, Monte Carlo, and western Italy on day excursions. The folks stayed a few days and left, and it was very special for the temporary expatriots to have them come all this way to visit. The children were thrilled to see the folks from home.

Darla had developed some sort of nerve disorder even before the departure from the States. This malady caused her to experience severe itching as well as creeping, crawling sensations in the skin of her arms and legs. The longer they stayed in Europe, the worse it got, and it was causing her some serious suffering. She got over the problem somewhere along the line after the family's return to the States, so it was probably a psychosomatic manifestation of her unhappiness with her life with Phil. Her dissatisfaction in living with a man who did not love her was understandable, but that was her own fault. She had decided many years earlier on a course of conduct that ensured that she would remain unloved, and that's what she got.

In France, Darla managed to find a homeopathic "doctor" through some sort of personal referral and started going to him for help with this itching. After a few days in a row of appointments with this man, Darla decided to tell Phil that the man recommended daily sexual stimulation followed by the application of acupuncture and acupressure procedures to affect a potential cure. The doctor also offered to provide the sexual stimulation. Darla did not like the man and regarded some of his conduct as improper and scary.

Phil and Darla agreed that she would stop going for this treatment and Phil suggested that they undertake the man's suggestion about daily sexual stimulation at home, although without the acupuncture, to see if it could help her. For the next eighteen days, Phil and Darla got together, and for the first time in fourteen years of marriage, Phil found out what it was like to be a married man having continual sex. That was the most married he had ever felt, at least in that department, and he found himself walking around with a new lease on life and a new spring in his step. The sex was about as good as it had been on their wedding night, but it was a good deal better than the mostly none Phil had been having for the last fourteen years. He was happy to be doing something to help Darla that was also giving him some pleasure and satisfaction. It was a pretty remarkable time for Phil, and it actually gave him a little hope that this disastrous marriage might yet have something positive to be said about it.

Then came the moment of reckoning. After eighteen days of newly-wedded enjoyment for Phil, during which time he thought he was also providing tender, caring help to this ailing person, Darla lowered the boom. On the morning of the nineteenth day, the children were off at school, and Darla was no longer able to contain the rage she felt at what was happening between them. She started off speaking in a cold fury, but was soon spewing hate at Phil so fiercely that her spittle splattered his face as her words tore through him like none of her many other outbursts had ever done in all their years together. Phil had opened his heart and had begun to feel the first inklings that he had ever felt of what the physical part of real marriage might be like, and this fact made what she was doing now all the more awful and catastrophic for him. She called him a vile monster who was getting his jollies at the expense of a poor and suffering victim of an awful illness. She roared at him her hatred for someone who would take such despicable advantage of someone in need. She was very successful in finding words to fully express the enormous depth of her contempt for Phil and for the disgusting torment and abuse he was putting her through. She set astounding new records for how much hatred she was able to direct straight at her husband. It was the last time he touched her for a couple of years. Man oh man, the crap a father will put up with and endure to be there for his children.

Not long after this, Darla decided that staying in France was more than she could stand, so she borrowed $5,000 from her parents and she and Sylvia went to Alaska to spend the rest of the summer there with the Oldburgs. Her stated reason for leaving was that the nude beaches were so offensive to her and made her so uncomfortable that she couldn't stand to be at the beach. The Temples lived one block from a beautiful Mediterranean beach where topless bathers were seen, but were a relative rarity, so there was clearly a greater reason for her choice to leave, namely, how miserable she was living with a bastard like Phil Temple.

Phil and Cole remained in France, where Phil continued his language studies, and the two of them had a good time just being the two of them.

It became one of the sweetest times of their lives for both of them. They spent a lot of time together, exploring that part of France and having fun. Cole had made friends with an English boy who lived nearby and whose mother agreed to look after Cole while Phil was in class, and then father and son spent the rest of their time together. It was great.

During this period, Phil had a number of opportunities to further explore the realm of extramarital sexuality. The instructor of the French-language class he was taking was an attractive, single woman in her thirties whose favorite subjects in conducting class discussion in French were sex and romance, and she made no secret of her interest in discussing those things more fully with Phil after class. There were also a number of young single women who were students there from several countries, and Phil had invitations to spend time with a couple of them. His choice was to provide a good and wholesome example for Cole about the way a father is supposed to behave, which does not include screwing around with other women while the son looks on or while the boy sits and waits until his dad shows up, having completed his extramarital fun. Phil devoted his time to Cole, and they both had very happy memories of that period together.

The Temples heard many stories from people who lived through the German occupation of France about the incredible brutality inflicted on the French by the Nazis. Coming from a country where respectful conduct and civility were the norm, the Americans found it difficult to comprehend the monstrous nature of the acts committed by the Germans as a matter of ordinary course during those days. The enormous numbers of graves in the vast number of graveyards containing the remains of people who died in the World Wars in Europe are sobering things to see.

Paris is famous for how rude and unfriendly the people are to foreigners, and Phil's experience in Paris when he was there with Silver and Darla confirmed that legend, but the people of southern France were mostly warm and welcoming. They were one of Phil's favorite features of the experience in France. Darla and Sylvia came back to Antibes at the end of August of 1980, and two days later the four of them got on a train to Salzburg, Austria, to begin the last portion of their European experience. A lovely river ran through the Austrian valley where the city was located, and the beauty of the location was overwhelming. Phil was now capably conversant in both Spanish and French, and German waited to be added to his list.

24

AUSTRIA

The Temples spent four months in Salzburg, which Phil found to be such a beautiful place that he could scarcely believe what he was seeing each day. The Tyrolean Alps tower above the valley, and the majesty and splendor of that setting is truly stunning. The mountains soar upward from the valley floor so steeply that hiking them requires extra special caution. The lush greenery puts one in mind of western Washington State, and Austria is truly one of the most perfectly beautiful places in the whole world. The family had an apartment in a farming village called Gotzens, near Salzburg. Phil enrolled in a language school in Salzburg and made reasonably good progress in his study of German, but it is much more grammatically complex than English, Spanish, and French, and is just harder to learn. By the time the Temples had been there four months, Darla was chomping at the bit to go back to the States, and winter was coming on in that seriously cold place, so they decided to return home. Phil's mastery of German was, while quite respectable for the amount of time spent in this German-speaking country, still not as good as Phil had been able to achieve with the other languages. He could communicate very effectively, and had to hope that this would be enough for his purposes.

Phil left Austria with a few indelible impressions, some good, and some bad. One of the good ones is what an incredibly beautiful place it is. Another good one came from the lady who owned the apartment where the Temples lived and from a woman friend of hers as the two of them spoke to Phil of their experiences as children following World War II. What they told him made Phil as proud to be an American as anything he has ever heard.

Salzburg is located in the portion of Austria that became the American zone of occupation following the defeat of the Third Reich. Similar to what happened in Germany after the war, Austria was divided into four zones, each administered and occupied separately and uniquely by the French, the British, the Soviets, and the United States. The part of the country taken over by the Soviet Union was subjected to the age-old practice of rape and pillage by the victorious power, and the people who lived in that area suffered greatly at the brutal hands of the Russians. The French and British were not as cruel and criminal as the Russians, but they were historic colonial powers who had very well-established attitudes and behaviors when it came to treatment of conquered peoples. Austrians who lived in the French and British zones found themselves greatly resenting the hostile and disrespectful treatment they typically received from the representatives of those countries who manned the occupation forces.

The landlady's husband, whom she married after she grew up in the years following the war, had been an Austrian member of the *Wermacht*, the German army, and had been captured by the Americans as they advanced across France toward Germany. He had been sent to a POW camp in the United States, where he lived out the war. He returned to Austria when peace came, and the landlady was confident that the reason he survived the war was that he was captured by the Americans. He received good treatment, including good food, satisfactory lodging, and high-level medical care while a prisoner, and came home very much an admirer of America as a place where goodness ruled.

Even more impressive to Phil, however, was the admiration and affection with which these people spoke of the American GIs who had been the occupiers of Salzburg. The GIs treated the Austrians with kindness, respect and restraint, and our American boys conducted themselves with honor and decency. The legacy they left behind was one of which all Americans can be proud. The Temples were able to discern and avail themselves of the fondness and positive feelings for Americans that many of the people carried as the result of the exemplary conduct of American GIs as they related to the population of Tyrolean Austria. The distortions and exaggerations spread by the irresponsible and reprehensible American press about the conduct of American military personnel are a continuing outrage. Similarly outrageous is the feeding frenzy that the press goes into when they find something negative to report about American military forces that is true. What they put out is disgusting, because the truth about how almost all Americans do, and have always done, is what the Temples learned in Austria. We can all enjoy a justified and powerful sense of pride as citizens of the United States because of the history of Americans in Austria.

Something that was not so wonderful about Austria for Phil was initially learned about when the Temples met an American family in Salzburg who had been there for several months when Phil, Darla and the kids arrived. The Temples received a warning from them about the necessity to count their money every time a transaction with an Austrian was made. The warning turned out to be very, very true. Short-changing tourists is such an entrenched practice there that you can expect to experience attempts to cheat you out of your money just about every day. Bus drivers, cab drivers, store clerks, food service people, shop owners, tour operators, just about all commercial workers can be counted on to behave this way. Even those who like Americans are happy to cheat them. If the short-changers were challenged, they always gave the money back, but twenty apologies a week for the same thing start to ring pretty hollow. Seldom has a more valid warning been given anywhere and it is unlikely that there are many places in the world where this practice is more pervasive.

When the Temples left Austria, the tour operator who was taking them to Munich, Germany, to catch a plane stopped in the mountains north of Salzburg and demanded more money to continue driving them to Munich. It was not enough to break them, and a small enough amount that Phil just paid her rather than risk missing the plane, but it was a very chicken-dung thing to have pulled on them as their last memory of Austria. If thousands of people read this, then adequate payback will have been accomplished.

25

BACK IN THE U.S.A.

The Temples caught their plane in Munich and flew to London, where they spent a few days. London is a fascinating place to visit, and after so long being surrounded by the sounds of other languages, it was great to hear good old English everywhere they went in that city. Finally, on November 6, 1980, the day Ronald Reagan was elected fortieth president of the United States, the Temple family landed in New York City, and their European adventure was over. They rented a car and drove around Manhattan to see the sights. They somehow found themselves in a neighborhood near Coney Island, where they saw junk-filled vacant lots, boarded-up derelict buildings, lost and broken-looking people leaning against lamp-posts, and a general atmosphere of decay and ruin everywhere. Sylvia looked at all this and observed, "Gosh, I didn't think there was any place like this in America." It was pretty grim. Maybe that part of New York is better now.

It was clearer than ever that the marriage between Phil and Darla was a failure, but the devotion of both of them to their children was still strong and unwavering, and the children did not know about the wreckage that was their parents' marriage. Both parents continued to try to do their best for the children, except for the part about loving their other parent.

They went to Cheyenne and spent a couple of months living in Phil's parents' basement apartment. Phil got a job selling solar heating equipment and did all right at that, but did not like selling. A good salesman can agreeably force a sale, and Phil is happier having people do what they think is best for them, not what is best for Phil. The tenants in the house in Vallejo cleared out after Christmas, and the Temples headed back to California.

The family was happy to be back in the good old U.S.A., but Darla's stress over how they would get along financially made her harder than ever to deal with, and life with her was bad. She found work as a part-time marriage counselor at a facility in Concord, California, and Phil got two jobs, one driving a school bus and another selling fire extinguisher service. They made it all right in the finance department despite Darla's unending fear of poverty, but there was a recession going on, and Phil's idea that his language skills, in concert with his degree in business, would open up broad, new vistas of employment opportunity in the Bay Area did not develop as he had hoped.

Phil's job as a school bus driver lasted only a few weeks because of his response to how badly behaved some of the young passengers were. He found himself once again protecting children from bullies, as he had done when he was a boy. Having grown up being a good kid who tried to do what was right and to be a good citizen, Phil had no tolerance for mean, troublesome, bullying, antisocial people, youngsters or otherwise, and was soon issuing citations and evicting passengers who became repeat offenders. It wasn't long until the bad apples were either off the bus or had learned to restrain their conduct while on Phil's bus. Peace and harmony were going to reign on that route. When offenders interfered with that objective, they straightened up or they were gone. Problems were quickly coming under control, and there was a chance for Phil to start enjoying this job.

Then came the day when the supervisor came to Phil to say that the school had decided that he was kicking too many kids off the bus and that he had to let them back on. Phil said that the ones who were off deserved to be off and that he was not interested in taking them back until a reasonable amount of time had passed for them to thoroughly think over how their behavior had impacted their lives, so he refused. He thought that took care of it. But then the supervisor came back to Phil a day or so later to say that the school administrators insisted and that Phil was required to let the troublemakers back on the bus. He responded that this amounted to undermining his authority and that the school was reinforcing the problem by rewarding bad behavior.

Phil said, "I am the captain of that ship and what I say and do to cause people to be orderly and civil is the law." Phil said that if they did not like that and would not support him, then he would not work for them, so they could get somebody else. They insisted, so he quit.

That is to say, he quit driving the school route. Phil stayed on the payroll as a charter driver hauling athletic teams, conventioneers, excursions, and tour groups, and the need to control ornery children was mostly at an end. There were a couple of trips taking kids to camp and bringing home other kids who were finishing their camp experience. The ones going to camp were subdued, probably homesick and not inclined to cause problems while missing Mama. The kids coming home were a different story. They had recovered from their homesickness and were raring to go. Phil discovered that when some of them would not follow orders to sit down and behave themselves as he was going down the road at sixty miles an hour, a public address microphone keyed in front of the speaker produced such a fiercely ear-piercing screech from the feedback that nobody could stand it, and the kids rode like good little citizens. An occasional snap on the mike key was sufficient to get hard-core testers to reconsider and sit down. Phil told the boss about his effective system, and they quit asking him to haul camp groups.

Hauling athletic teams and conventioneers was fun, and Phil got to see some good ball games and some interesting meetings. Not long after he left the school route, the supervisor came to him to say that the first day on the route after he left was a zoo on the bus, and she gave him a look as if to say that he caused the problem. Phil said to her, "What the hell did you expect? You just demonstrated in no uncertain terms that they can do anything they want without consequence. If I were still on the bus, there would be no problem." The supervisor had no response.

Darla was having trouble at work of a sort that became a pattern in other jobs that she got later on, and Phil came to believe that the same mental condition that made her unable to carry on a reasonable and healthy relationship with him affected her in the same way in her employment. Just about every job she ever had after that time became an ordeal in which she believed that she was being persecuted, picked on, and mistreated. The main difference was that she did not inflict her hate on her bosses face to face, as she did with Phil. They had the power to fire her so she kept it to herself. As long as Phil and Darla had the kids, Phil had voluntarily relinquished the power to fire Darla as his spouse, and she had free reign. The quality of her work in these jobs was all right, as far as anybody knew, but she suffered greatly in her conviction that all her bosses were awful to her. Even long after Phil divorced Darla Cole reported that she was still going through the same stuff in each new job she found.

California was not a happy place for the Temples, and Phil really missed Alaska, although as long as he and Darla were together, no place was going to be that great. After some discussion with Darla, Phil learned that she, too, thought about going back to Alaska. By the time the family had been back in the States for about six months, Phil and Darla came to the joint decision to return to the far north. The recession caused them to be unable to sell the California house by the time they wanted to leave, so they rented it out and headed north, Darla in June with Cole in the car, and Phil in July with Sylvia riding with him in the pickup. That trip is another of the sweet memories Phil has of just himself and Sylvia. She was as sweet and good a child as ever lived on the earth and was a delightful traveling companion. They had a nice time together traveling up the Alaska Highway. The California house eventually sold a year later, at a very large profit, as housing costs in that state had begun to skyrocket.

26

HOME TO ALASKA

The Alladists of Alaska had told Darla that an additional adult Alladist was needed in Seward, on the Kenai Peninsula, to fill out a seven-member assembly, and for that reason, Darla wanted move to Seward. Phil, too, found this fishing town on Resurrection Bay to be an especially beautiful and charming spot, with its spectacular views of nearby mountains and seascapes, and Phil was happy to choose this place as where the family would live. Seward almost rivals the Tyrolean Alps with its amazing level of natural beauty, and the spirit-lifting splendor there felt like a reason to go. Phil knew that finding good employment there might be difficult, but he was willing to give it a try in exchange for the privilege of living in such a marvelous place.

By the time Phil and Sylvia arrived in Seward, Darla and Cole had been there for several weeks and had settled in an apartment that Darla had found and rented. It was small but affordable and just roomy enough for the four of them if the adults slept on a fold-out couch in the living room. The kids each had a private bedroom. Phil began looking for work, and on his first day on the search he found a job as a deck hand on a crab fishing boat. That turned out to be an interesting adventure, which Phil is glad to have experienced, but which he did not like in the least. After spending most of a year on a Navy aircraft carrier, Phil had come to think of himself as a sailor, at least in the sense that he never got seasick in all the time he was aboard that ship, regardless of the weather.

Unhappily, being on a forty-five-foot fishing boat is a much different deal than being on a 1,000-foot-long, floating airport when it comes to motion sickness. The work on the fishing boat was hard and dangerous, although the perils that one faces while working on a day-boat operating in the relatively sheltered waters of south-central Alaska pale compared to the incredibly dangerous Bering Sea king crab fishery. Phil had several chances to contemplate his mortality or the prospect of being maimed aboard that crab boat, and didn't like anything about that. Between fouled lines, flying steel hooks, swinging crab pots, and leaking exhaust systems, the bad stuff that could happen to a crew member aboard that boat was legion, and close calls were frequent. Phil had heard about the extreme dangers of going out on the big, deep-sea crab boats, all even more hazardous than what he was involved with, and he knew that working out there was something he would not have even considered getting involved in.

Fishing Boats

The skipper of the boat Phil was on was an alcoholic whose wife had just left him, and initially, Phil felt sorry for the guy with all the troubles he had. This skipper turned out to be pretty much of a jerk that deserved most of the crap he brought on himself, and Phil's sense of pity abated. After Phil had been working on the boat for a couple of months, there was a day they went out when the skipper was in an especially bad frame of mind and became very impatient with the way the other deck hand and Phil were doing their job. The guy got very nasty and verbally abusive, which Phil was unwilling to tolerate, so Phil told his boss where to stick the job. The problem with that was they were twenty miles from port and had six hours of work to do retrieving their lines of crab pots, so walking off the job was not an option. They eventually finished the day and Phil stayed quit, so that was the end of his commercial fishing career. Phil had the sense that with all the crap he tolerated at home just so that he could stay and raise his kids was more than plenty, so was not interested in lying down for abuse from anybody else. That policy has gotten him into several near-scrapes over the years, and it has now been many years since he left his number one abuser, but Phil still chooses not to take crap from anybody. Life is too short. That skipper was not seen around Seward for much longer. He needed to find something else to do.

After Phil left the fishing boat, he took a job selling advertising for a little while, but his long-standing wish not to have to try to brow-beat people into doing with their money what Phil wanted instead of what they wanted to do with it caused him to fervently wish for another way to make a living.

Phil hired on at the biggest fish processing plant in town and found himself working at a conveyor belt picking fish, rocks, seaweed, and whatever else went by out of the shrimp that had been caught in trawl nets and delivered for processing. The pay was low, although it added up with the extremely long hours. Conditions were cold, the work was tedious, and by the time fifty thousand pounds of shrimp had gone by on the belt during a shift, Phil's body was ready for a rest. Twelve or fourteen hours bent over that belt, even though Phil worked at the high end of a sloping conveyor assembly designed to accommodate workers of every height, was enough to make his neck and back beg for mercy. But then there were four hours of cleanup to do on the machinery that moved, cooked, and processed the shrimp. Shrimp and fish goo got into every nook and cranny in that place, and cleaning was a nightmare. Exhaustion was the order of the day, every day, by the time Phil got home.

It was quite an adjustment for Phil to find himself working at this menial and grimy job after having been a hot-shot air controller making good money, saving lives like crazy, and telling airline and military pilots what to do. What a comedown. Phil decided that he was going to be the best fish picker they ever had, and it also occurred to him that he must be at least somewhat mentally healthy to be able to take this tremendous plunge in status and not get suicidal.

Phil worked hard, earned his way off of the fish-picking line, and was promoted into unloading boats, running forklifts to feed processing machinery, and doing general warehouse work, and enjoyed the strenuous physical character of what he was doing. After the required number of hours on the payroll, Phil became a participant in the employee medical insurance program for himself and his family, and was glad about that. Phil did a good job for the employer, and it was not long before he was recognized as a high-level performer and promoted to machine operator and eventually process foreman on the night shift. Phil was feeling positive about making the most of this undesirable job situation, and really appreciated it when Cole took the opportunity to tell his dad that he was proud that his old man was one of the bosses out at the cannery.

After Phil had been a foreman for a year or so, Darla found the appropriate moment to inform him that she was ashamed to tell people where her husband worked. There was no screeching or shrieking this time. In fact, there was no disagreement or trouble on the docket at that moment. She demonstrated a pretty cheerful demeanor as she said this to her hard-working spouse. She just enjoyed doing it. Phil was profoundly offended that she should say this to him. He figured that he was entitled to a little appreciation and respect as he busted his hump in that awful job so that Darla and the kids could be comfortable. It was clear that hoping for appreciation from Darla was a complete waste of time and effort, and Phil would have to be content with his son's admiration and provide his own respect. The plan to leave when the kids were grown was still solidly in place.

Phil ran crews in the processing of shrimp, which was his primary job, and he also supervised crews in processing king crab, Dungeness crab, tanner crab, halibut, herring, and cod, and unloading at the docks. Salmon was also a big feature of life in the plant during summers, but Phil worked in the other fisheries and not that one. It was all stinky work, the hours could be incredibly long, and Phil's wife was ashamed of what he did for a living. Phil shuddered at the idea of having to do this for the rest of his working life, but it was honorable work and he took pride in doing it well. There was the hope that the gut-level meanness shown him by the mother of his children would earn her just payment someday, somehow.

After Phil's second year as foreman, the shrimp fishery in the area was being overfished and was showing signs of collapse, so the state government agency in charge of monitoring natural resources shut down the shrimp fishery. That turned out to be a favorable development for Phil because in place of running the shrimp process during the summers, he got the job of driving a refrigerator truck filled with fresh product, mostly salmon, to Anchorage for air shipment out of the international airport there to destinations demanding fresh Alaska seafood. The work as a driver was not nearly as hard as running process crews, although the hours were plenty long. Driving all over the road system in Alaska was a very agreeable job, and Phil thoroughly enjoyed it.

Phil's favorite memory of working for that employer was his selection by the employee representative committee, two years in a row, as the best boss to work for in the whole plant. Phil really cared about the workers put in his charge, and he did everything he could to make that rugged job humane and tolerable for them. The first year, Phil did not even know that the committee made a best boss selection until he was chosen, but he knew that he treated his people well and was pleased at the recognition. It was nice to have his efforts appreciated. Similar to what he had experienced in the navy, people liked working for Phil because he was fair to them and considerate of their needs. They did quality work for Phil, and they helped make him look good to his superiors.

After a couple of seasons of shutdown, the shrimp fishery was reopened and Phil resumed his position as shrimp foreman. It was still a nightmare job despite all his best efforts to put a positive face on it. It was a situation in which the two realities of life in shrimp processing, namely, quality of finished product versus quantity of raw product purchased from the fishermen, were always working at odds with each other. It was never possible to get them both right at the same time. The best that could be done was to continually fight the good fight to achieve the best possible combination of the two.

The game in the food processing business is to turn out finished product from the raw material coming in the door. In shrimp, if twenty thousand pounds of high-quality, packaged, finished product is realized out of one hundred thousand pounds of raw shrimp purchased from the trawlers, a 20 percent rate of recovery is in effect, and the operation is making big money. If the recovery rate is 15 percent, the operation is paying off but the company is not making a killing. When recovery is anything below about 12 percent, the operation is losing money and management gets nervous.

The other side of the processing equation was the question of quality. If the entire volume of product delivered by the fishermen ended up packaged for sale, you would have a 100 percent recovery rate, presumably a good thing. No one would buy what was offered, however, because it would contain not only the delectable and nutritious shrimp meat, but also legs, heads, shells, rocks, seaweed, and all manner of other stuff that nobody wants to eat, not a good thing.

The battle to maximize and balance both the rate of product recovery and quality never ends, and leading that battle falls primarily on the shoulders of the foreman. The quality assurance people are constantly sampling the finished product to see if the fish pickers, the peeling machinery, and the packers are getting enough of the junk out of the shrimp to keep quality high. If the process is going great guns and there is a high recovery rate, it is almost a sure thing that QA is going to find a quality problem and might even force the reprocessing of some of the packaged shrimp to get the shells and heads out. For sure, the whole operation has to slow down. If QA determines that the finished product is practically perfect, then it is virtually certain that processing had been too meticulous, causing greater than acceptable loss of meat and product weight. Recovery is therefore reduced, and the operation has to speed up to reestablish a profitable rate of output.

The process foreman is answerable for bad recovery, for bad quality, or for both at the same time, which can occur. What is being sought is, of course, excellent quality and high recovery all at once, which can also happen, but the stress of that job, which is a constant fight, is extreme. Phil learned that of the last three people who had held that job before him, one died of a heart attack, one died of cancer, and one suffered a nervous breakdown and had to be hospitalized. Phil had thought when he left air traffic control that he would find work that did not eat him up with stress. How in the hell did he fall into this nasty job which, while not life and death every day like he had been concerned with before, was nonetheless another man-eater?

What made it so tough was that the foreman had no control over most of the factors that affected how the shrimp went through the process. If the fishermen did not properly layer the right amount of ice into the catch as they harvested it, the quality was affected. If the shrimp was unloaded on the first day, it was too fresh to peel well in the peeling machinery. If the shrimp had been on one of the last boats unloaded a few days later, it had aged and softened, and at some point might have become so soft that much of the meat was lost in the process. All the foreman could do was try to anticipate what was coming, try to react quickly and appropriately with adjustments in the process, make changes according to what actually came next, and deal with changes, surprises, and emergencies all week long. It was a gut-buster.

This job was discouraging because it was so stressful and unpleasant, but Phil was fighting the good fight and making a good account of himself. Then came the abdominal pain, constant diarrhea, and rectal bleeding. A visit to the doctor and some diagnostic testing revealed that Phil had developed a case of ulcerative colitis, an inflammatory bowel condition that makes life pretty unpleasant at times. Phil was informed that, because of his having manifested this malady, he was now at a 1,000 percent increase in his risk of developing colon cancer, as compared to someone who did not have colitis. The symptoms worsened on the longest and most stressful days of processing when Phil, as the foreman, was chasing around like crazy in the never-ending search for good recovery and good quality.

It occurred to Phil that the years of grinding his guts out on air traffic had generated the potential for him to contract this illness, and then the new pressure of this horrible job had provided the impetus to turn that potentiality into a life-threatening disease and wreck Phil's intestines. He remembered that during his time with the FAA, he used to think about the possible effect on his innards of all those days of stomach-knotting traffic, and felt lucky that his guts stayed intact. Well, the cumulative result of all that finally showed up in this ailment, and Phil was one very sick cannery man.

27

THE FINAL STRAW

By the time Phil had become a process foreman, Darla had made contact with a local psychiatrist who had a modest practice going on in town, and she was able to come to an agreement with him establishing her as his intern. This made possible her going to work as a family and marriage counselor and bringing in some money. She was basically a contract worker whose services drew eighty or ninety dollars an hour into the practice of the doctor. By the time he charged Darla for his supervision, office space, and attendant expenses, she was getting around thirty dollars an hour, before taxes. That was good wages in those days, although not a lot for a professional person. Darla had to travel to several communities in that part of the state, so travel expenses came out of her earnings. She only got paid for client hours, which was around half the time she actually put in, so what she was doing was strictly part-time employment. Between Darla and Phil, they were making enough money to get by just fine. It wasn't good enough for Darla, but it was just fine.

Within about two weeks of his receiving the diagnosis of colitis, Phil found himself going down once again into the powerful misery of clinical depression. News as bad as this can take a little time to sink in and create its psychological effect. The horrible sense that life is hopeless and that no matter what you do, there is no way out of your misery and suffering, is enormous and overwhelming. Living in a failed and abysmal marriage, having become unable to do the job he loved, finding himself in an awful

185

job that was eating him up almost a badly as the career he had lost, and now losing his wonderful good health with the specter of cancer down the line, Phil was in complete despair about his life. The evil of depression made him unable to see any hope. It was bad.

Phil started seeing a psychologist for some counseling and reached the conclusion that he needed to find another, less stressful way to make a living. He decided to leave the cannery job, and when Darla learned of Phil's intentions, the deep fear she felt from having spent her childhood feeling neglected and unloved by her father, and learning to find her comfort from the fact that he made good money, came surging to the surface. Despite living in a very small house and driving inexpensive cars, Darla's family bought nice things while she was growing up and were allowed to spend, within limits, on fairly well whatever they wanted. Darla's greatest fears in life were of becoming unable to spend however she cared to, of having to answer for her expenditures, and of running out of money.

With the combination of Darla's part-time professional earnings and Phil's working a million hours a week in that nightmare seafood job, they weren't doing as well as they had when he was an air controller, but they had no real money worries. Darla's shame about where Phil worked notwithstanding, they were really doing all right financially. They would have had to tighten their belts while he sought other work, but they still had money in the bank from the sale of their house in California, and it was clear to Phil that his own health required that this change be made. He believed that saving himself was worth a little temporary budgetary tightness. Darla, in her fear of financial deprivation, thought otherwise.

Darla chose one Alaska September afternoon when the two of them were home alone together to give to Phil the most up-to-date, precise details of her true feelings about him. Phil had spoken to her of the despair he was feeling and of the utter hopelessness he was experiencing, even though they were financially okay. This would have been a good opportunity for Darla to put her psychological training and her master's degree to good use for the benefit of the marriage and their family, but her hatred for Phil had long since obviated any such possibility.

Darla's choice was to take this time to tell Phil that she thought of him as nothing but a loser. She told him that she believed that he was a bum who could not hold a job, that she considered him not to be a man, and that she regarded herself as the only thing resembling a man living in that house. All the hate and venom she had unleashed on Phil over the years, as she destroyed any chance that marriage might have had, paled in comparison to this onslaught. In Phil's disbelief at what he was hearing, Phil pleaded with her not to speak to him in this way. His heart was already breaking as he felt his life slipping away from him, and to be assailed with this level of viciousness was more than he could stand. Darla, however, insisted on this course of conduct, repeating her opinion that Phil was not a man and declaring that she had no regard for anyone as worthless as he was. He begged her again not to speak to him in this way and found Himself weeping brokenly at what was happening.

As this monumental ugliness from Darla reached its crescendo, Phil looked into her face and realized, with utter horror, that she was thoroughly enjoying this experience and that watching him suffer like this was proving to be an enormously satisfying and pleasurable event for her. For Phil, it was as though he was looking into the heart of evil, and Satan himself was smirking at him through the face of this hate-filled person. It was the single most savage, most awful, most searingly horrible moment of Phil's entire life,, either before or since that time, and to this day, when he wishes to visualize the vilest, ugliest, most evil sight he has ever seen, Phil sees that disgusting grin on Darla's face. . Phil finally knew how much his interlude with Silver had advanced, for Darla, into this incredible hatred for him.

Not surprisingly, Darla has denied ever saying that she was ashamed to be married to a cannery foreman, denied that she said the things she said when Phil saw all that evil enjoyment in her face, and has no sense that she created all of the trouble and strife in their marriage that she did, in fact, create. She tells her children that their father was impossible to live with, that he was moody and mean, that he was unpredictable and scary in his treatment of her, and that he was a bad husband and a bully. That is all completely untrue.

These assertions by Darla would more accurately be described as the imaginings of the person who really brought all those characteristics to the marriage, and the fact that Darla is the only person in Phil's whole life who has ever thought of him as even slightly troublesome. It appears that Darla has lied shamelessly to the children about their father, but the saddest part is that she does not know that she is a liar. Because of the emotional damage she incurred growing up, she believed all the awful things she said to Phil and about him through all those years, and she has convinced the children that they are true. Cole has said that his mother does not spend time bad-mouthing Phil and says that Darla is completely indifferent to the fact of Phil's existence in this world, but her hatred of Phil is so clearly apparent when they are together and her comfort with the estrangement of her children from their father is so unmistakable that it is obvious to anyone that she fostered their rejection of him, whether she spent time on the project every day or not.

Shortly after Darla's horror show, Phil approached her with the suggestion that they seek marriage counseling. He was still devastated by what she had said and done, but his many years of enduring what she was capable of left him in the habit of trying to find ways to make it bearable to continue living with her. She immediately refused the suggestion, and she gave no reason for the refusal except to say that she would not consider such a thing. Phil's interpretation of this was that she would be embarrassed to reveal to her counselor colleagues that there was trouble in her marriage, and it could be that she was ashamed of the awful things she was guilty of and did not want anyone else to know about them. In any case, there was no doubt about her intentions concerning Phil's suggestion.

A few days after that, Phil came to the decision that he was done living with Darla for the benefit of the children. No amount of benefit to them was enough to justify paying the price of continuing to live with that evil. In Phil's depleted condition, he could no longer sacrifice himself to that degree, even for love of his kids. They were worth almost any cost, but Phil could no longer be helpful to them while continuing to submit to Darla's hatred and cruelty. Phil made the determination that he would stay long enough to get the house he was building up to a level of completion such that the three of them could be comfortable in it and have reasonable and decent living conditions without him around to fix and improve things.

Phil quit working at the cannery and set about making serious progress on the house. Over the next few months, he constructed the kids' rooms and finished them with carpets, wallpaper, closets, and trim; finished the kitchen with cabinets, countertops, flooring, built-in dinette, and pantry; brought the laundry area to a fully functional and usable condition; completed one bathroom and brought a second bathroom, including a hot-tub and walk-in shower, to a state of satisfactory functionality; installed heat sources both upstairs and down; and got the main living room to a state of respectable and reasonably attractive completion. He used up the money they had from selling the California house and actually had to borrow a few thousand dollars to get as far as he did with the project. When Phil's intended point of completion and habitability was reached, it was time for him to clear out.

Phil's decision to leave had brought him to enough of a sense of control over his life that the depression abated, and he undertook a program of vigorous exercise and dietary discipline to combat the digestive disorder that was causing him to hurt and bleed. Between escaping that awful job, enjoying the progress he was making on the house, his efforts toward better health, and the anti-inflammatory medication prescribed by the doctor, Phil's condition improved and his sense of hopelessness eased. He spent a few days in Anchorage in February to buy building materials for the house, and upon his return, Phil found that the mere fact of having to come back to that house of hatred caused him to become depressed again. What he had learned over time, however, was that vigorous work and accomplishment was the best cure for depression, and within a couple of days, was better. Phil left home in May without telling his family that he was leaving for good, because he would not have been able to bring the house to the point he intended to if Darla had known what was coming. Phil was never to live with Darla again, and interestingly enough, he has never been depressed again in all the years since he left her. That says a lot.

28

PROFILES OF THE TEMPLE CHILDREN

COLTON

The earliest days of Colton's life have already appeared in this book, beginning with the pregnancy, wherein, as a little passenger inside his mother, he became known to Phil as Hercules, Phil's yet-to-be-met child, whom Phil loved with all his heart, and whom Phil regularly told of that love through the mother's tummy, in the months before the baby was born. When Hercules emerged as Colton, later called Cole, he became the source of one of the most amazing experiences of Phil's life, and Phil learned from this what truly selfless and unconditional love felt like. It was wonderful for Phil to love that little person so much that he would not have hesitated to lay down his life for him or do anything to save and protect him. Phil learned of the meaning and existence of God by becoming a parent to this marvelous and precious little person. Being a dad was the best thing that had ever happened to him, and until the crazy behavior of Cole's mother made it necessary for Phil to change his plans, that great love for Cole led Phil to want to be the father of six children, so that he could have the miraculous experience of loving five more little ones with the same life-changing love that he had for Cole.

As Cole grew, he blossomed into a sweet, affectionate toddler who demonstrated extreme cautiousness as he related to the world, and also a great wish to be pleasing to his dad and mom. He did not learn to walk until he was almost fourteen months old, even though he seemed to have the physical capacity to perform that function many weeks before he actually accomplished it. He was daunted by the challenge, and Phil's perception of him as cautious by nature evolved from the child's strong preference for sitting down on the floor or hanging on to furniture or someone's supporting hand rather than striking out on his own to walk. He never got into exploring and damaging things the way many toddlers do, and although Phil and Darla certainly did not do it, they actually could have left dangerous weapons and deadly poisons lying around with impunity. Cole absolutely never got into anything.

Learning tasks that required him to use his hands proved to be challenging for Cole, and teaching him to button his clothes, open doors, use a spoon, and later on tie his shoes, comb his hair, or other ordinary manual functions was surprisingly difficult. One day when Cole was two, within a few months of his third birthday, Phil came upon Darla in the bathroom, whipping Cole with a folded electric extension cord because she was trying to get him to flush the toilet and he could not, or would not, do it. She was extremely angry at him, and he was crying very hard as Phil picked him up and brought an end to this rather shocking scene. Darla and Cole soon calmed down, and Darla seemed to be a bit ashamed of herself, although she never said so, because while she often spanked Cole with her hand, Phil never again witnessed her abusing the child in anger as she had on that occasion. Cole later would tell of his mother's hitting him with various household items that happened to be at hand after he became a big, husky teen-ager who would laugh at her while she punished him, but none of that occurred in Phil's presence. A day or so after the whipping scene, Phil attempted to get Cole to flush the toilet and learned what Darla's frustration with the boy was about, although Phil refrained from the punishment and demonstration of anger that he had seen from Darla in this connection.

There was something in the messages being sent from Cole's hands to his brain, concerning the sensations he was receiving from the flush lever, that scared him, and he could not bring himself to push hard enough to make the mechanism operate. A similar thing occurred when his parents tried to teach him to operate a door knob to open doors. The snapping feeling, or the sudden change in the tension of the mechanism when the spring-loaded latch in an ordinary door knob released, or some other sensation as Cole experienced it, was frightening to him, and it was a long time before he finally learned to operate these items. Phil and Darla stopped trying to teach him how to operate these things, allowed him to approach them on his own terms, and it eventually came out all right.

What Phil developed from these difficulties was a belief borne out as time went on and as Cole had other difficulties with matters of manual dexterity. The Temples thought that perhaps there was some deficiency in Cole's neurological development that interfered with the information he got from the feelings in his hands. This may have had something to do with what happened at the time of his birth, including the violent contractions of the induced labor, the mere four hours of labor that pushed him out so fast, and the use of forceps and other implements. The distorted shape of his head was evidence of the difficulty of what he went through, and there was likely some interior damage, as well.

Cole had great trouble learning to write with a pencil, and even when he reached adulthood, his penmanship was so bad as to be scarcely decipherable. When he was in college, he had a summer job with a home appliance dealership; he worked on a delivery truck, helping transport and install home appliances. He was a big, strong kid, and an athlete, so he was very fit, and he was a star performer when it came to muscling around the refrigerators, freezers, stoves, home entertainment items, and other heavy things that he and his coworkers delivered with their truck. He was very likely as good an employee as they ever had when it came to being able to handle the weight. But when it came to hooking things up, especially washers and dryers, which had small nuts, bolts, screws, clamps, fittings and so on, to deal with, his value declined. He had so much trouble handling those tiny items, because of how fumble-fingered he was, that they stopped letting him hook anything up. It just took him too long and he needed too much help. Even when he was in high school, he still held his spoon in his fist to eat, much as a small child does. He continued to hold a comb with his fist, instead of with his fingers, until he got old enough to decide how he wanted to wear his hair, at which time he began wearing a buzz cut. He never had to comb his hair again.

Cole was very difficult to potty train and was still wearing diapers to bed when he was in the first grade. Even as an infant, he did not mind in the least having wet or dirty diapers, and never cried to tell his parents that he needed changing. When Phil was a student at BNAO School in Pensacola when Cole was first born, one of Phil's jobs in the domestic division of labor was to do the laundry at the Laundromat and hang the clothes on the clotheslines at home. As a rookie dad, Phil did not know about the concept of "harsh laundry detergents" versus "gentle Ivory Flakes." He was washing everything, including Cole's diapers, in some industrial-strength laundry soap, and it wasn't long until they began to notice diaper rash on the baby. They generously applied baby powder, ointment, burn remedy, baby oil, and who knows what else, but nothing helped. By the time they got Cole to the Navy doctors, his rash was a flaming burn, and his diaper area looked like he had been roasted on a spit. It had to be painful. The medics suggested Ivory laundry soap, and within mere days, the problem cleared up. Phil and Darla were very relieved but Cole didn't seem to care. During the whole time this was going on, that baby never complained a peep. He cried when he was hungry, he cried when he wanted company, he cried about other stuff, but he never made a sound to say that he was uncomfortable in the diaper department. They speculated at the time that he must be numb down there and that he might be tough to toilet train. He never cared how totally rotten it got in his pants. He was a happy baby, even when he stank to high heaven.

As a school-age bed-wetter, Cole continued to need his parents attention as they tried to help him get over this problem, but when it became clear that it was not going to be easily done, they did not make a punishment issue out of it, and by the time he was in second grade, Cole only occasionally had an accident, and he finally quit wearing diapers to bed. Cole was a sweet boy who loved lots of affection and cuddling, and was not a behavior problem at all. He wanted very much to please his parents, and Phil thought of his son as very easy to raise.

As he got older, Cole demonstrated a great love of books, and by the time he was in the second grade, he was devouring everything he could get his hands on to read. He liked to curl up with the encyclopedia, almanacs, natural history books (especially about dinosaurs), adventure books, and science fiction, and his favorites were military books on air power, warships, and weaponry, and later on, even military theory and tactics. Phil had been assigned to Naval Air Intelligence when he was in the service and was deemed to have the brains and aptitude for the field. He had a wide array of knowledge, largely because he, too, had been an eager reader growing up, so was smart enough for the job, but Phil had no interest in warfare and military matters until he was compelled to develop such an interest by joining the Navy in time of war. Cole had that stuff in his blood and could not get enough of it even as a small child. Phil was amazed that someone could have such a powerful devotion to military subjects and still be related to him.

Cole never did particularly well in school, except for reading, but it was not because he wasn't smart, he just didn't like school and didn't like the work it required of him. Even though Phil and Darla thought he was beautiful and had ceased to notice the asymmetry of his face and head, children he encountered at school certainly noticed, and he was subjected to merciless teasing and name-calling throughout his years in school because of it. He grew up to be a very tough guy, and being required to endure that cruelty was probably part of the reason why. It definitely did not do anything to make him like to go to school. A few times, he got picked on so badly that Phil had to intervene, either with the teachers and principals to get them to observe what was going on and protect the boy better, or in a few cases, when Phil directly confronted some of the bullies who were making Cole's life miserable. Phil threatened to come after them and come to their homes if he heard any more about them picking on Cole, and that stopped them. Phil was certainly not able to confront most of the people who were cruel to Cole, and the boy became very resourceful at dealing with the problem. He chose to ride his bicycle or walk to school rather than take the bus when possible, thereby removing a lot of the unpleasantness. As he got older, Cole became a weightlifter and a varsity wrestler, and became tough and strong enough to physically stop the unkind treatment that he had faced all those years. The last teaser/bully or two went down hard, as they learned that it had become unwise to be cruel to Phil's boy.

One of Phil's favorite stories about Cole is the one in which, while attending junior high, Cole became the student of a social studies teacher who liked to have weekly competition among the kids in his class to test their overall general knowledge and their awareness of current events. Cole turned out to be the best in the class at this competition, and it wasn't long before the contests turned out to be Cole against the entire rest of the class, and even then he always won. All those hours and years with the encyclopedias and almanacs really paid off for him in that setting. In high school, he participated in interscholastic college bowl competitions and held his own in history, geography, literature, and current events. Other team members carried the load when it came to math and science. Cole came out of high school with thoroughly average grades, but went on to college and graduate school, attaining a master's degree, so he's a smart cookie, good grades or not.

Cole had an enormous imagination, and he could mentally carry himself away to places far from where he might physically be at any given moment. It touched Phil's heart to see how much fun Cole could have with nothing more than his brain for a toy. He loved dinosaurs, bugs, and the game of Dungeons and Dragons growing up, and he never stopped being a sweet and well-behaved youngster, although after he grew up, Phil learned from him of a number of adventures he had been through as a kid that would have scared his dad if he had known about them at the time. Cole never gave Phil any trouble, and Phil took a lot of joy in being the dad of such a good kid.

Cole had an athletic career that was a very interesting one, indeed. From the time he was very small, Phil and he played a lot of catch with ball and glove, practiced fielding fly balls and grounders together, shot hoops with a basketball, and threw a football to each other. Much as was the case with Phil, Cole was not a gifted athlete, but he was not a bad one either, and he got a lot of enjoyment out of athletic activity. He played tee-ball baseball and kiddy soccer when they lived in California, and he swam and played soccer while they were in Europe. After the family's return to Alaska when he was thirteen, Cole's interests turned to wrestling and football.

Initially, Cole was a terrible wrestler, and one of the greatest tributes to the strength of his character through all those years, from eighth grade through twelfth, was that he never quit. He hung in there year after year until he finally succeeded. He won not a single interscholastic match during the first two years he was a wrestler, and after that, he won a few, but not many, and Phil never saw him win a match until he was a high school senior. It became so painful for Phil to watch Cole get pinned and slaughtered and humiliated, time after time, that Phil stopped attending every home match, although he still went to most when he could. More than once, Phil and Darla received calls to tell them that their son had been injured in a wrestling incident. Seeing him on a gurney in the emergency room with a cast on his neck, arm, or leg did nothing over the years to add to Phil's enjoyment of wrestling as Cole's sport of choice.

Early in the wrestling season of Cole's junior year, he came home from practice with another heavily wrapped wrist from another injury. Phil took that occasion to tell Cole that he was fed up with all these injuries, and that if he came home injured again, he would not be allowed to continue in the sport. Sure enough, within a week or so after the wrist healed enough to resume workouts, Cole came home with his foot in a brace from an ankle injury. Consistent with what Phil had said, that was the end of the season for him, before it had really begun. Phil thought it was the end of his wrestling career. Cole was very unhappy about this and put in a lot of time and effort pleading with Phil to reconsider his ruling. Cole would not give up, although he was always respectful and reasonable, as well as passionate and sincere in his attempts to persuade his father. Phil was moved by the heartfelt character of the boy's approach and eventually relented, part way. Phil told Cole that he could resume participating with the team, but only as a manager, and that he could not compete. Further, he had to limit his workouts in such a way as to ensure no more injuries, and that Phil would communicate with the coach to see that this was exactly how it went. Phil said that if he completed the year as manager without further injury, he could compete again when he was a senior. Cole agreed, coordination with the coach was accomplished, and Cole rejoined the team as manager.

The wrestling season ended without any further injuries to young Cole, at least that his parents knew about, and he performed his job as manager with dedication and reliability. He also must have gotten some important further training and experience without actually competing, because the following year, when he was a senior, an entirely different scenario took place. He wrestled in the 180-pound category that year, and when Phil attended Cole's first match of the year, the young wrestler's dad got to see him make a good account of himself, actually doing better than Phil had ever seen him do in the years of watching Cole lose every match Phil ever attended. He was winning and outperforming the other kid throughout the match until the very end, when Cole made a mistake that allowed his opponent to reverse and pin him. That part was the same as ever, but even Phil, who knew very little about the art and science of wrestling, could tell that his son had shown some real skill and ability out there, and things could very well be different this season.

High school athletic competition in Alaska goes on among all sizes of schools, but is, to some degree, restricted so that similar-size schools compete mostly against each other. Seward High School had almost four hundred students, so was among the bigger of the small schools. Cole competed against wrestlers from all over Alaska and from all sizes of schools that year, and he encountered two or three kids from big schools that he could not beat. But he beat almost everyone he met from the small schools and most from the big schools, and Phil got to enjoy watching him win a lot that year, which was much better than all the stuff it had hurt so much to watch for all the years before.

When the state finals wresting tournament came around, Cole wrestled in the small school tournament and came up against the only small school wrestler who had beaten him that year, a boy from Nome. That loss had taken the form of a forfeit because Cole had been injured in that match. Cole had been behind on points when the injury and forfeit occurred. In the state tournament, Cole was seeded second in the small schools 180-pound class, and the kid from Nome was seeded first. Cole was still wearing the rib wrap and brace he acquired after the injury. Those two competitors defeated all their state tournament opponents until they faced each other in the championship match. The other kid was faster and more naturally talented than Cole, and was overconfident, having beaten him before. Cole won that match through sheer guts and dogged determination, and the final score was 1-0, as low a score as it is possible to have. Phil's son was small schools 180-pound State Champion, and Seward was team small schools State Champs. It was a wonderful moment.

Cole's amazing rise from being the worst wrestler who ever lived to winning a state championship is attributable to three things. The first is that his wrestling partner in practice for that whole year, and for much of his high school experience, was a kid who was so gifted and skilled a wrestler that he was undefeated throughout his entire high school career. As a senior, this boy wrestled at 191 pounds, and fortunately (or unfortunately) for poor Cole, he had to wrestle that guy in practice for hundreds of hours, getting beaten and tied in knots more than anybody should have to endure in a lifetime, but he learned from it, he toughened up from it, and he became a genuinely good wrestler because of it.

The second reason for Cole's success was his coach. The man was a dedicated teacher who loved his athletes and knew how to coach. He was able to take a not-very-talented, but very coachable kid like Cole, and turn him into a champion. The third factor was that Cole had the heart of a lion and let no amount of failure and discouragement deter him. He made his dad very proud.

Cole went on to wrestle in college at an NAIA school in Oregon, where he met limited success, because most of the people he wrestled had greater natural talent than he did, and because he did not want to train year round, but preferred to train only during the wrestling season. Phil visited him and attended his college wrestling practices a few times, and came away absolutely awestruck by the rigor of those workouts and the toughness of those athletes, including Cole. Those were rugged, painful workouts, and rugged, rugged guys. Phil could not blame his son for not wanting to continue that grueling schedule year round, but the guys who became national champions did just that.

Cole's football career started out somewhat like his wrestling career, that is to say, rather lacking in luster and glory, but ended up with a fair measure of success, and Phil has an enjoyable memory of how that football career began. Seward High was very rural and backwoods, and as such had a football club rather than an official, school-sponsored team. Students who wanted to turn out for the team had to join the club and pay dues to be in the program. Cole expressed an interest in turning out for football when he was a fourteen-year-old freshman, weighing about 120 pounds, and Phil said that he could turn out if he wanted to and that the family would pay the costs for him to participate. Strangely, Cole said no more about it, and as the day approached for the turnout, Phil began to wonder what was going on with him, since he had become silent about the matter. Phil asked Cole about it, and he sort of shrugged the subject off, without saying anything.

The Saturday morning arrived when the turnout was to take place, and still no information was forthcoming from Cole about his plans. It looked to Phil as though he was just going to let the moment pass without doing anything, so Phil confronted him about what he was going to do. Phil said that if he decided not to turn out, that was up to him and it would be okay. But if he was going to do that, the requirement would be that he make an affirmative decision one way or the other. What Phil would not allow was for Cole to piddle around without acknowledging his fears or misgivings, and let the hands on the clock make the decision that he ought to be making. If he was going to go, then let's get it together and go over there. If he was not going to go, then look his dad in the eye and say he decided not to do it. Then it was his decision, and not, "Oops, time got away from me and then it was too late."

Given that ultimatum, Cole decided to go, and they made it to the turnout. Cole was the smallest kid there, and after he got his gear, the workout was no-contact and he got all hot and sweaty but did not get beat up. Phil attended a practice the following week where there was some blocking, tackling, and hitting going on, and gained a new respect for the littlest guy out there. Poor Cole was getting scrunched every time he went up against anybody. He encountered people weighing anywhere from ten to one hundred pounds more than he did, and he looked like a feather getting blown out all over the field. It was like watching him wrestle, only with a helmet and shoulder pads. Nobody tried to hurt him, and he came out uninjured, but he was no match for anybody in sight. What he did was to never give up and to never quit. He just hung in there for all that punishment. Phil really admired his funny little punching bag boy for taking it like a man and coming back for more. He was tougher than Phil had imagined.

Cole played football all four years of high school, and when he was a sophomore, the football club changed to an official school-sponsored activity with paid coaches. Cole was never on a team that had a winning season, but he was named second team All-Conference as an offensive lineman when he was a junior and honorable mention as a defensive lineman when he was a senior. He played with courage and pluck, and did himself proud, although he was no threat as a college football prospect. He did turn out for football when he went to college, but found himself reliving the scrunching experiences of his first year of football when he was fourteen, and after a couple of weeks of that, he withdrew, deciding to focus on wrestling as his college athletic endeavor.

Both of Phil's children, with his acquiescence and approval (because Phil believed that imparting a strong moral code to children was important), were raised under their mother's tutelage as devout, observant

Alladists. Cole took a fairly typical college kid step when he found himself breaking Alladist law and drinking like a fish during his first couple of years away from home. After it was all over, he had some very funny stories to tell about his adventures as a drunk. Thankfully, he did not hurt himself or anyone else with these antics, and by his junior year he had reverted to more circumspect behavior. After he graduated, he adopted his mother's faith wholeheartedly and became a teetotaler. That was a good many years after Phil had also become a teetotaler because of his alcohol-related misadventures as a youth and because of his inflammatory intestinal condition. Because of Darla's crazy treatment of him, Phil never considering adopting her faith, as discussed earlier.

Consistent with his lifelong interest in the military, Cole decided to join the U.S. Army after he graduated from college and opted to enlist instead of pursuing a commission, as his degree would have qualified him to do. He worked for a while as a nightclub bouncer before he reported to the Army, and he had his dad in stitches on several occasions as he regaled him with hilarious stories of what bouncers do to drunks in a wild and crazy bar. Cole was well qualified to be a bouncer because of his years as a wrestler, and the kid can really entertain with his storytelling abilities.

Because of his degree, Cole was advanced in rank to E-4 after he completed Army basic training and was sent to the Defense language school at Monterey, California, where he learned Arabic.. Upon completion of language school, he got orders attaching him to a unit of the Hundred and first Airborne Division at Fort Campbell, Kentucky. He earned his jump wings at Fort Benning, Georgia, and then became a member of an intelligence-gathering team whose mission was to be inserted behind enemy lines and to set up secret listening posts to covertly gather electronically transmitted intelligence. He was proficient at combat arms and had a great adventure as a soldier.

Cole never had to go to war while an Army soldier, as the bombing of Baghdad in the first Gulf War began the week he reported to basic training at Fort Leonard Wood, Missouri, and that war was long since over by the time he achieved operational readiness. He attained the rank of sergeant while in the Army, and except for some problems with his weight, which delayed his promotion, he was an excellent soldier. His difficulties with weight were the result of the horrible habits he developed as a wrestler, where he learned to cut pounds to make weight for his matches, and then gain weight like a crazy person until it came time to cut again. He could gain and lose twenty pounds in a week, and his body's metabolism got

202 | James C. Wilson

very screwed up because of it. The military has a special weight-to-height proportionality chart especially for weightlifter/athlete types, and Cole had to rely on that to get him to meet requirements to stay in the service. He is far shorter than his dad, at six feet, one-half inch, but he weighs about the same as Phil does, 240, although he has weighed as much as 280, which the military likes not at all. To see someone as massive as he is with his burr haircut and his bull neck, who is also physically fit, running on an oval track for exercise is impressive indeed. He is one awesome dude.

By the time he had nearly finished his four-year Army hitch, Cole was sure that he wanted a military career, but he had developed the belief that he would like it better as an officer, and that the remote assignment duty that characterized his Army service was not conducive to married and family life, to which he aspired at some point in the future. He was a good soldier, with high efficiency ratings, and so when he hit upon the idea of getting into an Air Force Reserve Officer Training program, both the Army and the Air Force backed him up. He got himself released from active duty four months early and was accepted in a master's degree program as an AFROTC cadet at Oklahoma University at Norman, Oklahoma.. He spent two years as a cadet, earned his master's degree, and was commissioned a second lieutenant in the U.S. Air Force.

After his commissioning, Cole attended the National War College in Washington, D.C., for over a year, and while there he met a local girl whom he decided to marry. He was then sent to the same intelligence school Phil attended when he was in the Navy, except that it had been moved to Kelly AFB in San Antonio, Texas. Cole got married while stationed in Texas and asked Phil to be best man at his wedding in Washington, D.C., which Phil was honored to do.

It was not long until the Air Force recognized that they had a high performer on their hands, and while Cole was a captain, he was recognized as being among the top 5 percent of junior officers in the Air Force and was on the fast track for promotion. His first duty station as a lieutenant was at a Royal Air Force base in England, from which post he served in Kosovo and Italy during the Kosovo War. From what he told Phil, it seems that his job was not unlike the one Phil had aboard ship during the Vietnam War.

Command assignments for Air Force junior officers are rare and given only to those recognized as special, and when he made captain, Cole was given command of an Air Force detachment aboard a Naval Communications Station in Ohio. After that, he served in Kuwait in support of the Iraq War effort, and then in Belgium, at NATO headquarters. He is a major now, and will no doubt be a lieutenant colonel soon, could very well end up a general, and is having himself a fine career.

Phil's impression of the Air Force, gained while he was in the Navy stationed at an Air Force base, was that the Air Force is the least military and therefore the least harsh and most civilian-like of the four services: Army, Navy, Air Force, and Marine Corps (which is actually part of the Naval Service). Because the Air Force is a lot like a civilian job, except that the people wear uniforms and salute, when a tough-guy Army veteran comes on the scene who is good at militarily hard-assing people under his command, as well as motivating them in more subtle and thoughtful ways, they have a real leader on their hands. He gets things done, and they find him to be among the best they have. That explains Cole's success in the Air Force, and that is probably a good object lesson for that service in how to develop their officer corps.

Phil believes that Cole is a good man, a good soldier, and will be a good father to his children. As a son to Phil, Cole is disloyal and he dishonors himself more than he does Phil with his behavior toward his father, but Phil only partly blames him for the shameful character of his conduct. When a person is born, as Cole was, to a woman who harbors as much hatred of men in general, and who hates with a passion of monumental proportions one good and decent man in particular, namely Phil, it would be a very difficult disadvantage to overcome for anyone. As much strength and virtue as Cole has shown in his career, he falls far short of the best he can be, and that can be laid directly at the feet of his mother. He may someday grow beyond her effect on him, forgive Phil for the mistakes he has made, and accept Phil's forgiveness for the wrongs he has committed, with Darla's approval, against His father.

29

SYLVIA

"Phineas" was the name Phil gave to the little passenger in her mother's tummy, much as he had called their first child "Hercules" before Cole was born, and Phineas also received frequent messages from Phil of Phil's love for him/her in the months before that little being emerged as Sylvia. Sylvia was the most beautiful sight Phil had ever laid eyes on when he first saw her, moments after her birth, and proved to be permanently beautiful as time went on. Both children were very good natured and pleasant babies, but otherwise, Sylvia was a much different child than her brother in the sense of being adventurous and curious where he was cautious; squirmy and resistant to affection where he was cuddly and loved being hugged and nuzzled; admired for her physical beauty, where he was odd in appearance and was later on treated with cruelty for this; very fussy and fastidious about her personal hygiene, while he could not have cared less, and many other differences that made it seem strange that two such different children could come from the same parents.

Sylvia raised Cain whenever she was even slightly in need of a diaper change, and she was extremely easy to potty train. She wanted nothing to do with messy diapers and got herself trained and out of them as soon as humanly possible. Phil found it strange that ordinary or unfortunate looking parents such as he and Darla could produce such an incredibly beautiful child as Sylvia, but produce her they did, and Phil continually marveled that such a beauty could also be so sweet and good natured.

Sylvia was walking by nine months of age, compared to Cole's waiting until he was nearly fourteen months old, and she was a curious one. Cole had never been one to get into stuff. He always left everything alone, and Phil and Darla had become less attentive than they should have been to questions of access to items around the house that were dangerous to little ones. A couple of trips to the emergency room, after Sylvia ate dishwasher soap on one occasion and had a sip of some caustic liquid another time, were enough to train them that this was a different kid and that they had to be more careful. Once when Sylvia was two, she got exploratory and fell ten feet off a porch onto a concrete slab, which could easily have killed her. Phil witnessed the fall and ran to her with virtual certainty that he was going to find her terribly injured, but she was not. It seemed like a miracle, but not feeling comfortable counting on a miracle every time, Phil promptly built an impenetrable wall barrier around the porch to prevent any further such mishaps. Falls taken by children that were from much shorter heights than this one, have caused grievous injuries. But Sylvia was spared. Thirty-five years later, this episode still feels to Phil like a miracle.

Sylvia had golden, curly hair and twinkling blue eyes that bespoke her happy heart, and among the favorite sounds ever to reach her father's ears were the little, tuneless, humming songs that Sylvia would intone to herself while she played alone, unaware that anyone was listening. Also precious to Phil was the almost silent little laugh that would emerge from Sylvia when she was riding piggyback on him or horsy-riding on his foot as he sat on the living room couch. "Daddy, give me a horsy ride," was a very frequent request from her, which gave Phil lots of chances to hear that happy little laugh. Sylvia's fifth birthday party was a time when Phil was nearly overcome with emotion at the miracle in his life of being allowed to be the father of this wonderful little angel. He had many chances to marvel at what God had wrought in his precious girl.

Another of Phil's favorite memories of Sylvia is of how much she enjoyed having him make up stories to tell her at bedtime while tucking her in. She would say, "Tell me another story about Loosky, Daddy." Loosky, a figment of Phil's imagination, was a little girl about Sylvia's age who had many adventures and was the heroine of all the stories. One of the love names Phil had for his beloved Sylvia was "Boosky the Proosky," so it was not hard for her to make the connection between herself and the star of the stories. The requests for new stories soon began to tax Phil's limited creative imagination, but he made the effort because he found this time with Sylvia to be so wonderful. Phil loved to provide the safe and special tucking into bed for his children that were such happy memories for him from his own childhood.. Maybe Sylvia still has someplace in her heart for the memories of bedtime hugs and stories. Phil certainly does.

As Sylvia grew, her sweet and loving nature grew and increased along with her. She was cheerful, generous, happy, caring, considerate, and smart, and was a marvel to see in action. She became a little girl who sought ways to be helpful, cooperative, and kind, and when she reached school age, her teachers, every one, absolutely adored her. The Temples became very accustomed to hearing teachers praise Sylvia for all her virtues, and she was a teacher's pet in every class she attended. When she was in about the fourth grade, one of her teachers, with whom Phil sang in the community chorus, took the trouble to approach Phil and offer his opinion that Sylvia must come from a wonderfully loving and nurturing home, because she was such a remarkably sweet and thoughtful child. The teacher thought that her parents were sincerely to be commended for having produced such a special girl. Phil thanked him and refrained from explaining that although both he and Sylvia's mother loved their daughter dearly and did their best for her, the mother restrained herself from showing her contempt for the father until the children were not around.

Sylvia began to show at an early age that she possessed great strength of character and firm ability to be decisive. Once, when she was about five years old and the Temples were living in California, there was an episode involving their swimming pool that illustrated this. A little kindergarten friend of Sylvia's who lived a couple of blocks away was visiting at the Temples' house, and the two little girls and Cole were playing in the back yard near the swimming pool; Phil was close by, but was addressing himself to chores around the house. Suddenly, Phil heard Cole shouting and screeching at the top of his lungs, which brought Phil, within seconds, to poolside. What he found was Cole dancing around in a state of complete panic and still exclaiming with great volume, while Sylvia lay quietly on the concrete deck at the edge of the pool, holding onto the arm of her little friend, who had fallen in the water at the deep end. Cole had provided an excellent alarm, but Sylvia had quickly done what was necessary to save her friend, who could not swim, from going under. As Phil extracted the little girl from the water, she was a bit upset but none the worse for wear, and all ended well. The cool head and presence of mind shown by Sylvia to handle that situation being found in one so young was very impressive.

When Cole was fifteen and Sylvia was twelve, they spent part of a summer working with Phil in a food stand business he started up to try to find a way to escape from his awful job at the seafood plant and to capitalize on the tourist trade where they lived in Alaska. Because Phil was also working at the seafood plant, the two kids ran the store for much of the time during his working hours. Before long, when it was clear that this was not going to be Phil's ticket out of the cannery, he had to resume putting in the long hours on that job, and the kids then ran the stand almost on their own except for Phil's showing up for a few minutes every so often throughout the day when he could get a break from work. This went on for a few weeks until Phil closed it down. When it got busy, Cole would panic and freak out, and Sylvia was the one who maintained a cool head and would help her brother rein in his fear so that they could get things taken care of. Heavy customer flow was not a frequent problem, so Sylvia did not have to take care of Cole all the time, and she was even better than Phil was at dealing with the stresses of being hit with several customers at once. She was very adult in her ability to deal with those situations, and Phil began to predict great things for this unusual child. She possessed a calmness and ability to deal with difficult situations that was amazing.

It was during this same summer, and thereafter, that the sweet, happy, and loving child that Sylvia had been since birth began to change. She was entering puberty, and it may have been hormonal changes that brought about what happened, but whatever the cause, the days of teachers loving her and praising her to the skies were over. Teachers began to complain that she was sullen and unpleasant in class, although she committed no outright rebellion or defiance; she just became withdrawn and uncommunicative, and it began to be apparent that her teachers disliked her. This was an extreme change from what Phil and Darla had been accustomed to with all the accolades over the years, and Phil could perceive the difference at home, as well. He tried repeatedly to reach Sylvia in a loving way, but she would have none of it.

There were any number of occasions when Phil would say, "Please talk to me, Sweetie, your old Dad loves you and I want to help you. Where did my happy, joyful, little Sylvia go? What can I do to get you to share your feelings with me so we can work on what is bothering you? Please, please, Precious Girl, tell me what is happening with you."

Her responses were the same, every time. Arms crossed, glaring straight ahead, she would snort, "Nothing's wrong, what do you want me to say? Forget it. Leave me alone." She never confronted her father, sassed him, or became disrespectful. She was just completely withdrawn and unreachable. The last real communication of Phil's life with his beautiful girl was already in the past. One hears it said that such extreme changes as this in behavior or demeanor are often indicators of the child's becoming involved in drug or alcohol abuse, becoming sexually active in scary or dangerous ways, becoming a victim of sexual abuse, experiencing fear and alienation resulting from bullying or personal attacks at school, or some other such personal trauma that can completely alter what the child's life has been. At the time, and even several years later, Sylvia thoroughly and vigorously denied that anything resembling any of this stuff had happened or was happening to her, and Phil never saw any evidence, whatsoever, to indicate that she was lying. The reason for the change in her is unknown, but it certainly did happen.

It was at the end of the summer in the food stand that Darla demonstrated her satanic hatred of Phil by enjoying the profound suffering he was experiencing, and Phil decided, without telling anyone, that he was going to leave as soon as he could get the house into comfortably habitable condition for them. It was Phil's consistent belief that his children had been spared any knowledge of the depths to which the relationship between their parents had sunk. Phil's policy was to fight Darla as little as possible, and not at all in the presence of the kids, and her vile attacks on him were virtually all committed when the youngsters were absent. Phil had ample reason to think that the children were unaware of the true state of affairs, but what happened with Sylvia might indicate that this very special and intuitive girl somehow sensed, even without overtly witnessing anything, how bad things were and that she had been turned by the poison of her mother's hatred for Phil into a creature unlike anything she had ever been before. She most likely could not have articulated any knowledge or comprehension of what was going on, but maybe her soul, her inner spirit, knew and was harmed by it.

By the time Phil left, the following May, Sylvia had withdrawn so completely, and was so utterly unavailable to all his efforts to reach her, that it was clear to him that there was nothing he could do for her and that his leaving would at least save him. He relinquished his oath to stay until both children were grown, and although it hurt him deeply not to be able to keep his commitment to himself, leaving was the best thing for him to have done. His staying would have made no difference in how Sylvia turned out, and it was the best decision he ever made in the interest of his own health and sanity.

Phil had regular, if frustratingly barren and cold, contact with Sylvia for the fifteen months she remained in Alaska after he left the house. She participated in girls' volleyball, and although Phil was living in Anchorage, then later Kenai, somewhat closer to Seward than Anchorage was, he traveled to watch Sylvia play in several volleyball matches. She was tall, eventually reaching six feet in height, which is an advantage in that sport, but she had inherited the leaden jumping ability that plagued Phil's athletic career, so she was not a star. Sylvia demonstrated no pleasure in her father's attendance at her games and could clearly not have been less interested in whether he showed up or not, but he came anyway, to show his love. She discontinued participation in athletics after she left Alaska.

Phil continued to try to pursue a relationship with Sylvia for many years after she and her mother moved to California, just before Sylvia's fifteenth birthday. They moved so that Darla could attend school in Los Angeles and earn a doctorate in psychology. Phil traveled to California numerous times over the next six or seven years and paid for Sylvia to come to Alaska, Wyoming, Oregon, and Washington on many other occasions during those years to visit him, or his parents and him, or her brother and Phil, but she never stopped being the cold and sullen person that she had become before Phil left her mother.

One of the trips Phil made to California was a February road trip during which he flew from Alaska to Oregon, where he took delivery on a new pickup truck. He visited Cole, and then drove south to visit Sylvia. Phil and she traveled in the new truck from where she lived near Los Angeles out to Death Valley, where some relatives of Phil's were having a reunion.

That 300 or 400-mile round trip was the longest, loneliest road trip Phil ever took in his life, even lonelier than the times he drove the Alaska Highway to the Lower 48 and back by himself. Phil's efforts to engage Sylvia in conversation about her life, his life, the world, current events, politics, philosophy, religion, and anything she cared about met with monosyllabic nonresponses that cried out how little interest she had in relating to her father. The two of them slept in the back of the new pickup, out under the desert stars, and Death Valley was interesting and amazing in February, but Sylvia never gave any indication that she enjoyed even one minute of that lonely trip.

Sylvia graduated from high school in Southern California in June of 1989, and Phil traveled there to witness the event. By that time, Darla had remarried, and her new husband supported her while she continued to work on her doctor's degree. Their wedding took place the same month that the spousal support payments Phil was making to Darla came, as per the divorce agreement, to an end.

Sylvia attended college for two years at Cal State University at Northridge and then attended acting school in Burbank for a year because she wanted to try acting more than she wanted an academic degree. Phil sent her a good deal of money during those years and visited her at each of the places she lived. He tried very hard to get a feel for her life, but she shared nothing. The amazing thing to Phil about all this was that he never stopped showing her love and caring and never stopped trying to share his heart with her and make her know the great depth of his love for her. She never responded in any way to any of that. There was just no one in there. Something had killed her heart. In all the years from the time she started to change as a twelve-year-old until the last time Phil visited her in Burbank, he never heard her say a nice or positive thing about anything or anybody. She despised her mother's new husband, who seemed to Phil to be a simple and harmless guy. Sylvia seemed to have no friends and had nothing in her life that Phil could see that she could smile about or enjoy. It made his heart ache to see this lovely girl with such a cold, hard, and dead way of relating, not just to him, but to the whole world. The acting school did not invite her back after her first year, so her acting training came to an end.

In Phil's final visit to Sylvia, during her year at acting school, she at last took the opportunity to tell him that she had no regard for him, no use for him, and no respect for him. There was no particular context for that revelation. They were just sitting around Sylvia's living room and she made that announcement. Phil did not know what to say, so did not say much. After he returned home to Alaska and had some time to think it all over, he wrote her a letter saying that he was very hurt and offended by what she said, and that he had been trying for many years to get her to talk to him and to feel his love. He said that she had gone out of bounds on this occasion, so he wanted to start at the beginning and, in a civil and respectful manner, address issues. Phil insisted that as her father, he was entitled to respectful treatment, and that he was not interested in being abused. He said that he wanted to talk with her, share with her, and get her grievances against him out in the open and work them out. Phil was firm that they had to talk like decent grownups, with no hatefulness or abuse, and that he would not take any crap. On that they had to agree. He never heard from her again.

Phil tried for a couple of years to get Sylvia to respond to him but she never did. All he knew about her from then on was what he heard from other relatives. She stayed in touch with Phil's parents, but never saw them again and showed them only minimal interest. Sylvia's brother continued to be loyal to her, but expressed the sense that she was a very difficult person to have a relationship with. What Phil learned from Cole about Sylvia was that she had two or three careers in business, each of which lasted two or three years. She worked in banking, in office management for a construction company, and in some other field. In each of these, she started at a modest entry-level job, quickly showed how smart and capable she was, advanced to a highly responsible and well-paid position as manager or girl Friday, became indispensable to her employers because she worked so hard and effectively, worked herself into exhaustion, with her job as all there was to her life, and quit because she had nothing left to give and could no longer take the punishment she inflicted on herself. The employers were devastated to lose her and would beg her to return, but she was adamant and stayed quit. She would rest, recuperate, find another job, and repeat the scenario. It was a very unhealthy way for anyone to live, and in 2000 or 2001, seven or eight years after Phil's last contact with her, Sylvia came down with cancer.

Phil was notified by Cole of what was happening to Sylvia, and he attempted to connect with her to see if he could help at this time of crisis, and to see if such an emergency might open the door to doing something about their lost relationship. She responded with some written communications and accepted money Phil sent to help with her health care costs, because she had quit her last job before she was diagnosed and had no insurance, but she refused to see him and would talk only very little on the phone. Phil attempted to talk to Darla in an effort to get her to try to get Sylvia to be reasonable and see him so that he might be able to participate and help in what lay ahead in Sylvia's battle with illness, but Darla's hatred for Phil came spewing forth in the one face-to-face meeting they had.

Phil showed up unannounced where Darla worked one day to try to get her to see how Sylvia's attitude toward him might be contributing to Sylvia's illness, and how a change in that attitude might be helpful to her in fighting for her health. Darla would not talk to Phil, and when he spoke of how Sylvia's health might be helped by repairing her relationship with him, Darla snarled at him, hissed that anything like that was strictly between him and Sylvia, and stalked away with nothing else being said. It was clear that her revenge against Phil, taken by insuring that his position as a father remained lost, was more important to her than allowing him to reenter Sylvia's life, even when it was endangered. At the time of their divorce, Darla had issued a threat, initially laughed at by Phil, to destroy his relationship with his children. That threat was fully accomplished with respect to Sylvia. What was most amazing to Phil was that this credentialed mental health professional refused to see any value to Sylvia in efforts to get a father's love back into her life. It seemed to be stunningly ignorant and unprofessional, but registered as completely consistent with all the stuff she had directed toward Phil for all those years.

Sylvia continued to refuse to see Phil, so he sent her a letter denying that he was the villain in the breakup of her parents. He admitted mistakes and apologized, as he had already done very thoroughly in his earlier attempts to connect with Sylvia, declared his love and devotion to her, and provided to her a description of his life with her mother to show what had really happened. Phil heard from Sylvia one more time in a very nasty letter and then never again. As far as Phil knows, Sylvia survived her cancer, but he is dead to her, and if she is still alive, she is determined to be that way without her father. Sadly, it looks as though Sylvia must be as hate-filled as her mother seems to be, and the last Phil knew, the two women lived together, almost as married people, sharing that bond. Sylvia may be another world-class man-hater, and it is unlikely that she would ever to be capable of sustaining a loving relationship with a man.

Phil attempted to get Sylvia's brother Cole to intervene with her on Phil's behalf, but he refused, not wishing to go against his mother, and the relationship between Phil and Cole was damaged because Phil slowly began to realize that Cole also believed that Phil was the evil one who had destroyed the marriage, and although he was willing to have a relationship with his father, Cole had no sympathy for Phil's position. The huge damage came because Phil repeatedly tried to get Cole to change his mind about what a bastard Phil was, but Cole just resisted more. There will be more, later, about what happened between Phil and Cole.

Something that comes up now and then when the subject of paternal estrangement from daughters is discussed, is the question of molestation, incest, and sexual abuse. People who know Phil and know his character have no problem in dismissing the possibility that he could be guilty of anything like that, but people who do not know Phil might wonder, and why they might is understandable.

What is probably a substantial fraction, possibly even a majority, of cases of total paternal estrangement like this were ones in which sexual abuse did occur, and the daughters separated themselves from the offending or complicit fathers, justly so. It could be argued that such egregious circumstances as that are the only ones that provide a perfect and iron-clad justification for a child to completely evict a parent from his or her life. There are other forms of misconduct that could also be reasonable bases for such alienation, and few would argue that a wife beater, a habitual womanizer, a drunk or drug addict, or other miscreant parent should be spared the consequences of his bad behavior. But there are fathers who are far more deserving of rejection like this by their daughters than Phil is, Pop Oldburg being the best example to come to mind, and whose daughters have relationships, to one degree or another, with those men. That seems very unfair, but who says that life is fair?

After Darla began working as a family counselor, one of the most common tasks she faced in her job was dealing with men who were court-ordered into counseling because they were guilty of sexually molesting their daughters, other relatives, or other children. Darla never disclosed identities of people like this with whom she came into professional contact, but after a number of months of hearing about how many such men there were, Phil sensed the horror in Darla of learning how common this is and he was horrified, as well. Phil never even had a molesting or child abusive thought cross his mind, but finding out that this stuff is everywhere, he became curious enough about the phenomenon to undertake a self-evaluation to see if such a thing is possible in a normal man, which is what Phil most certainly is.

One night, as Phil was tucking Sylvia into bed, he intentionally paused and tried to inject incestuous, sexual thoughts about his daughter into his mind to see if such a thing was possible in a normal, healthy, loving father. The instant disgust, horror and revulsion he experienced as he performed this mental test told him all he needed to know. Behaving in such an abominable way was utterly out of the realm of possibility for Phil, and anyone who could do such a thing to a daughter, or to any child, is clearly very sick indeed. Child molesters and incestuous fathers should be put in prison forever. Or perhaps, better yet, put to death.

Another realization Phil came to during this process is that, knowing the popular awareness about how damaging such abuse is to its victims, even if he were inclined toward this sort of unacceptable sexual conduct, which he most certainly was not, he could not do it because of the harm it does to the children who experience it. Phil cares too much for the well-being of God's children to ever play a role in doing this kind of harm, even if he were mentally unwell enough to contemplate it.

There is an interesting connection between what is expressed in this last paragraph concerning self-control of personal demons in the interest of protecting others, and Darla's conduct toward Phil throughout their marriage. For someone crazy enough to experience impulses to do harm to innocent others, common decency would demand that such a person refrain from acting out on those impulses. Even unbalanced people who have the intention to do good in this life for the world, their greatest wish as human beings and loving souls should be to do harm to no one. Rather than gratifying inappropriate impulses and harming others, they should restrain themselves and protect people. All the damage that Darla did in her treatment of Phil over those years would have been spared him if Darla had shared such a commitment to doing no harm, personal proclivities notwithstanding. Darla had no such internal restraint, and the harm she did will last forever.

Also interesting is how clearly this story bears out the conventional wisdom which surfaces when the subject of people's decisions to take degrees in psychology come up in group discussions or at parties. That wisdom says that the craziest people decide to major in psychology because, whether they are conscious of it or not, they carry an inner wish to find out why they are crazy and to learn how to cure themselves.

It would seem that this is true of poor Darla. What is very sad about this is that she never got a clue about any of that. It seems clear that she never addressed her inner demons, and never learned to recognize them. Proof of this is her enthusiastic embrace of her revenge on Phil through approving the destruction of his relationship with their children. The appropriate reaction of someone in Darla's shoes would be to know how harmful to the children a ruined relationship with the other parent is, and how valuable a forgiving, positive, healed connection with the other parent could be. The children should be vigorously encouraged by both parents, no matter what those parents may have thought of each other, to do the best the children could to love the other parent, honor him or her, appreciate what he or she has done for them, and show him or her those feelings. Darla has done no such thing concerning Phil, even slightly, and continues to believe that he is, and always has been, the monster that she perceived him to be. It all proves how consumed Darla is by hate.. She had the power to make this all better for her children and chose not to do so.

Phil regards the choice that his children's mother made to join the Alladist religion very early in the marriage as bearing a significant part of the blame for what has befallen him with respect to his children. A reasonable analysis of the situation would be to break it down as 80 percent the result of Darla's upbringing and 20 percent her religion. Phil's own actions have certainly played a role in what his children have done, but fathers who have loved their children less than he did, who are guilty of far worse conduct than he was, and who are far less virtuous people than he is, have not been ruled out of their children's lives. A big difference is that their children are not Alladists. Phil's conduct is therefore not considered when establishing the above-estimated, percentile equation. There are many wonderful and honorable people who are Alladists, and it is entirely possible that the grossly wrong and unfair positions held by Phil Temple's children against him are the result of their improper interpretation of the rules of their faith.

The final letter received by Phil from Sylvia was especially nasty and filled with absurd assertions about Phil and about how she believes he thinks. Phil had been trying to find a way to be helpful to Sylvia as she dealt with cancer, had been vigorously resisted by Darla in his efforts to do so, and was then shunned by Sylvia. This was when he began to fear that, because of the extremist people he was dealing with, some sort of outrageous action might be taken against him. Phil contacted the National Governing Congress of the Alladists of the United States in an effort to get protection and assistance from the leadership of the religion in dealing with this situation.

The Alladist religion has a process by which adult children who have disagreements with their parents can petition the leadership for a ruling that declares the parent to be morally, ethically, or spiritually unfit and therefore ineligible to continue being the parent of the petitioner.

Alladists who wish to marry are required to obtain parental permission to do so before the faith will perform and sanction the marriage. This is true whether the marriage candidates are 20 years old and their parents are 40, or the engaged couple are in their 80s and their surviving parents are 110 years old. For this reason, adults who consider their parents unworthy can be found, at any age, seeking a declaration that their parents are unfit.

Cole was already married when, somewhat later than when the letter came from Sylvia, he became completely estranged from his father, and so unless he becomes divorced or widowed, such a scenario is unlikely for him. Sylvia, however, never even had a boyfriend that Phil ever knew of, so if she decided to marry, Phil's permission for her to do so would be required unless Phil were declared unfit by her religion. The protection Phil sought from the leadership of the religion was for the purpose of preventing such a vile smear as this from being committed against him without his having at least an opportunity to present his side of the story to those making the decision.

The National Control Board of the Alladists of the United States told Phil that they would notify him if they became aware of any such actions taken against him, but otherwise, they declared that they were without jurisdiction in this matter. They declined to provide Phil with any other help and referred him, if he wished to get his concerns addressed, to the ruling assembly of the region in which Darla and Sylvia lived at the time. The problem with this is that Darla was, for many years, one of the leading lights of the religion. She has been a member of one or another ruling body on a number of occasions, and she is very likely still functioning in that way. She or Sylvia, or both, or friends of theirs, are likely to be members of an authoritative conclave from which it was recommended Phil seek redress. For that reason, his chance of getting a fair hearing, or any hearing at all, could be severely limited, or nonexistent.

It is highly likely that an Alladist kangaroo court may have already found that Phil is morally, ethically, and spiritually unfit to remain Sylvia's father. Darla enjoyed so much telling Phil once that he was a no-good bum, a worthless loser and less than a man, that she may have again had the pleasure of telling the same thing to a group of decision-makers gathered to consider Phil's merits. A gathering of ecclesiastical decision-makers may well have taken such testimony and determined that Sylvia does not have a father. Phil has never received notice from the Alladist faith of any such steps taken against him, but that is not a reason for him to be confident that nothing like that has happened.

If Phil were still considered by the Alladist religion to be Sylvia's father, she could not get married in the faith without his permission. If Phil's permission were sought, he would not grant it unless and until he had an opportunity to let all concerned evaluate him and the situation as it exists, and to at least allow the potential husband to observe the details of what he was getting himself into. Motivation is therefore in place for Darla, Sylvia, Cole and the Alladists to sneak Phil out the back door and get him excised from Sylvia's parental roster without his ever knowing about it.

Some time ago, an acquaintance of Phil's saw the announcement of the marriage of a woman named Temple. She asked Phil if it might be his daughter. Phil did not, and does not, know the answer to that question. If Sylvia were indeed the person getting married, that would mean that Phil had already been removed as her father. That would be such a monstrous affront, would have required so much lying and distortion of facts about Phil, and would be such an abomination, one committed without giving Phil any opportunity to offer his side of the story, that words fail in an effort to describe the enormity of the insult. It would constitute some serious backbiting, to say the least. Thus, one can see the need that someone in this situation would have for protection. Fighting against such brutality is necessary and honorable. There is no requirement for a good, decent and honorable man, such as Phil Temple is, to prostrate himself so that people like that can kick him.

Phillip Temple is 100 percent deserving of respectful and decent treatment by his children. He merits far better than he got from them and their mother, but, as a group, they are capable of conduct against him as wrongful and reprehensible as the possibilities just mentioned. This fictionalized story is, in part, an effort to bring to fruition, by separate means and in a public arena, the fair hearing that this good man deserves but is certain they would deny him.

30

LIFE AFTER DARLA

The chronology of this story was interrupted in order to provide some information about Phillip Temple's children. That task having been accomplished, the story now resumes at the point when Phil had reached a stage of completion on the house he was building that would allow the three he was leaving behind to be safe and comfortable. By the day Phil left, in May, 1985, the house was ready. It was by no means finished, but completely livable, and it was time for him to go. Phil told Darla and the kids that he was going to Anchorage to look for work, and that he would keep them posted on developments. Within a week, Phil had a temporary job selling advertising, which wasn't much, but when compared to the cannery job he had left a few months earlier, was, at least, not a nightmare. In all the years since then, when Phil's work life got a little tough, he would reflect, compare the situation to working in that cannery, and realize that things could be a whole lot worse. That was the great value of his cannery career.

Anchorage was a much larger city than Phil had become accustomed to in Fairbanks or the small town of Seward, but having grown up in Cheyenne, which was bigger than Fairbanks, he had no difficulty in adapting himself to a this medium size city. Anchorage is located on a triangle of land surrounded on two sides by salt water and on the third side by mountains. Many Alaskans who do not live in Anchorage have uncomplimentary things to say about the city; one of the most common slights heard is that when you get to Anchorage, the real Alaska is not far away---you're getting close. Phil found it to be a pleasant enough city, but agreed that, for his taste, the boondocks of Alaska were preferable. He connected with friends who set him up with a couple of house-sitting jobs in Anchorage for the summer, so shelter was taken care of, and he continued to look for work even while he was selling advertising space for an organization that was publishing a one-time circular in a fund-raising effort.

Phil had come to the decision a year earlier to abstain from alcohol following his colitis diagnosis, and so spending a few evenings in bars and dance halls in Anchorage that summer opened him up to some new information. Feeling like a fish out of water as he watched the booze-enhanced, or more accurately stated, booze-diminished behavior of the bar denizens while Phil drank soft drinks established for him that hanging around in such places was never going to be something he wanted to do. He just felt lonely and out of place, and watching skilled womanizers as they tried to take advantage of drunken women just saddened him. Phil found the process distasteful, and as a neophyte single guy, had no inclination or skill to prey on foolish women who would allow themselves to be picked up in bars. He mostly avoided the bar scene. Those weeks reminded him of that lonely summer in Seattle when he was in college before Darla came back from Hawaii.

By the time the Fourth of July had passed, Phil had not been home for nearly eight weeks, and Darla finally asked him in a phone conversation when he was coming home. The time had come to break the news, and so this was the point at which he said to her, "Never. I'm never coming home. Never." Phil told Darla that his horrible life with her was over. The surprise and shock of this revelation hit her hard. Despite their history, and as much as she hated Phil, Darla seemed to have no idea that Phil was having a problem being married to her. She floundered around for a while in her state of unbelief, but then asked Phil to come home soon to discuss it, and he agreed. Phil dreaded having to return to that place, but at least he felt as though he was finally in control of his life and going there would not cause him to descend into depression the way it had before.

Phil went home in mid-July to find that Cole was in as much shock as Darla was about Phil's decision to leave Darla. Cole was not a boy notable for his observational powers, and in Cole's case at least, Phil was correct in his belief that his refusal to fight with Darla in the presence of the kids, and Darla's waiting to commit her hate scenes against Phil until they were not around, had kept Cole completely ignorant of how bad things were between his parents. Cole had no idea that Phil wanted to leave Darla and had no idea why he should want to leave her. Cole was deeply stricken by all this and was eager to persuade Phil to change his mind.

Sylvia was another matter. When Darla told her what Phil had said and that Darla was completely surprised by it, Sylvia's comment was, "Yeah, right, he is living in Anchorage and you are here and there's no problem." That kid continued to be amazing in how she could demonstrate such perceptiveness, and in her ability to get right to the root of what came up in life. She also said that she could not care less whether her parents stayed together or not. Her insightfulness and the new, stony cold heart she had acquired were an interesting combination.

Phil and Darla sat down to talk, and Phil learned that she was completely blindsided and mystified about why he would want to leave her. Phil told her about all the horrible stuff she had made a habit of saying to him during all their life together and she seemed not to believe it or understand why he felt so abused. He had put up with her crap for so long that, as far as she was concerned, it was all just normal human interaction with no consequences. She was not ready to deal with this and would prefer that Phil reconsider his decision. She also wanted the kids, or at least Colton, to provide input.

Sylvia said that "whatever" was all right with her, taking pains to demonstrate that she could not care less about the whole matter. Cole was the one who made the difference. His impassioned expression of how heart-breaking this was for him was very compelling and was more than Phil could withstand. Cole's entreaties to Phil to come back impacted Phil so strongly that he relented and agreed to do what Cole wanted. When Phil finally said that he would return to Darla, the joy and happiness Cole showed were enough to make Phil forget, briefly, what a nightmare he was agreeing to start living again. This seventeen-year-old jock actually danced around and clapped his hands.

Darla's reaction was relieved rather than happy, and Phil sensed that this reconciliation was more a chance for her to assuage the massive return of her old fear about not having plenty of security and money, than it was anything to do with wanting to be around him. It was a mistake for Phil to agree to come back, but Cole's ecstatic reaction was irresistible and unforgettable. Phil ended up reneging on his agreement to return, and this may be a part of the grudge Cole carries against his father, although the two of them were very close for many years after all this happened, so Phil believed that Cole had forgiven him.

Phil returned to Anchorage and continued making his rounds, selling advertising space, not liking it much and knowing that when the publication came out, the job would be over. Phil also continued looking for a better job. In very short order, he realized that the idea of going back to Darla was just going to be more misery and punishment for him and that he could not see how he could do it and still find life worth living. Phil was unsure how he was going to resolve all this, and Cole's joyous response to his decision to return remained a clear image in Phil's mind, so he was conflicted and troubled. For the moment, at least, he was away from Darla and would go slowly and play it by ear.

In mid-July, Phil was hired, because of his degree in business and his knowledge of several languages, as a teacher of English as a second language. The employer was a trade school in Anchorage, and he was scheduled to begin work in mid-August. The school was adding a new department to its program to take advantage of the generous student loan program that had recently been enacted into law by the Alaska Legislature. There were vast quantities of dollars flowing into the state of Alaska's coffers from the production of the Prudhoe Bay oil fields, and the state was making some of that money available for loans of various kinds to Alaskans, including student loans. Lots of entrepreneurs were figuring out ways to tap into this unbelievable gusher of money, and Phil's new employers were among them. Phil now had a good job lined up, was ready to finish his ad sales job, and looked forward to beginning work in August. The new job turned out to be a much different experience than Phil had anticipated, but for the moment, it was great to be solidly employed.

31

SILVER

One of the last calls Phil made in his sales job brought him to the office of his old friend Silver Hampton, who, a few years earlier, had divorced her first husband, moved to Anchorage and started a new life. Silver was now the marketing director for a major company in Anchorage, one of the largest employers in Alaska at the time. Silver made the firm's advertising buys. Phil had known that Silver was in Anchorage, although she was in no way the reason that he went there from Seward. Anchorage was simply the nearest large job market to where his children were. Phil delayed calling on Silver even though he was pretty confident that she would buy advertising from him. This delay was because Phil was unsure what might happen between himself and Silver. He had now agreed to return to Darla and was trying to deal with all his own inner turmoil about was going on in his life. It seemed to Phil the complication of coming face to face with Silver could only increase his turmoil, and it was with serious hesitation that he contacted Silver's office. He needed the sales, however, so that helped him overcome his conflict about seeing her.

Since Phil's return to Alaska, Silver had been remarried, moved to Anchorage and then divorced again. One of the times Phil had seen her was around three years earlier, and it was then that she informed him that she was engaged and would soon marry. Phil had the feeling that Silver's reason for taking the trouble to tell him this was to see, given what their experience with each other had been, what he might do, or at least, what he might have to say on the subject. Phil's response at that time was neutral, for even though he still dreamed about Silver, his focus remained on trying to stick it out in his marriage for the sake of his kids.

Silver told Phil that her intended was a successful local businessman and that they had great sex together, something Phil imagined that he and Silver could accomplish, as well. He did not get the sense that she was telling him about a great love story, and although by that time Phil was still about as inexperienced in love and sex as any pushing-forty, nonordained man on the planet, he hoped that she had more reasons to marry someone than great sex only. Phil just wished Silver every happiness and let her go, believing that she would be married for all time and knowing that his situation did not permit him to seek his own gratification in this drama at that juncture. Down deep, however, Phil realized that he had been harboring the secret wish that Silver would wait for him until he could complete his pledge to stay with Darla until Sylvia was grown. Phil wished that it could have been he who was having the great sex with Silver, but she was lost to him now.

After Silver's marriage, Darla had encountered her a few times and visited with her, having apparently gotten over her overt rage at Silver, but never getting over her anger at Phil. Darla was aware that Silver's relationship was not working and told Phil, on two or three occasions as soon as she learned it, about what she had learned. Presumably, this was to see what Phil's reaction would be, but whatever Darla's motivation, Phil knew a bit about what was going on with Silver.

Silver's marriage lasted for two years or so, and she had been divorced for well over a year by the time Phil came around selling ad space. When he showed up on his sales call, Silver was glad to see him and made one of the biggest buys of Phil's time doing this temp job. The two of them agreed, for old times' sake, to get together soon, for a meal. Silver called Phil a few days later and they made a date to meet for lunch the next day at a Denny's restaurant near where she worked. She said that she had a very busy job, and that she spent a lot of time away from the office, but that she was glad for a chance to visit and this was a handy place.

Phil showed up on time for the appointment, but after waiting about fifteen minutes in this pre-cell-phone era, he left. He felt somewhat angry at Silver, anger not being a familiar out-front emotion for Phil, and was a little puzzled about why he would feel so strongly about something as almost rinky-dink as this lunch date. There was clearly still plenty going on inside him about her. Silver called Phil the next day to apologize vigorously and to say that she had been held up by work commitments, arriving about twenty minutes late for lunch. Phil had apparently only just departed the restaurant when she got there. Silver suggested that they get together for dinner that evening, and Phil, his anger completely suffused, quickly agreed. Not until this moment had there been any genuine and easily realized opportunity for Phil and Silver to reopen the door Phil had not passed through during his visit from California seven years earlier, but, at last, the time had come and open it they did.

Phil had almost no frame of reference for knowing what to expect in a situation like this, so he was without any conscious notion of what might happen or how things might go, and in his uppermost thinking, at least, he was just happy to be getting together with someone he had known, been attracted to, and cared about for thirteen and a half years. Down deep, he probably knew what he wanted to happen, but it was all new to him. Amazingly, or maybe not so amazingly, it went like clockwork.

After dinner, Silver agreed to come to the home where Phil was house-sitting for friends, and after some time sharing a soft drink and visiting, there was some foot massaging (reminiscent of their time in Amsterdam), some head massaging (something new), and then lovemaking, and then more, and then more, and then more. A whole new world opened up for Phil that evening, and his life was never the same after that. To find himself experiencing such passion, such pleasure, such engulfing emotion, wonder, surprise, amazement, and spiritual joy was overwhelming, and from then on, any question about returning to Darla was resolved forever. Phil was, at last, with the person he regarded as the most perfect alive, experiencing the most perfect togetherness it was possible to feel in this world, and he could never go back. The only question was how to bring about the final break. He should have done it immediately, but contemplating the unpleasantness of dealing with Darla, and worse, the disappointment that it would cause Cole, gave Phil pause.

Phil and Silver got together once more at a Safeway store before the weekend. They spent time visiting and necking in the car in the parking lot, but more very private time was not possible that week because she had other commitments and kids at home, so Phil departed for Seward on Friday to fulfill his promise, made before his big evening with Silver, to go home for the first time since being persuaded by Cole to come back. Phil was unable to decide just how to break the news to Darla and spent Saturday hanging out with Cole and working on the house. Sylvia was around, but was not interested in interacting with her dad and just kept to herself. Darla was cool and sort of noncommittal, but not awful, and Phil actually sort of enjoyed his time working and being with Cole. But Phil was troubled, because this had to be resolved soon. Darla even wanted to have sex with him Friday night, a rare experience during the last nineteen years, and he initially went along, but couldn't do it, did not get the job done, and the last time for Phil and Darla to do that turned out to have been already well in the past.

Phil headed back to Anchorage on Sunday without disclosing the new reality to Darla and the kids, but with full knowledge that he had to get that done very soon. He contacted Silver that evening, she came over to his temporary home, and that was when the busiest two weeks (which turned into the busiest two years) of loving and sex Phil had ever lived through began. That was the week he started his new job, and he worked from 4 in the afternoon until 10 PM because he taught classes that began at 5 PM. That same week, Phil's house-sitting job ended and he rented an apartment not far from the school. He furnished the place with just an easy chair and a mattress, which he put on the floor with no bedstead, and soon Silver was coming to his place for her lunch hour and would be there again when he got off work at ten, and the two of them reprised, many times over, their first time together.

The world had now become completely new for Phil and Silver, with Silver saying that the same wondrous epiphany of love took place for her that had happened for him. As the father of two children, married nineteen years, and as the veteran of three or four brief extramarital dalliances, spread out over the six or so years since his life got so miserable in so many ways, it is remarkable that Phil should reach this advanced age having never experienced anything even remotely close to what this love affair was finally doing in his life.

Within a few days, Phil talked on the phone to Darla, and they agreed that he should come down to Seward and that they should talk when he got there. Phil was so busy experiencing the splendor of true love for the first time in his life that thoughts of a confrontation with Darla entered his mind only now and then, between hours at work and timeless trips to paradise with Silver. By the time he headed for Seward again, Phil had a plan pretty well worked out in his mind about what he would say to Darla. Phil was fairly apprehensive when he arrived, but he was also fully sustained by the beauty of the miracle that was going on for him, for a miracle was exactly what it felt like.

Up to this time, the two most perfect experiences of Phil's life had been feeling the love he bore for his parents as a child growing up, and the incredible love he felt for his children as he entered and lived the great joy of parenthood, which was a higher order of experience than the child's love for his parents, wonderful and beautiful though that was. Phil now had a third most perfect experience of his life to add to the list. After all those years, Phil finally knew what it was like to realize and consummate true love for a woman, instead of just daydreaming and wishing. Sadly, this great joy had been a possibility for Phil and Darla, and they might have been able to build such a thing if Darla had not opted for horror instead of love. It was her choice, or her disability, that caused the potential wonder never to be realized.

Phil picked Darla up at the house he had built for her to live in, and they drove down to the Seward shore to have their talk and to watch the evening lights sparkle on the water. They parked, and as they prepared to bring the marriage to its complete and final end, Darla got straight to the point and beat Phil to the punch by stating that she thought the two of them should divorce. Phil was surprised, but also impacted in a positive way, because this was why he was here, and this made the process quicker and easier. Since this was just the ticket, Phil quickly agreed, saying that he was thinking the same thing.

Later, it occurred to Phil that, between the time he first broke the news that he was leaving her and the moment when she suggested that they divorce, Darla must have come up with a plan to end the marriage and get on with her life that included serious financial support from her parents, because her congenital fear of being short of money and her belief that not being comfortably well-off was the same as poverty, all seemed to have disappeared. There was no way she wanted to stay with Phil any more than he wanted to stay with her, and it just took this long for her to collect her thoughts, make her contacts, and come up with a plan. She was as happy about their splitting up as Phil was. They came to an agreement that Phil would pay all the bills while continuing to work in Anchorage and would send Darla money for her and the children to cover daily expenses. The conversation came to a fairly amicable end .

Phil and Darla returned to the house and broke the news to the kids. Cole was crestfallen and saddened. Sylvia maintained her attitude of complete indifference, and the situation had reached a point of resolution, for the time being. Phil did not disclose his relationship with Silver nor mention her at all, and the visit ended peacefully. Phil returned to

Anchorage and his new life, and faced the future as a man entering middle age and finding true love for the first time. Except for Phil's feelings of regret for not being able keep his bargain with himself to stay for the kids as long as he had originally planned, he felt very happy. He was determined to keep showing the kids how much he loved them, but it could no longer be in the same house where their mother lived.

Phil felt that his love for Silver was equal in its power to the love he had for his children in its wonder, beauty, and amazing enormity, and thereby truly qualified as another of the most perfect experiences of his life, but it was very different all the same, and with other benefits he had only imagined until then. Phil's relationship with Silver came to a sad end after two years, but ultimately, eleven years after Phil left Darla, he married again and was able, at that time, to begin rewriting that other most perfect and wondrous experience, which has now become the single greatest, most wonderful, and most rewarding chapter of his life, that of being with the cherished and beloved woman who remains his life partner today. There will be more about her later.

By the time two or three months had passed since Phil's new life with Silver began, and with her spending lunch hours and evenings at his place, and their spending weekends together, Phil had been through more experience with lovemaking and sex than he had known in all his life, including the more than nineteen years of his marriage to Darla. He was pretty amazed at what he and Silver were able to accomplish. He had been saving up for a long time. God was in his heaven and for Phil all was well in his world, for a while.

One evening, Phil and Silver were together after he had gotten off work, and they were enjoying a sort of self-congratulatory conversation about what sexual athletes they had turned out to be together, when, somehow, they got into the subject of their past romantic history with other people. One of the few good features about Phil's marriage to Darla was, for him, the fact that Darla was not a worldly girl and was, as Phil was, sexually inexperienced and not inclined to cat around. As a youngster, Phil was severely disinterested in, and put off by, fast girls, easy girls, and bad girls. It was something that was in his blood.

Even as a small child, Phil was troubled by the fact that actors and actresses in the movies were always kissing many different people in different films. When he asked his parents about this, they said that the actors were just doing their jobs and that many of them were married to other people, for whom it was necessary to be understanding when their husbands and wives had to kiss and hug other people in the course of their employment. Little Phil was troubled by this, did not really buy it and had grown up sensitive to how hard it would be for somebody with the severe monogamous instincts that he was born with to be able to stand how life is in show business.

Once, when Phil was discussing with his mother the issues that had come up and which were causing serious problems between himself and Silver, Molly said, "Oh my God, you're just like your father!" When Phil asked what she meant, she said that some of the serious trouble between Loren and Molly went through earlier in their marriage had to do with the fact that Molly was a widow when she met Loren and that she had some sexual history that bothered him. That was probably what the arguing was about that Phil remembered hearing as he lay in bed some nights when he was small.

What happened was that Silver, in the spirit of good-humoredly sharing with Phil what had led up to where they were together at that time, disclosed to him some information about her sexual history that he was unprepared to deal with, and the die was cast for the effect of this on their relationship. When Phil heard what Silver had been doing since her first divorce, he was shocked, stunned, and profoundly stricken. This was not a reasonable or rational response on his part, for even though he had lived most of his life up to that time as a virtual celibate, Phil had at least dipped his toe into the sea of romantic adventurism a few times and was not without blemish in that department. The overwhelming and destructive reaction Phil had when he learned about Silver's sexual history was unreasonable, unhealthy and huge in its impact on Phil, and it destroyed the relationship. The experience was worse for him than the depression he had lived through. This was true in the sense that even though the depression was completely debilitating and awful, it did not include the very personal agony Phil felt about the history of his loved one. After Silver, Phil became involved with some women whose histories were considerably more varied, venturesome, risky, or even scandalous than what Silver told him about herself, but she was the only one whose past affected him so much, and she was the only one about whom he allowed knowledge or beliefs about the past to be so painful and destructive.

Some theorizing about the underlying causes of Phil's destructive reaction to what Silver told him about her past may be appropriate here. First, it was in his blood. Phil was bothered, even as a small child, by all the different people kissing each other in the movies. He worried about their spouses at home and how they could possibly bear to watch their husbands and wives kissing other people on film. No one taught Phil that. It is just the way he was.

Once, when Phil was eight or ten years old, his parents had some neighbors over for some early New Year's Eve drinks, and after they toasted, they all shared a holiday kiss, on the lips, which, as Phil watched, burned into his memory for all time. The kisses were just light pecks, no passion, infidelity, or romance involved, but it was not a suitable thing for the boy to have seen, given how he reacted, and he never forgot it. It was mentioned earlier that Phil's mother told him how horribly Phil's dad suffered from knowing about some of his wife's past, and Phil was afflicted, without any intention on his part to subscribe to such views, in exactly the same way as his father.

Point number two, Phil married the second girl he went out with more than twice, and when he married, he was utterly naïve and ignorant of the ways of the world. Neither Phil nor Darla was equipped to become part of the sexual revolution and sought refuge from it in each other, so when Phil emerged from that awful marriage, he had not grown or changed in his reactions to the same things that had bothered him so much as a young person. Phil was the adult in his marriage to Darla, insofar as he was the one who attempted to bring reason, rationality, negotiation, good sense, and responsibility to the relationship, but when it came to being the kid who wanted his virgin, after all those years Phil was forty-one going on twelve.

Point three, after spending almost twenty years in a marriage of complete disappointment, where the participants never found any sexual compatibility or common frame of reference for that portion of the relationship, Phil probably had a subliminal belief that he was still entitled to what he had wanted to start with, namely a bride with whom he could learn, love, grow, and find perfection. That may be naïve, but it must have been going on with Phil, because it sure seemed to own him.

Fourth, after more than a decade of carrying a torch for Silver and imagining a life with her someday, finding out that she had been getting together with this assortment of other men must have felt like betrayal, although from a reality standpoint that is unreasonable and foolish, because Phil had no hold on her and she had made no pledge to him.

For the rest of the two-year life of that relationship, Phil lived a sort of schizophrenic existence, on the one hand loving this remarkable and gifted person so much that it felt like a miracle, and on the other hand, obsessing about her having been with other men to an extent that was nightmarish, both for Phil and for Silver. They were together so much during the first six months of the relationship that Phil was able, to some degree, to sort of drown his destructive obsession about Silver's history in his magnificent intoxication with her and the magic they made together. But then, Phil's employment situation changed quite abruptly, and he went to work for the State of Alaska Department of Labor in Kenai and moved away from Anchorage. When that happened, he suddenly had more time alone to obsess full-time about what bothered him, and he really went down the drain.

The startling end to Phil's job as a teacher of English as a second language came when the state of Alaska shut down the operation because there had been reports that the operators of the school were using fraudulent incentives to persuade immigrants to enroll in the school and borrow money from the state to take the course. The ESL program was shut down, and the school was eventually closed. One of the entrepreneurs who developed this scheme was a scoundrel from the Dominican Republic who ended up fleeing Alaska with warrants circulating for his arrest for sex crimes against children. Phil disliked the guy and told him to stay out of his classroom, but Phil only had an inkling of what a low-life bastard the guy really was. There were three other ESL teachers, good people all, who were victims of this racket at the same time Phil was and who ended up looking for work as well. Fortunately for Phil, just as that job came to its abrupt end, he got hired by the Alaska Department of Labor. Not so fortunately for his relationship with Silver, Phil moved to Kenai, and the end of the relationship came into view.

Silver had access, through her job, to minimum cost, space-available air transportation to Kenai, so she flew there to spend nights with Phil two, three, or four times a week, and he drove to Anchorage most weekends. Cole was a senior and Phil went to most of his football games and, later, his wrestling matches, but was still able to see a lot of Silver. Phil attended some of Sylvia's volleyball games, as well, but she could not have cared less whether he was there or not. In November, Phil revealed to the kids his relationship with Silver. Their reaction was muted, but that was when it may be that they came to the conclusion that Phil's leaving their mother was a low-life play on his part, intended from the beginning as a way to be with Silver. They decided that the only reason their father left was because he wanted to disengage from his responsibilities as a father and husband in the interest of fooling around and having a good time. The fact that

Phil was no longer able to stand the abuse that Darla dished out was not within their frame of reference. They persist in their mistaken belief today and for all time, encouraged by their infuriated mother, who no doubt considered her soul to have been raped again by Phil. The truth of his soul having been raped by Darla for two decades is not on their radar screen, and they won't consider it.

Even though Phil's reason for leaving Darla had nothing to do with Silver, his connecting with Silver after agreeing to reconsider his decision to leave Darla leaving was poorly done on Phil's part. Phil long ago recognized his error and apologized to the kids for that. But they consider themselves to be deeply spiritual, enlightened, and superior beings, and are not inclined to understand, forgive, or empathize with their father, nor will they discontinue their vengeful treatment of him or apologize for their wrongs, so that is where things stand. Phil has endured all the abuse and injustice he intends to take from their mother or from them. Phil told Cole in the last communication between that Phil has forgiven Cole and Sylvia for the wrongs they have done against their father, just as they should forgive him for the mistakes he has made. Phil further stated that he will put up with no more crap from anybody. If they were to approach their father with a wish to patch things up, he would be available to them, but Phil says that he has kissed the last ass he'll ever kiss in that family and has been abused by them for the last time.

Darla's nature was clearly revealed when she informed Phil that, if he stayed with Silver, Darla would destroy his relationships with his children as punishment. Phil did not believe that Darla had that power, and the end of his time with Silver had nothing to do with that threat, but Darla is very happy with the familial rupture, and that is wrong of her.

After two years of struggling, separating, making up, and Phil's finding that the problem still ate at him, Silver became fed up with his inability to let go of the obsession with her past and she ended the relationship. She was wise to do so, and Phil regrets very much all the heartache and hurt he caused her. Phil believes that Silver loved him very much and began to force herself to break the attachment because Phil couldn't fix his obsession. As much as Phil cared for Silver, it seems clear in retrospect that he loved even more the fantasy he carried about his untouched woman. One of Phil's greatest regrets is how much suffering he put Silver through, for she was a good and gentle person and did not merit all the sadness this sad tale brought to her. The great benefits Phil was able to derive from his relationship with Silver were 1) that at long last he had confirmation that he could truly and beautifully love a woman, and 2) he learned how much his own negative thinking could cause himself and someone else to suffer, and he determined not to ever again allow such unhappiness to be the result of his actions and his unbridled negativity. If Phil could erase the great hurt he created in the life of a good person who did not deserve it, he would do so, but except for that, the great lesson he learned from this experience was so important and valuable to him that it was worth the pain he went through to learn it.

32

PHIL'S NEW LIFE

Phil's new job with the Alaska Department of Labor was a good one, and he was glad to have it. It was not as exciting nor as much of an ego trip as air traffic control, and did not pay as well, but it was satisfying, demanding, interesting, and far less punishing when things got out of kilter. Even when Phil retired from it, everything was just right. All the time Phil had that job, he looked forward to going to work each day and really liked what he was doing. When he retired, Phil did not miss it a bit. That's about as cool as it can get.

Phil went to work for the Department of Labor in Kenai, Alaska, as a veterans' services representative, but he actually helped all kinds of people, including veterans, find work. Phil got hired because he told the interviewer that he knew how hard it can be and what it is like to be unemployed and looking for work, and that he knew the extent to which hope is a big factor in what keeps a person going. Being someone who provides hope to those looking for work would be a privilege, and to actually play a role in helping many of those hopeful folks find new jobs would be even better. Phil felt that, to be a real contributor, facilitating a way for Alaskans to improve their lives by obtaining honest employment, would feel more like a calling and a mission to him than a job. Phil said that one of the best religious tenets he ever heard of was the one that declared that honest work, performed in a spirit of service, is equivalent in God's eyes to worship of God, and that Phil would bring that approach to this job, should he be chosen. The man liked what Phil had to say and gave him the position.

In this job, Phil gained computer skills he had not possessed before, and found that his organized, systematic, and dedicated approach to providing the service being offered, both to clients seeking work and to employers in search of workers, allowed him to be extremely effective at his job. Phil really loved it when one of his referrals got hired, and when lots of them got work, he was in hog heaven. The growing number of Hispanic workers in Alaska gave Phil ample opportunity to make use of his Spanish-language skills, and he became accustomed to receiving outstanding performance evaluations. Phil spent those years as happy in a job as a person can reasonably expect to be. It was nice to reflect on how this job compared to the nightmare cannery job, and how much better life can be when you enjoy how you make your living.

Phil learned when he was a Navy officer and when he was a processing plant foreman that he was a good boss, that people liked working for him, and that he got good performance out of workers because he cared for and looked after them. Phil received great personal satisfaction from that, but he liked even better the gratification he got from putting together jobs and people seeking work and feeling every day that the world was better off because of what he did that day. The prospect of becoming a supervisor, simply watching other people in his position do the anointed work that he loved, instead of actually doing the work, was an unattractive one to Phil, for which reason he never applied for promotion to supervisory levels.

In later years, a reorganization of the department caused the Job Service function to be combined with the Unemployment Insurance side of the house, and Phil became a UI adjudicator who evaluated the circumstances surrounding applicants' reasons for being unemployed. He made legal determinations as to applicants' eligibility for unemployment benefits. The work was not as heart-warming as helping people find jobs, but it was like being an investigator or detective and very interesting because of the fact-finding involved. It also required Phil to have a strong knowledge of labor law and the ability to write clear, concise opinions concerning the decisions he made, so he liked the job very much and was good at it. Phil received praise from his superiors for his skill at crafting factual, comprehensible, thorough decisions that gave complete and accurate information to the claimants and employers for whom they were composed.

Phil encountered thousands of interesting cases and stories over the years, and has the opinion that a book of some of those stories would be fun to write and interesting to read, so plans to write one. By the time Phil reached a point where he was thinking about seeking advancement to boss level so he could watch others do the work instead of doing it himself, he had attained an age and level of financial security that allowed him to retire in modest comfort, so he retired without ever applying for a supervisory job. Cole once expressed disappointment in his dad that Phil had not sought higher office, but Phil chose being happy in and loving his job over advancement to jobs that did not interest him. It was better when Cole was a kid and was proud of his dad for working in that nasty old cannery.

Following Phil's break-up from Silver, he had a couple of girlfriends whom he dated for around a year and a half each, one following the other in chronology, who were both sweet, gentle, utterly untroublesome people with whom Phil got along easily and without strife, and whom he remembers with respect and kind thoughts. With the singular exception of Phil's experience with poor Silver, his relationships with women since Darla are evidence of his contention that a trouble-free existence with him has always been possible for anyone who is willing to try to get along, as Darla was not. To spend three years in which not a single harsh, unkind, nasty, hateful, troublesome, or bitter word was spoken between Phil and each of these nice people, with each of whom he had very active, satisfactory, exclusive, and monogamous physical relationships, is testament to how easy Phil is to have peace with, and anyone who thinks that the ugly character of his long, lonely life with Darla was his fault is blind, ignorant, and utterly misguided.

The two relationships spoken of here failed, in part, because of fundamental disagreement Phil had with the women concerned in such areas as child rearing, abortion versus life, emotional intimacy, and opinions on cultural and societal change and decay. Phil learned after many months of seeing each of these women that both had undergone abortions while they were married, and neither seemed to carry any negative feelings about having done so. The women were clearly both good and decent people, but having had the experience Phil did in which he loved and cherished his children from the moment he learned of their existence, he was unable to understand how anyone could choose to destroy the life they had created. Unfortunately, both of the women had been married to scoundrels, and the choices they made were not unreasonable, given the law that permitted what they did, but Phil could not abide the knowledge of what they had done.

One of these women had a daughter who, as time went on and as Phil got to know the child better, turned out to have a vicious mouth and a surly attitude, which Phil found to be completely out of bounds. The child's mother was such a nice person and not troublesome at all, so where this ugly streak came from was unclear to Phil, but Phil's children were never allowed to behave that way, and he disliked finding it necessary to stop the girl from being disrespectful to her mother in his presence. Phil could not see marrying into that situation, and in marriage was the only way he wanted to have a long-term relationship.

The woman whom Phil dated after he ended that relationship had a son in his late teens from whom she was estranged in a manner similar to Phil's circumstance. The woman described her ex-husband as a tyrannical bully whose rage at her when she left him forced their son to make a choice about which of his parents to despise. The boy chose to reject his mother, who was clearly a gentle and loving person who deserved better. The description of the ex-husband reminded Phil of Pop Oldburg, and the ugliness of the son's attitude and the encouragement of his father in hating his mother were reminiscent of Phil's experience with Sylvia. Both parents definitely had in common their sad stories about their children.

The problems Phil had with this relationship were not insurmountable, but they bothered him. One was that they had met in a bar/dance hall. Phil seldom went to those places and he never picked up women there, and this woman was the only person he ever dated after meeting in a bar. After they met there, they exchanged phone numbers and then started going out together in a respectable way, but the idea of spending the rest of his life saying that he had met his wife in a bar was a bad one for Phil, and this was a small part of his decision to end the relationship.

Because of how badly she was treated by her ex, this woman indicated her intention never to marry again, which was the opposite of Phil's hopes and aspirations. He had been equally ill-treated, but Phil knew that he had the capacity to succeed in marriage if he found someone with similar capacity, and he always intended to marry again. This woman might have been susceptible to persuasion to think otherwise, but the relationship never reached the point where the effort needed to be made.

The other problem Phil had about this woman was that, after the third date, she invited him to spend the night with her. He accepted, but was still working on getting over being the obsessive prude who had destroyed his relationship with Silver, and he realized that this was probably a pattern for this woman and that there had very likely been plenty of other invitations issued. Three dates did not seem to be enough time to get the information needed to make a decision as important as who you are sleeping with. Phil never got any details about the woman's other men, and did not suffer or obsess the way he had before about what he thought she might have done, but Phil never liked the fact that three dates was all it took. Phil was still trying to figure out where he fit into this new morality and social code, so immediately rejecting this sweet and gentle person for this one reason seemed unfair and premature, and he did not do it, but this ended up being one of the reasons he did not stay with her.

After years of the opportunity to reflect upon why Phil chose not to stay in either of these peaceful, strife-free relationships, he has come to believe that the main reason for his dissatisfaction with them had to do with the pathology that accrued from all his own years of living with difficult people like Loren and Darla. Perhaps the reason Phil did not find himself deeply in love with Darla before they married was that he thought she was peaceful and untroublesome. Perhaps Phil had a distorted need to deal with a complicated, temperamental, angry person like Loren in order to feel comfortable in an environment similar to what his life had always been. Consciously, Phil had the belief that Darla was as peaceful and determined to have a civil relationship as he was, so chose her despite not feeling a lot of love for her. It may be that subconsciously, Phil recognized how difficult life with her would be, although to say what would have revealed that to him would be guessing. Also, Phil's need to be a repairman for an angry person, so that she could stop being angry, found in Darla a potential outlet for his repairman imperative. Darla ended up being so mean and unreachable that Phil's hoped-for fix-it skills were totally insufficient, so the marriage failed.

Concerning the two gentle women mentioned earlier, there was still that same dynamic going on with Phil as he related to them. Despite caring very much for these sweet people, Phil experienced in those relationships a persistent and nagging dissatisfaction that could not be explained by whether or not the women were pleasant to be around, because they were. Phil was probably damaged enough by life with Darla and with his father that he must have still felt the need to save somebody from themselves, and those women did not need saving, at least not from destructive behavior resulting from lifelong anger. Thus, the dissatisfaction Phil felt. It's sad to say that Phil's own scars caused him not to be able to capitalize upon the goodness available to him in those women. One can hope that they were ultimately able to find someone loving and evolved enough to appreciate the virtue and peace in living that they had to offer. They both cared deeply for Phil, and he cared very much for them, but he had already once married someone whom he did not love with all the power in his being, and he was not going to do that again, so he moved on.

33

PSC

About five years after Phil was diagnosed with ulcerative colitis, he received a disturbing letter from the Anchorage Blood Bank, where he had become a blood donor on a regular basis. The colitis had gone into remission and had stopped being a problem for Phil about three years after he was diagnosed. During those years, Phil had transferred in his job from the Kenai office to the Anchorage office of the Alaska Department of Labor, His relationship with Silver had ended, and he was approaching the end of his time with the second of the two peaceful women mentioned above.

The letter from the Blood Bank informed Phil that they would no longer be able to accept blood donated by him because the mandatory testing they performed on all blood received from volunteer donors had revealed abnormalities in his liver enzyme measurements, which required that his donation be rejected. Abnormal readings such as these can be explained in a number of ways, one of which is that the potential exists for the presence of liver disease or other blood-borne anomaly which, in the interest of protecting public health, cannot be allowed into the blood supply. The numbers were only just slightly outside the normal range, so Phil was not thought to be profoundly ill or in grave danger, but he was advised to consult with his physician about this matter.

Phil saw the doctor who had been treating him for colitis, and this doctor referred him to a specialist in gastroenterology and liver disease. After a thorough work-up, this doctor produced the diagnosis of primary sclerosing cholangitis (PSC), a serious and potentially fatal autoimmune condition in the liver that slowly destroys the ducting system in the organ through persistent inflammation. The cause for the development of this self-destructive condition within the body is not known, and a primary concern for patients with it is that the chronically inflamed ducting can often develop into liver cancer, which is as bad as it gets. Even if the persistent inflammation does not cause cancer, the damage it does to the liver can eventually destroy the ability of the organ to do its job, and the patient may require a liver transplant. Some years after Phil's diagnosis, the famous NFL player Walter Peyton died of liver cancer caused by primary sclerosing cholangitis, and PSC became known as "Walter Peyton's disease" in a manner similar to another case involving a famous athlete in which amytrophic lateral sclerosis, or ALS, became known as "Lou Gehrig's disease."

Phil was informed that colitis patients, even those in remission as he was, have an increased likelihood, compared to people who do not have colitis, of contracting PSC. The reason for this is unknown, but both conditions are autoimmune, that is to say, they are diseases not transmitted by contagion, and are maladies in which the body damages itself because of some genetic, hereditary, or organic disconnect within the person's DNA. It is annoying to Phil that his own physical being would betray him in this fashion. It is possible that all the stress he went through as an air traffic controller and as a seafood process foreman provided a trigger for these autoimmune illnesses to ignite, but that is not known for certain, and people who do not have such murderously stressful jobs also come down with these diseases. Research is ongoing, and someday science will find the answers and produce a cure. Genetic engineering is presently where the greatest hope lies for finding a cure.

Phil's specialist told him that some people die or require a liver transplant within two or three years of diagnosis, and some people are still doing all right many years later. The average time period between diagnosis and death or transplant for PSC patients was thirteen years. The longest the doctor knew of at that time for a patient to continue to be alive and well with the disease was seventeen years. The specialist knew of no way to predict how it would go for any individual patient, so the only thing to do was watch Phil carefully and see what happened. The doctor prescribed medication that returned Phil's slightly elevated liver enzyme measurements to normal levels, and so far, twenty years later, he's doing fine. Many people with this disease have probably had it for years by the time they are diagnosed, because it does its insidious work with very little in the way of symptomology for a long time before it is obvious. In Phil's case, his regular blood donations showed no problems over an extended period, so when the abnormality showed up, the disease had just manifested at a measurable level and was promptly detected. That would explain, at least in part, why Phil's illness has been more like no illness at all for such a long time.

Another portion of the explanation for Phil's healthy longevity with this disease is that he has a happy life. He is joyfully and securely married to someone he loves with all the power he possesses, and the two share a wonderful existence as a real team. Phil has a positive outlook and an excitement about life that causes him to be able to greet each new day with eagerness and optimism. Living life in that way is well-known to be a boon to good health, and this is very likely what has slowed the progress of this killer disease. Phil has, in recent months, established a relationship with a well-respected liver transplant clinic, whose assessment of him is that he does indeed have PSC, although cases are rare in which the people remain as healthy as Phil has after such a long history with this malady. They say that Phil's condition is still much too mild and undeveloped for him to expect to need a transplant any time soon. After this much time, however, things could change rapidly, so closer than ever monitoring is required and is now ongoing. It is possible, but also relatively rare, to have PSC without it ever becoming so advanced that the patient enters end-stage liver disease. Phil has plans to be one of those rare cases and expect that when he dies, it will be at a very advanced age, and it will be from something other than PSC. As a common-sense and conservative planner, however, he is covering all eventualities just in case and is enjoying life to the fullest in the meantime.

Phil was born with an innate sense of optimism and has always had a natural-born inclination to find and focus on the best he could make of most any given situation. After encountering so many potholes in his road of life, which his inborn positive outlook could not stop from appearing, and after experiencing all the resulting depression that he went through, Phil was pleased that, four years after leaving Darla, he remained depression free and was no longer experiencing any of the despair and hopelessness that is attendant to depression. This was certainly a good thing, but it was clear to Phil that he had not managed to fully regain the overall "glass is half full and not half empty" way of addressing the world, which had been characteristic of him in his earlier life.

Phil was very aware that his internal, emotional health was a lot better since he no longer had to deal with Darla and with punishing, killer jobs. Still missing, however, was the always upbeat and positive sense about most everything that had been present in him before all that other stuff happened. In an effort to recapture that, Phil began a campaign to find out what he could do to get back that good, old, positive Phil. It was a growth process that took a couple of years of searching, reading, studying, attending seminars and groups, and reflecting on what he was learning for Phil to find his answer, but he found it. He discovered what it took to regain his old way of being positive, incorporated what he learned into his daily existence, and has been living his life in an outrageously enjoyable way ever since. Phil plans to share what he has learned and how to apply it when he's done with telling this story, so stay on board.

34

ALONE

While Cole was attending college in Oregon, Phil made a number of trips there to visit him, and on one occasion, when Phil had decided to buy a new pickup truck, He found that an auto broker in Portland could get him just what he wanted, a four-wheel-drive, stick shift Dodge pickup with a few upscale accessories, for a much better price than he could get in Alaska, so Phil arranged to buy the vehicle and to have it waiting for him at the Portland Airport when he arrived there on one of his visits to Cole.

The dealer had mailed Phil a key to the new pickup truck, and he found the vehicle waiting for him in the airport secure parking area, so he drove on out to where Cole attended school outside of Portland, found Cole in the dorm where he lived, and began a visit. Phil got to observe a wrestling team workout and learned what a really tough dude his son was. Phil arrived there during the school week, so while Cole attended classes, Phil got his new truck rust-proofed and bought a bed-liner for it, after which he and Cole went out to dinner, got together with some of Cole's friends, explored suburban Portland, and had a fun visit.

Cole's wrestling team had a three-team meet scheduled for that weekend at Western Oregon College, a school in Monmouth, Oregon, the town where some of Phil's mother's relatives had lived when Phil spent the summer of 1958 in the northwest, and where he had met the girl for whom he carried a torch all through his high school years. Phil learned that this girl, now a middle aged woman, still lived in Monmouth, and he decided to look her up. Her name was Temperance Hannity, she was a somewhat distant cousin whose grandfather was kin to Phil's mother, and she had been divorced for years. Phil found her number in the phone book at the college library and called her. He told her that he lived in Alaska, had a son attending college in Oregon, was there visiting his boy and buying a new truck, would be in Monmouth on Saturday to watch Cole wrestle, and would like to see her. She remembered Phil, was surprised to hear from him, and agreed to meet him at a restaurant in Monmouth on Saturday morning after he drove the sixty or so miles down from where Cole attended school. Cole was traveling on a bus with the team, so Phil made the trip alone.

Phil was seeing someone at the time and had no expectations of anything romantic developing with Tammy, as she had been called when they were kids. He had a girl friend, lived very far away and had no interest in a long-distance relationship. Besides, Phil and Tammy were shirt-tail cousins, and you don't usually date relatives. Phil's thinking was that, having been secretly loved for as long and as truly as she was by him when they were teenagers, it would be a nice thing to know about all these years later. It would be a shame to have been cared for that much and to never even know about it, so Phil wanted to tell her. He thought that if someone had secretly cared for him that way at some point in his life, he would have liked to know about it just because it is rare and special to be loved, and not to know about it would be missing out on something good.

Phil and Tammy met at the restaurant, and he was impressed to see that she was still beautiful and graceful in appearance, and that she looked very fit and healthy. She had dark hair (streaked with some gray), dark brown eyes, and a very cool, low-key, and guarded demeanor. They had coffee and shared a nice visit, and when Phil told her of the love he had carried around for her so long ago, she seemed pleased to learn of it, but it was certainly not a big deal.

Later that day, Tammy met Phil at the college gym and they watched the wrestling meet together. They looked on as Cole won one match easily and was then easily beaten in his other match. .

After the wrestling meet, Phil and Cole hung around Monmouth for a while and then later, with Tammy and her two teenage kids, had dinner at the house of some of Tammy's cousins whom Phil did not know, but who were also some distant relation to him. After that, Phil and Tammy shook hands, agreed that it had been a nice day, and said that they should get together again some time when Phil was in Oregon. Then, Phil and

Cole headed back to Cole's campus in Phil's new truck. Phil contacted Tammy and visited with her once or twice more on other trips he made to Oregon to visit Cole in the next couple of years, and the two developed a small, platonic friendship, but there was no romance and nothing more than visiting and saying howdy.

After they returned to Cole's college, Phil and his son spent the next day together and really had fun. By this time, they had become very close, and Phil was getting as much pleasure out of him as he had experienced when Cole was such an affectionate and loving little kid. Phil had actually begun boasting to his parents and others about what a terrific relationship he had with Cole now that he was grown. As they visited on this occasion, Cole regaled Phil with hilarious stories about life on a wrestling team with a bunch of Neanderthal college apes. There is no one alive who can tell a funny story better than Cole could. Phil and Cole threw a football around, Phil met some more of Cole's friends, and then the following day, Phil headed out for California.

Phil made it the first night to Vallejo, where he had lived when he worked at Bay TRACON, and stopped to visit the old neighbors there, then got a motel room for the night, and the next day, he pressed on to Los Angeles, where Sylvia was. Phil spent a few days with her, including the sad and lonely trip with her to Death Valley mentioned earlier. This was the occasion during which Phil met, for the first time, Darla's new husband, whom Sylvia despised, but who seemed to Phil to be a harmless sort.

Phil drove to Phoenix, Arizona where through mutual friends in Cheyenne he had learned that Kara, his first girlfriend, was living, and stopped to see her there for the first time in twenty-five or so years. Kara had been married, divorced, and had one daughter, now a teenager, and Kara was just about to remarry her former husband. Phil and Kara had a nice, very platonic, catch-up-on-old-times kind of visit, and Phil headed on toward Cheyenne where he visited his many family and friends there. Phil has never seen or heard from Kara since and presumes that the remarriage was successful and that she is doing fine.

As Phil's Cheyenne visit was ending, his old high school friend Fritz Marsden, who lived in Portland and worked for United Airlines, and whom Phil visited whenever he went to Oregon to visit Cole, flew into Cheyenne, where Phil picked him up at the airport. After Fritz spent some time visiting Phil's folks, who had always been very fond of him and were glad to see him again, Fritz and Phil hit the road for Alaska in Phil's new Dodge truck. Fritz traveled to Alaska regularly in his work, and was curious to experience the Alaska Highway as a way to get there instead of flying. The trip together with Phil was Fritz's idea, and Phil was grateful for the company and the help with the long drive. Fritz is a dear friend to Phil. This trip took place in February, so they went through lots of darkness and far-below-zero temperatures on the way north. They had a nice trip because they enjoyed each other's companionship, but it's actually more fun to make that trip in the summer, when there is maximum daylight and warmer weather.

When Phil and Fritz arrived in Anchorage, Fritz was the first friend to whom Phil was able to show the small house he had just bought there. This was somewhat less house than Phil could have afforded, but because he wanted to keep his options open rather than being stuck with a big house payment, Phil chose small. The big, worldwide crash of oil prices that occurred in the late 1980s had dramatically driven down the prices of homes in Alaska.

The house Phil constructed in Seward had sold for a sickeningly low price after the plummet in home values, but Phil was able to turn that money around and buy the small Anchorage house in a similarly cratered market and came out pretty well. Phil and Darla had a lot of equity in the house Phil built because their California house had sold for such a big profit, and Phil was able to turn his share of the Seward house equity into an accelerated payment schedule and pay off the Anchorage house, in full, in six years. Phil believed that there is real advantage in minimizing personal debt, because then you don't end up underwater on your home mortgage and you can come out of a crazy economic time like that in decent shape.

After Fritz went back to Portland, Phil ran across an Anchorage friend named Bud Morris, who had just lost his job and gotten divorced, and was in a very bad way. Phil let Bud move into Phil's new house with Phil, rent-free, until Bud was able to get back on his feet. Bud lived with Phil for more than a year and a half and was able to get himself squared away. During his stay with Phil, Bud got on "The Oprah Winfrey Show" as a result of his appearance in *Alaska Men* magazine when Oprah did a show on the magazine and the men featured in it. Bud met a number of women because of being in the magazine and being on that show, married one of them, and moved to Canada to start a new life. He has done very well there and is still enjoying life as a Canadian.

In all the time Bud lived in Phil's house, not one unkind word, not one spiteful, angry, troublesome, bitter, or even simply irritable word passed between the two men, even though they saw each other daily. This is another example of how easy it is for someone living with Phil Temple to get along with him, if they just want to. Of course, living expense-free with someone, as Bud was, is good motivation to treat them well, which Bud did. But Phil had no other motivation to treat him well except that Phil treats everyone well. A damaged wife just can't spot that. Morris was another very mellow guy, much like Phil, who had married someone with a lot of hate in her soul, just as Phil did, and who had spent years as the verbal punching bag of a demented woman, just like Phil did. Both men were free of that now and glad of it.

35

TAMMY

Cole was completing his college undertaking and was graduating in May of 1990. Phil traveled to Oregon to witness the event, much as he had traveled to California in 1989 to see Sylvia graduate from high school. Everyone in the broken Temple family but Phil had left Alaska, but he still made the very strong effort to show his kids his love for them by being there for them in their lives.

Phil contacted Temperance (Tammy) to say hello and that he was in Oregon, and she expressed an interest in sharing the experience of Cole's graduation with Phil. She could not go to the commencement ceremony because seating was limited, there was no way to get her a ticket, and her presence at the event was a last-minute development. There was, however, a banquet afterwards where no such limitations existed, so, with Cole's permission, Phil invited Tammy to come to the banquet with them. She accepted and showed up on campus after the graduation ceremony, and the three of them had a nice meal and visit together. It was fun to observe the dynamics of a bunch of college grads on their big day. Cole said good-bye to Tammy and went off with his friends for a while, so Phil and Tammy went somewhere for coffee and a last visit. Phil told Tammy that now that Cole had finished with school, Phil would not be coming to Oregon to see him anymore, and that he had enjoyed getting to know her and wished her well. Phil had made nothing of the attraction he still felt for her and could see no point in continuing the periodic visits because, even though he still had friends and relatives there, his biggest reason for coming to Oregon was ending. Phil and Tammy said good-bye, , went their separate ways, and as far as Phil knew, that was that.

He went back to Alaska and resumed his life, tame though it was. The house Phil had bought turned out to be typical of what it has always been possible to find in the cold country. That is, houses built by people who came from warmer climates who don't understand or care that it can really get cold in Alaska. It is better if the house is built so that the occupants can stay warm even when the temperature plunges outside. What Phil found when he moved in there in early 1989 was that when it got below zero outside, it was not possible keep the first floor of that house any warmer than fifty-five degrees, even with the natural gas furnace cranked up to ninety degrees on the thermostat. Phil set to work that summer, and continued for the next couple of years, solving the many deficiencies in that place that caused it to leak heat and suck cold.

The process of upgrading the house took so long because when Phil finished one or a few of these projects, he assumed that the problem would be solved. Winter came back and he found that things were better, but that the situation was still unsatisfactory, so did another upgrade and hope that would do the job. Phil performed the first three improvements that first summer, did one more the second summer, which he was sure would do the job, and then had to do the last two upgrades the third summer, and that finally did it. The place had, at last, become a real Alaskan house in which it was possible for the occupants to stay cozy and warm. The jobs Phil did included 1) furring out the sides of the house to make them thicker and then adding insulation and re-siding the building. The house was framed with two-by-four lumber, a stupid thing to do in Alaska, which requires two-by-six construction so that adequate insulation can be installed in the walls; 2) reinsulating the attic and 3) putting fiberglass batts under the floors; 4) plumbing in new heating zones to the gas-fired hot water heating system; 5) tearing out and completely rebuilding the fireplace, which had been constructed with no insulation at all; and 6) digging up the earth all around the outside of the house and insulating the concrete foundation and installing drainage so the crawl space would stop flooding. When Phil was finally done, the house was at last able to retain warmth. It was a much better place to live, and he was proud of it.

One day after getting home from work, a month or so after Phil had returned from Cole's graduation in Oregon, he was outside installing furring on the house when he heard the phone ringing. By the time he got inside, the caller was leaving a message on the recorder, and Phil was surprised to hear that it was Temperance, calling from Oregon. (She told Phil that since becoming an adult, she preferred to have people call her by her given name instead of Tammy, which was how she was known to Phil all those years ago when they were kids and he was carrying around that torch for her. Even now, decades later, calling her Temperance was difficult for Phil and seemed strange. He could not get comfortable calling her that rather formal, slightly imperious name, so just called her Tammy, as he had done so long ago.) Anyway, it was Tammy; Phil answered before she ended her message, and when they spoke, Tammy suggested an idea that was a real surprise to Phil. She proposed that she come to Alaska and be his guest for a week. She did not say what her intentions were, but Phil could not think of a reason to say no. Besides, he was intrigued. What did this beautiful but very cool and withheld lady have in mind?

Bud Morris had been living with Phil for well over a year by this time, and as two peaceful guys, they were still getting along fine. When Phil told Bud what was up, Bud got a sort of knowing look on his face and said that he would stay at a friend's house when Tammy got to town, so that he would not be around to interfere with anything. It was only a two-bedroom house, and there was nothing going on between Phil and Tammy that would put them in the same bedroom, so Bud pretty much needed to do what he suggested, because putting Tammy on the couch did not seem very hospitable.

When Tammy arrived, Phil picked her up at the airport and brought her home, and they visited like the friends that they had become during the few times Phil saw her on his trips to spend time with Cole. When Phil asked what her objective was in coming to Alaska, Tammy said that the younger of her two kids was finishing high school, so her job of raising her children was coming to an end, and she was examining some options about getting on with her life that did not include staying in the somewhat rut-like existence she was living in Oregon. Tammy wanted to look in some new places to see where else she might want to live and to explore career change possibilities in other localities.

Phil said that he would take his truck to work and that Tammy could use his car to get around and get acquainted with Anchorage and its surrounding area, and that she was welcome to do all the fact-finding that she cared to do about jobs, living situations, the local market, and whatever else she wanted to learn about. They agreed that this seemed like a plan, and Tammy settled in for her week-long stay, using Bud's room as a guestroom.

The next day, Phil went to work and Tammy took his car and looked around Anchorage. That evening, they went out to dinner and Tammy disclosed to Phil a little more about herself. She said that she had been a pretty wild woman when she first divorced, some dozen or so years before, but that she had been celibate and unattached for six or seven years by this time, and that she was interested in expanding both her professional and personal horizons, now that her kids were grown. Tammy had a master's degree in counseling, and made her living working with developmentally disabled people. This, of course, did not necessarily represent anything particularly strong to Phil, given his experience with Darla, the last holder of a master's in counseling he had known. Phil had been divorced some five years or so by this time.

When Phil asked Tammy what she meant by "wild woman," she said that she had gone through a "rocking divorcee" phase and had been rather promiscuous and unwise in some of her choices as they related to sexual behavior and the men she had associated with. She dated married men, had affairs when she was married, had lots and lots of sex partners, and thought that wild woman was a fairly good description of the way she had lived. Phil was pretty taken aback, but was not horrified, which surprised him a bit, because what she was saying would have qualified in his book as horrifying for most of Phil's life.

Tammy then said that part of the reason for her visit was that she wanted Phil to consider the possibility of the two of them becoming a couple, with the long-term ramifications that might entail. Phil's disclosure, a few years earlier, that he had been so much in love with Tammy as a teenager had caused her to reflect about those days and to dredge up a recollection that she had experienced similar feelings for Phil. That was a surprise to him, because his belief had been that she had not given him a second thought, but he saw no need to debate the subject. Tammy said that she had been alone and celibate for years, having recognized that the life-style she had adopted earlier was not a particularly good one, either for her or for her children. She said that she was now ready to look into getting involved with someone, since her primary responsibility of raising children was fulfilled, and Phil looked like a good prospect to her. It seemed that Phil was actually more than just part of the reason she was here.

Tammy's interest in examining the possibility of a relationship with Phil made more sense to him than thinking that she would come all this way just to look for work. No mention of anything romantic between them had come up during the small number of times Phil visited Tammy in Oregon. Tammy now said that she wasn't proposing that they start sleeping together, but only that they spend some time together and see if this seemed like a good idea. Phil said, "Well, okay, why not?"

Phil was not seeing anyone, and his intentions included marriage as the ultimate objective of starting any serious relationship. Phil and Tammy did not know each other well enough to contemplate marriage at this point Their distant cousin, not first-cousin status and the fact that they were past child-bearing years, made that a possibility. Phil was able to remember, and to find that the potential existed for him to reconstruct, the love he had felt and carried around for years for Tammy when he was a teenager, and he thought it would not be difficult to recapture those feelings for her, even all this much later. Phil did not know her very well and could not pretend that this suddenly, he was head over heels for her, but he could certainly see merit in the idea of exploring the possibility of a life with this smart and attractive person.

Phil requested and received approval for a day or two off work as the weekend approached, and he and Tammy traveled and camped out around south-central Alaska for a few days and got better acquainted, still with no sleeping together. It seemed to Phil to be a bit like a sort of civics research project or something, and a little odd, but Tammy was nice company, good-looking, and Phil was flattered to be considered in this way, somewhat academic though it was. They talked about how something like this would go, given how far apart the two of them lived, and about how there was no likelihood of Phil's moving to Oregon. It looked as though if it were going to happen, it would be because Tammy moved to Alaska.

They completed their car trip during which they took advantage of all the hours together speculating and postulating to get a picture of what their future together could be like. It looked favorable to both of them, and Phil was getting excited about this unexpected and potentially wonderful turn his life had suddenly taken. By the time they had reached this point in Tammy's visit to Alaska, the week was more than half gone, and after they had been back home for a day, Tammy suddenly suggested that they "give it a whirl," meaning she thought the time had come for their first sexual encounter. This was a new approach for Phil, but he was not nearly as much of a veteran of the love wars as Tammy was, so he decided to make no negative judgments. They gave it a whirl (or more accurately, two or three whirls), and Phil thought it was great. The love he had felt for

Tammy as a youngster was proving very easy for Phil to reignite, and he was experiencing the sweet magic of new romance. After they got together, it was unclear to Phil just what was going on with Tammy. She seemed especially contemplative afterwards, and Phil was puzzled as to just what might be happening with her. She was quiet, thoughtful, and not at all expressive of the same kind of beautiful, loving, happy feelings that were coming up for him.

After a few hours of this, which Phil found a bit peculiar, at last Tammy came to him saying that she wanted to talk, and Phil agreed. They sat down and Tammy said that she had been thinking over all that they had discussed and all that had happened, and that she had a plan to propose.

Tammy's idea was that she return to Oregon, spend several months getting her affairs in order, get her youngest lined out on a college career, dispose of her house, and then come to Alaska permanently and move in with Phil. They could travel back and forth to visit while all this was going on, and find out during that time whether there was any reason not to do this. Tammy did not mention marriage at any point in the plan, but Phil indicated that marriage was his ultimate objective, with the right partner, and Tammy registered no objection to that.

One problem Phil had with this idea was that, as his kids were growing up, he had impressed upon them very strongly his belief that shacking up was a bad idea, that it should not be an option for them, and that if they were to do such a thing, it would be without Phil's approval. Now, here he was, contemplating doing just what he had made a pretty big point of telling them not to do, and was uncomfortable with the equivocalness of it. The other side of the argument Phil was having with himself said that Tammy represented a strong chance of being an excellent life partner, with whom violent temper tantrums would never be a problem, but that getting to know her as well as he would need to in order to consider marrying her would not be possible from a distance of thousands of miles. The only way this could be accomplished would be for them to live in the same city. She would be broke and unemployed when she came to Alaska and her moving in with Phil made good sense from a logistical and managerial point of view. Phil's kids were adults now, and Phil would explain to them that this was not just a way to get it on for fun, but was part of a long-term plan that required some variation from regular procedures. Phil sort of sold the argument to himself and hoped that he could sell it to them, as well.

Phil was also uncomfortable with what Tammy had told him about her single life before she changed her ways, because indiscriminate promiscuity, which was how Phil interpreted her description of the way she had lived for several years, was anathema to him, and he had no wish to be tied to someone whose values were that much different from his. On the other hand, people can change and reform, and Phil had learned and grown enough to be able to avoid the judgmental, unreasonable reaction to this kind of information that he had inflicted upon Silver several years earlier, which caused so much pain to both of them. Phil was encouraged to note that, while he did not like what he had heard about Tammy's former life, there was a complete absence in him of the gut-wrenching, heart-slashing, unbearable agony because of what he knew, tossing and turning all night long, night after night about it, that he had experienced before. Nothing in the world is worth that much emotional pain, and somehow, Phil had learned his lesson. Thank God, he was not going to ever do that again, to himself or anyone else.

Phil seemed to have somehow created a new compartment in his mind and heart where he could file that sort of knowledge without its causing pain and damage. Having once been forty-one going on twelve, Phil was now forty-six and going on with living.

Phil told Tammy about the nearly celibate life he had lived with Darla for almost twenty years and made sure Tammy knew that such a thing was not a possibility for him in any future relationship. It would be best for Tammy to plan for a maximum of that type of interaction, even at their advanced ages, and there had to be perfect clarity as to Phil's intentions concerning the physical part of the partnership. Tammy seemed intrigued by that more than stimulated or pleased, but raised no objection. The idea of lots of going for it for years with one exciting, interesting, committed, loving person had lots more appeal to Phil than years of short hook-ups with dozens or hundreds of strangers and assorted acquaintances. Tammy's assertion that she now had years of celibate devotion to her children behind her sparked Phil's respect and approval but it also made him think that maybe there could have been some sort of bad experience that made Tammy give up sex. Her odd behavior after their first time did nothing to change that thought.

Phil assented to the proposal Tammy made, and after she returned to Oregon, Phil redoubled his efforts to bring the house up to snuff, so that his new sweetheart could be warm in the home he would provide for her.

By the time the months had gone by in Tammy's plan to get ready to move permanently to Alaska, she and Phil had visited back and forth several times; Phil had taken two trips to Oregon and Tammy had come to Alaska twice more. They talked on the phone three or four times a week while apart, and when together, discussed their respective career objectives, long-term retirement plans and potentialities, relationships with their children (all of whom were now grown, as Tammy's daughter was getting ready to enter college), and what life ahead looked like for the two of them as they merged their futures. They learned that they shared a love of the outdoors and agreed that camping, hiking, traveling, and exploring the wonder of Alaska would be an important part of their lives together.

The subject of Tammy's past came up, and Phil told her what he had been through concerning that kind of stuff before, but that it seemed he was better now, and that he believed that he no longer represented a threat in that way. Tammy admitted to having had a lot of sexual partners and having made a lot of mistakes, but never disclosed any details or discussed what might have happened to cause her to so drastically abandon that way of living. Phil did not seek more information about the subject, because details had done him a lot of damage before, and he was pleased not to suffer about this stuff knowing this much, but he did not want to push his luck.

The main problem Phil had with the way this relationship was shaping up was Tammy's lack of excitement about the new love they were sharing. Phil was having a wonderful time with all the new planning and dreaming and doing things together and the fooling around, and while Tammy was a very calm, peaceful, compliant, and cooperative companion, there was a remarkable lack of playfulness, giddiness, or joy in her way of relating to Phil. He found that for Tammy to tell Phil she loved him, he would have to ask her to say it. She would always comply, but the words almost never came out of her spontaneously or without Phil's having to ask for them.

Tammy told Phil that she had loved him when they were teenagers, and that her love for him was probably the reason she never learned to love the man she married, who was her kids' father, but Phil did not really buy that. He had been madly in love with her as a kid, but those feelings were far in the past and nearly forgotten by the time Phil met Darla. Tammy had absolutely nothing to do with what happened to the love Phil should have had for Darla, whom he wanted to love and for whom he made a valiant effort to do so. Darla drove him away with her viciousness.

Tammy's husband, from what Phil knew about him, was not a troublesome guy, and it seemed that they just bored each other.

Tammy had reached out to Phil in a rather bold and stunning fashion to get this relationship going, but then it was as though once the reaching out was over, she was just going along. This was most evident when the day finally came for her to come to Alaska to stay. Morris had moved out, and Phil was excited and filled with anticipation as the big day dawned, because his new life, with the person who would probably become his life's chosen partner, was about to commence. It felt almost like a wedding day to Phil, and he was way, way up with happiness. When he picked Tammy up at the airport, however, Phil discovered a decided lack in her of the joy and excitement he was feeling. By the time they got home, and then after they spent some time together reuniting and being close, it was clear to Phil that Tammy was sad, depressed, and even heartsick. This was a real blow to Phil. Finding himself feeling so thrilled, excited, and positive about what they were doing together, and then to see how miserable she was about it was very discouraging.

Phil's thinking was that, were he in Tammy's shoes and moving away from his lifelong home, some nostalgic feelings would certainly come up, and there might even be a little sorrow in leaving his family and so much history behind to start a new life. But overriding everything would be the joy, the anticipation, the fun, the excitement, the wonder of new love and a new life, a life it had taken courage and boldness to create, plan, and bring into being. Phil's thoughts were that when this time for him was such a thrill, a gas, a great moment, a happy experience, why would it not be the same for her?

For poor Tammy, whatever the reason, it clearly was not a happy experience. She was one bummed-out, depressed, miserable lady. She moped around the house and around town on her own for several days and would share with Phil nothing of what she was feeling or what was going on inside of her. The way she seemed to feel reminded Phil of how he felt when he showed up at Indoc Battalion on his first day of active duty in the Navy. Of course, Tammy had Phil there being loving, supportive, and welcoming, instead of twenty jerks screaming, threatening, calling names, and deliberately making life hell. One would have thought she had the better deal.

What Phil began to realize was that Tammy's feelings for him might not be nearly enough to provide the lift she needed to deal with the big change she had made in her life. Whatever she felt for Phil was insufficient to help her in overcoming all the loss, the loneliness, the sorrow she was feeling. Phil was hurt by this, but he is what you call a "glass half-full instead of half-empty" kind of guy, and even though it appeared that for Tammy, Phil was more of a component, or a feature, in a long-term project to enhance her material well-being than he was a beloved sweetheart, he promptly got into his "positive focus" mode and was very quickly able to envision a way for this to come out just fine.

The fact that Tammy's love for Phil was lukewarm, at best, was not a hopeless thing. Phil knew that he was a lovable person. Phil had spent a lot of time wishing he could find someone with the enormous capacity for love that exists inside of him, and he had been loved very much by a few very good-hearted and lovely people in the years since leaving Darla. It would therefore be a mistake to conclude that some unlovability in Phil made it impossible for Tammy to have such an experience with him. Phil was aware of the enormous magnitude of the affection and devotion Tammy had for her children, and to him this was evidence that she had the capacity to develop and foster a similar great love for him.

As a result of this line of thinking, Phil came to the determination that he would give Tammy whatever chance she might need for that kind of love toward him to grow and thrive, and that he would do everything in his power to make it easy and proper for that to happen for her. Having made that decision, Phil let his hurt feelings go and went about the business of building a happy life with his beautiful Tammy.

The days and weeks went by, and Tammy's depression lifted as she became accustomed to the changes she had made and she got used to being farther away from her children. She had a pretty good deal going on with Phil, with room, board, and a car provided by an attentive, loving partner, and it was not very long until she seemed to enjoy her new life. Phil thought of this as the first step in creating the great love story that he believed he was destined to live. Tammy found work in a grocery store which, while it was not in line with her advanced education, was enjoyable enough for her, and she made the most of it. She shared with Phil a lot about what she experienced each day at work, and initially, he was pleased that she chose to engage with him in her lengthy and detailed descriptions of her daily adventures in the grocery business. Eventually, however, Phil began to wish that she would share with him more about her inner feelings, her philosophy of life, her political views, what was in her heart. Phil never learned any of that stuff about her, and even when he asked, she seemed uncomfortable talking about anything except daily minutia.

The most fun Phil and Tammy had together was camping, hiking, snowshoeing, canoeing, and exploring the outdoors of Alaska. Tammy was a more experienced camper than Phil was, and he learned some good skills from her that helped him enjoy that wonderful state even more. They took a couple of trips to Oregon together, one by driving down the Alaska Highway and back, and the other by air. Phil enjoyed both trips, but after they got back from the second one, they never took another out-of-state trip together in the several years they were a couple. Phil proposed several such trips, to Hawaii, to Florida, to Colorado, to New York, to Oregon again, but Tammy always declined. She preferred to travel to Oregon alone to visit her children. The two kids came to Alaska a couple of times, and Phil found them both to be very nice, personable, and completely likable. They seemed to be happy that their mom had a nice man to love her and with whom she could share the future.

During one of Tammy's trips to Oregon without him, Phil reached her on the phone, and she was filling him in on her daily activities when she happened to ask about Jazzy, Phil's little Maltese dog who had been his kids' pet when he left Darla, and who ended up with Phil because he was the only one whose circumstances permitted keeping a dog. Tammy asked because she missed Jazzy. Phil told her that Jazzy was fine and missed her too, and then Phil asked Tammy if she missed him. Her response was that, yes, in addition to missing the dog, she missed Alaska, she missed the house, she missed her job, she missed Phil's car, she missed camping, and finally, in seventh place, she missed Phil. He pointed out that seventh place was not an especially complimentary ranking, and she laughed and said she loved him. That was one of the handful of times in their years together when she said that without being asked, but it did not qualify as a spontaneous expression from her heart because of the guilt trip Phil laid on her after coming in seventh.

Phil's plans had been to love and cherish Tammy and watch and enjoy as her reciprocal love for him grew, and after they reached the point where their beautiful love affair was of world-class proportions, they would marry and live happily ever after. Phil did his part with the loving and cherishing, but by the time they had been together for a couple of years, it was clear that Tammy's share of the story was not coming out like Phil had hoped. Phil and Tammy got along fine, and there was almost no strife or discord, but Phil still had to ask for expressions of love from Tammy, and the separate vacations development was a real disappointment to Phil. There was a very large amount of lovemaking, and with that aspect of the relationship, Phil was very content. Tammy was very compliant and uncomplaining about it, but did not approach it with the same level of enthusiasm that he did. That was all right with Phil, because it was still great, but Phil wondered if the separate vacations might not be a way for Tammy to get a break from all that sex. Tammy never said as much, but Phil felt that this might be the reason.

Phil's view of the situation came to a place where he recognized that Tammy liked him, that she felt quite a bit of genuine fondness for him, and that she was satisfied with the lack of depth and emotional closeness that characterized how things were between them. Phil made every effort to show Tammy the love and devotion he sought from her, but she gently fended him off and kept it cool. As a result of her actions, their partnership was lightweight, friendly, cordial, and peaceful, but not rich, close, nurturing, or profound like Phil wanted it to be. The constant sex was the best part of the relationship, but more and more, it was turning out not to be enough for Phil.

During the second year she was with Phil, Tammy got a better job at a new, large chain grocery store that was opening up in Anchorage, and during her third year in Alaska, she finally got hired into a job where she made use of her advanced degree. She worked counseling and assisting, in their search for work, women who were receiving aid to dependent children. Her employer was the same one Phil worked for, the Alaska Department of Labor, although Tammy was in a different division and worked in a different location. It was the best job she had ever had, and she was very pleased to have it, although she managed, as with everything, to refrain from demonstrating any outward indications of joy. Up to this point in their lives together, the only sharing of her feelings Tammy would do with Phil was concerning her children and her work at the grocery stores. The kids were, beyond any doubt, the most important, and perhaps the only important, things in her life. After she got this job, Tammy began to share with Phil a great deal about the day-to-day accomplishments and experiences she was having at work, and it was clear that she at last had something extremely meaningful in her life besides her kids. Phil's hope that he would become one of those important items had not come to pass.

By the time Tammy had been with Phil for this long, more than three years, he had never again brought up the subject of marriage because Tammy never demonstrated a level of love for Phil that he thought met the requirements for getting married. It was obvious that Phil's optimism about how this was going to turn out had been unwarranted, and the time had come to lay it all on the table and see what Tammy had to say.

On the day that Phil confronted Tammy about where they stood with regard to his aspirations for their life together, Phil said that in his mind, the kind of love that, ideally, goes on between life partners is one where each recognizes the other as a soul mate; that they cherish each other with a strength and devotion that is enormous, unique, and special; and that they bear a reverence for the relationship that establishes what they have together as treasured beyond all else in the world. That was what Phil offered to Tammy, what he sought from her, and what he wanted between them. Then he asked what she thought about all that.

What Tammy said was that, no, she did not relate to the term "cherish" and did not think that she had in her the capacity for that kind of love. She said that she did not believe in "soul mates," and that while she cared for Phil and valued what they had between them, to call the relationship a "treasure" would be to seriously overstate the case. Tammy was very clear, without being angry or ugly about it, in her response to Phil, and he had to give her credit for her honesty. Phil believes that Tammy was never untruthful to him, but because she never shared her deepest inner feelings or thoughts, the need to stretch the truth rarely came up.

During Tammy's first year with Phil, her grandmother, who played a large role in providing care for Tammy when she was very small, and with whom Tammy had carried on a relationship throughout her life, passed away. The grandmother whom Phil had met had died many years earlier, and he had never met the more recently deceased grandmother. Tammy did not travel to Oregon to participate in her grandmother's funeral, and Phil was unable to detect any kind of emotional reaction in Tammy to the death of someone who had helped raise her.

About a year after her grandmother's death, Tammy's father died, and again, she chose not to go to Oregon for a last farewell. Whatever feelings, if any, she may have had about his passing were not apparent to Phil. Tammy's parents divorced while she was in college, and it seemed that their marriage had been dead by the time Tammy was old enough to go to kindergarten, so she had grown up witnessing a pretty cold relationship between them. Phil sensed that she did not like her dad very much but that she felt a duty to care about him. She took Phil to meet him during one of the couple's trips to Oregon, and Phil found him to be welcoming and pleasant enough. Once, when Phil was a teenager, he had met the father, but only momentarily, and had no real memory of him.

Phil was a bit troubled by Tammy's reaction (or rather, lack of reaction) when these close relatives died and found himself thinking that this would probably be how she would behave when Phil died. Phil wasn't planning on kicking over any time soon, but he had received his diagnosis of PSC not long before the time he first reconnected with Tammy, so wasn't expecting to live forever, and was hopeful that someone would care when he passed on. Phil's daughter Sylvia had executed her estrangement from him during the first year after Tammy moved in with him, so Sylvia was not going to lead the procession of mourners at Phil's wake. Although she never said so, Phil thought that part of the reason Sylvia chose to tell him how low her opinion of him was that he and Tammy were living together, unmarried. Phil's training to Sylvia about how to disapprove of that practice had been extremely effective.

The cards were now all on the table with Tammy, and there was no lack of clarity about how things stood between her and Phil. There was still no hostility around the house, and life remained quite peaceful, but by now it was obvious that this was never going to turn into the love affair of the millennium. Phil was glad that they had not decided to marry, and had come to believe that marriage had never been something Tammy had in mind from the beginning.

During the spring of the fourth year that Tammy was with him, Phil again suggested that they take a vacation together to Hawaii, to share the experience of that beautiful place. Tammy declined, preferring instead to go to Oregon alone to visit her children. One of the reasons Phil ended up in Alaska and loving it so much is that he does not like hot weather. It was now early spring and was probably not yet too hot in Oklahoma for Phil to go there to visit Cole who, having gotten out of the Army, was now an Air Force ROTC cadet at Oklahoma University in Norman, working toward a master's degree and a commission. Phil had visited Cole while he was in the Army at Monterey, California; Fort Campbell, Kentucky; and Fort Sill, Oklahoma, and decided to take advantage of the cool time of year to visit him again in the Southland.

Phil left a few days after Tammy departed for Oregon and, after spending four or five days and having a good time around Norman with Cole, flew on to Cheyenne to put in some time with his parents. By the time Phil's traveling and visiting were done, and he was on his way back to Alaska, he had not spoken to or heard from Tammy in two weeks, despite having given her phone numbers where he could be reached and asking her to keep in touch with him. The memory of seventh place remained strong in Phil's mind, and he wanted to see if he had done any moving up on the list. Phil had left the initiative with Tammy to make the contacts between them while they were apart. This was sort of a test to see how hard Tammy would try to keep connected with him as they vacationed separately. Phil's approach would have been to talk daily had he not been conducting this test. Clearly, Tammy had no wish at all to communicate with Phil, and there was absolutely no contact between them for the whole time they were apart. By the time Tammy met Phil at the plane, because she had been home for a day or two when he got back, Phil had made his decision. Phil was done waiting for Tammy to get involved in this relationship. Phil was feeling pretty angry but waited to tell Tammy about how he felt.

Phil went back to work the next day, and that evening, sat down with Tammy and told her that he believed that her two weeks without contacting him at all showed that she had not given him a thought during the whole time. Tammy did not deny it. Phil said that he loved her and had tried to get her to love him for years now, but at long last, he was done. Phil believed that he was worthy of more and better love than Tammy was willing or able to give him, and that since it was clear he was never going to get it from her, he wanted her to move out. Tammy had spoken to Phil's folks and gotten information about when to meet his flight after Phil left their place in Cheyenne on his way back to Alaska, so she was aware that he was pretty frosted at her, but she had not expected anything as drastic as this. She got in Phil's car and drove off for a several hours alone for contemplation of this development, and when she got back, she agreed that it was best that she do as Phil suggested and move out.

Tammy told Phil that the only people that she would ever truly love in any way close to what he was asking for were her children. She was not unwilling to love Phil that much, but she just did not have it in her. Phil was saddened to hear her admit that, because with him, she had a shot at being a part of the great love of all time, and she didn't want it. Love happens to people, but to a significant extent, it is also a choice, and Tammy's belief that she didn't have the ability to be part of a great love story was really a choice she was making, whether she knew it or not.

Tammy took a few days finding an apartment, and Phil helped her move into it. She said that it would be all right with her if they continued seeing each other, and Phil agreed that they could remain a couple for now, but he was very clear with her that this relationship was not doing it for him, and she needed to be aware of that. Tammy said okay, so they continued to get together a couple of times a week for a while, but after a few months Phil began going to church, responded to one or two singles ads, and was making a low-key effort to meet someone new. One day, Tammy saw Phil on a get-acquainted coffee date with a woman, and the next time he called her, she said that they should stop seeing each other at all if he was going to be going out with other people. Phil had not actually gone out with anyone except a couple of these coffee meetings, but he agreed with Tammy, and the relationship came to its end. All Tammy said to Phil as they parted was that she would miss camping with him.

36

MARIA

During the last couple of years before Tammy moved out, Phil decided to take instruction in martial arts. He was approaching the age of fifty and was keeping pretty fit, but it occurred to him that as one gets older in an increasingly dangerous society, becoming skilled at defending oneself seemed like a good idea. America is a country where more and more, young people are growing up with no guidance and no values, where gangs are replacing families in providing a place to belong, and where the judicial system has created a culture in which crime prospers and decent people are at greater and greater risk. The older one gets, the softer a target he becomes to attract evildoers who might wish to take his belongings and do him harm. Because Phil did not frequent places where trouble is to be expected, and probably because he is big, strong, and fit, he has never been assaulted by someone wishing him ill or wanting to take his stuff, but it is becoming ever easier and more usual to experience bad behavior and threatening attitudes from young people who, placing no limits on their ugly conduct, can be found acting out in places that used to be free of danger.

Phil lives by a code that directs him to look for the beauty, the good, the best in people, and he does that, continually. But looking for the best in someone becomes secondary when that person is loudly yelling the famous "f" word in a public place, over and over, is clearly demonstrating that he has no regard for the sensibilities and feelings of those around him, and threatens anyone who asks him to clean up his language. Phil has no more wish to get into combat now than he did years ago when he was astonished by the love of war and combat that was expressed by the warriors he met in the Navy. But today we find American culture descending into the commonplace ugliness created by secular progressive people who think that it is wrong to make judgments about personal conduct. Their henchmen, the judges, the lawyers, and the politicians, are causing this ugliness to become standard practice, supported and codified by the supposed "rule of law," of which Americans once had the right to be proud. No matter how disgusting, immoral, debased, or wrong it might be, bad behavior is now fostered, promoted, and legalized. Just lying down and enduring this putrification of America is something that Phil will not do without a fight.

Phil shopped around and decided upon a martial arts course called Hapkido. He began attending classes and found out that it was fun as well as potentially useful to roll around on a mat and practice fighting with people. Hapkido places emphasis on strikes and holds that can quickly bring a combat situation to an end. Phil learned ways to hit people and to react to aggression. This gave him a sense that even though he is getting older and may be more of a target, he will never, as long as he can control his body, have to be a helpless victim to anyone, no matter how mouthy, vulgar, aggressive, or disrespectful that anyone might be. There have been a few instances in recent years when Phil has been threatened by young men in public places and when he was ready to hurt them if he had to, and in which he was glad he knew how to hit someone in a way that will stop him cold. So far, they have all backed off, probably because Phil demonstrates willingness to do them harm if they try to hurt him.

Phil had advanced to a level in his Hapkido training in which he was approaching green belt level in his skill testing, but then something happened that made him lose interest in advancing further in his combat training. Phil met Maria.

During Phil's time living alone after he asked Tammy to leave, he began trying to get in better touch with the spiritual side of himself and went to various churches around Anchorage. He went to spiritually oriented gatherings of several varieties and was trying to learn how to pray. He established a schedule that included some praying, new territory for Phil, each day. Throughout his adult life, Phil had developed an inextinguishable connection to God that was associated with his experiences with love, initially with his parents, then his children, then with Silver, and oddly enough, most recently with Tammy. Even though Tammy never returned Phil's love in any substantial way beyond fondness, Phil felt a genuine holiness in the innocent love he'd had for her as a youngster and in the recaptured love he experienced many years later as an adult. Phil was now finding growing satisfaction in a belief system that starts with the premise that God is love. He was reaching a point in that credo where recognition that sincerely felt love, be it romantic, filial, familial, parental, the love of a friend, or general love of mankind, is the purest way that humans can experience God on an individual basis.

Phil had a skeptical side, and as a thinking person, found it very easy to see reasons to be doubtful about the existence of God. So many terrible things happen to people in the world, it is possible to think that no loving god would allow such things to happen to innocent persons who have done nothing to merit the catastrophes that befall them. There are evil people all around who deserve all the terrible justice one could imagine, and who seem to get off scot-free for years and who apparently never pay the price for their wrongful ways. Phil's experience with Darla enhanced his sense that life is not fair and that God must like to play tricks if he could inflict Darla on him. Phil had been a good kid and a good son growing up, and as a young adult, recognized that his intentions and internal motivation were those of a decent, respectable, honest man, the kind of man that any good person, would want to associate with. Phil had done nothing to merit the kind of punishment that Darla delivered continuously, and in a fair world, one would have thought that a good person would get good results consistent with the goodness present in that person, free of gratuitous torment.

What happened to Phil when he became a parent resolved for him his questions about the existence of God. The all-consuming and selfless love for his children that possessed him when his little ones were born settled the issue of whether or not God existed, and then it was just a question of trying to understand as well as he could why things are the way they are, and accepting what could not be understood. Phil transferred that miraculous experience into his understanding of all the different ways love can be expressed, and had no trouble simply accepting that God is there and God is love. Phil had the sense that if he were God, he would have done a lot of things very differently, and fairness would have held a much higher ranking in the order of the universe..

After the disappointment of what happened to Phil's relationship with Tammy, he decided to just put the question of a life partner in God's hands and began to include in his daily prayer program a request that God put such a partner in his path. Up until this time, Phil had taken upon himself the burden of seeking out a mate, and had done all right in later years, but without enduring success. With God's help, maybe he could do better than all right.

Phil Temple is a dutiful sort who sees it as his responsibility to do his share or more, and participating in an organization that exists to look out for the public interest is right up his alley. In connection with Phil's work for the Alaska Department of Labor, Phil had become a member of the International Association of Personnel in Employment Security, or IAPES, and now that he had more free time, he decided to look into becoming a more active member. This organization is not a union, but is a professional association dedicated to finding and improving ways to serve the working public. The group has numerous programs, projects, and activities that help people who work in employment security to do their jobs better and to more effectively be of service to clients. The pleasure Phil received in helping people find good jobs, and in helping provide support and sustenance when they were between jobs, was life enriching for him, and he wanted to take advantage of what this group could do to help him be better at doing those things.

A weekend IAPES workshop for Labor Department folks from all over Alaska was coming up, and Phil paid the tuition so that he could take part. The Saturday came to attend the workshop in Anchorage and, just as advertised, there were people there from an assortment of Alaska offices, as well as instructors and presenters from other states. Phil knew everyone there from Anchorage and several from Fairbanks, Juneau, and other places, but there were quite a few people whom he had not met before. One of them was a vivacious, dark-eyed lady with the most fantastic head of beautiful, curly, salt-and-pepper hair Phil had ever seen. This woman was full of joyful energy with which she embraced everyone in the room, and she seemed to spread the gusto she had for life into every corner of the building. The obvious pleasure she felt as she greeted old friends and interacted with new acquaintances was without artifice and was fun to watch.

When this woman got around to Phil, she smiled a beautiful, perfect smile and shook his hand. She said that her name was Maria Montoya and said that Phil was the only person present she did not know. She had been attending IAPES functions for a long time, and this was Phil's first workshop, so that explained why she knew everyone but him. When the workshop broke for lunch, Maria and Phil sat at the same table with about eight other people. The two were directly across the large, circular table from each other, so there were others on either side of both of them, but for each of them, it was as though no one else was there. Other people noticed the chemistry going on and spoke about it later, but Phil and Maria had a delightful lunch just visiting across the table as though they were alone.

It turned out that Maria was a recent transferee to a Labor Department office near Anchorage, that she had spent nearly ten years working in the Seward office (having moved to Seward shortly after Phil left his marriage), and that she was now about to transfer again very soon into the Anchorage office, where Phil worked. The department was going through a lot of changes, including centralizing unemployment insurance functions into three major telephone centers, one of which was in Anchorage, and closing down UI operations in the smaller cities around the state. So Phil and Maria were going to be working in the same office. When Phil went home from the workshop, Maria, the beauty with the incredible hair, the dazzling smile, and the personality that embraced everyone in sight, was still on his mind. He looked forward to meeting her again when she transferred into the Anchorage office.

The next week, Maria came to work in her new assignment, and Phil took the opportunity to get to know her a little better and found her to be a delight. She was cheerful, attractive, pleasant, and simply nice to be around. She later told Phil that she attracted the attention of more guys around the office than just himself, and that by the time he asked her to lunch the following week, she had been asked out by two other Anchorage men. This was no surprise, because she was uniquely attractive and fun just to be around, so she was certain to generate plenty of interest.

Phil took Maria to lunch during her second week in the office, and they had a very nice time. Phil had asked her at the office on her first day in her new job how it was going, and she was grateful for his kindness for asking. Any new job can be a source of stress, and Maria said that Phil was the only one who inquired about how she was feeling. She appreciated his concern. Phil and Maria went out few more times and found that they had a wonderful time together. Maria is full of vibrant energy, and Phil enjoys the vigor she puts into the atmosphere anywhere she is. She is one in a million, or more, and it did not take Phil long to become enchanted by this life force on two feet.

Phil was scheduled for a trip to Oklahoma to attend Cole's Air Force commissioning ceremony following his graduation from the master's degree program at Oklahoma University, so on his last date with Maria for a while, the couple went walking along the Anchorage Coastal Trail that overlooks Cook Inlet, a beautiful place to walk. They held hands and did some outdoor smooching as they enjoyed the beauty of Alaska and each other. Maria gave Phil a small framed picture of herself of a size just right for packing in an overnight case while traveling and said that she hoped he would think of her while he was gone. Phil said that there would be no problem with that.

Phil flew to Oklahoma City and stayed in a hotel in Norman. Darla had come to see Cole's commissioning, and it was the first time Phil had seen her since Sylvia graduated from high school, seven years earlier. Darla's hatred for Phil was still apparent in her clenched jaw, but she tried to downplay it and behave herself in the interest of making Cole's special occasion a nice one. Darla pinned Cole's second lieutenant's bars on him, and an Air Force general gave the keynote address, the subject matter of which took Phil back to his Navy days. The general's theme was the integrity of a U.S. military officer and, among other issues, touched on the importance of honoring one's marital vows. He spoke of the penalties that accrue to a military officer found guilty of adultery and encouraged all the newly commissioned people to be persons of honor. Knowing what he knew about the way most officers behaved when he was in the service, Phil was a bit amused that this façade was still being maintained, but since he agreed with the general's premise about the way things should be, he was glad they were still trying.

After the commissioning ceremony, Cole, some of his AFROTC friends, Phil's sister (who had come over from her home in Kentucky), Darla, and Phil all went to a nice restaurant and shared a meal. It was a very happy day for Cole. Somehow, the idea came up that Cole and his parents spend some time together, just the three of them, so they did. They went to a beautiful museum in Oklahoma City where public tours were conducted for a fee. They paid their way in, and took the tour. It was very interesting and informative to Phil to learn about Oklahoma and Indian Territory history, and Phil enjoyed the afternoon. Darla was so tense from being near Phil that one could almost cut the air around her with a knife, but Phil was interested only in trying to make Cole's special day a nice one, so disregarded the tense behavior of Darla. Phil was feeling very good about how two people who dislike each other can bury the hatchet for a day because they both love the kid. When the tour was over, the three of them stopped for a bite and a little visiting; Phil gave Darla a hug and returned to his hotel.

Later, Phil got together with Cole to say good-bye before he left to catch his plane to Cheyenne to visit Loren and Molly. Phil had already shown Cole the picture of Maria and expressed to him how attractive and delightful he found this new acquaintance to be.

As their visit ended, Cole told Phil that he hated the time he had spent with him and Darla so much that he would never consent to spending time like that again. Cole was so tense and uncomfortable being around both Darla and Phil at the same time that he almost could not bear it. It turned out that Phil was the only one who enjoyed the excursion. Darla's inability to stand being around her ex-husband was so obvious that it ruined the day for Cole, although, in retrospect, Cole probably blamed Phil because, as the guilty party who ended the marriage by leaving his mother, Cole apparently believed that Phil actually deserved the hatred Darla felt for him. Phil enjoyed the outing partly because it was interesting, but mostly because he was mentally patting both Darla and himself on the back for being good guys and trying to do right for their son. Right then, the writing was on the wall for the future of Phil's relationship with Cole. Phil was the only healthy person present on that excursion, and the poison in Darla, which had ruined Phil's marriage with her, was now seeping into what had been a very warm and close relationship between Cole and Phil.

Phil caught the plane to Cheyenne, spent a pleasant few days with his folks, visited some friends and relatives, went to a party being thrown by an old high school acquaintance, then got out of town just as Loren was starting to get ornery, and returned to Alaska. During the trip, Phil showed his picture of Maria to all his friends and relatives, and called her almost every evening. It was clear to Phil and to everyone that he was very interested in this warm, vivacious, and fascinating woman. When Phil was back at work, he and Maria went out a couple of more times after his return from Oklahoma and Wyoming.

Maria told Phil that she was planning a trip to celebrate a special occasion in his old hometown of Seward, where she had lived for nine years. She said that she would tell him later about the nature of the special occasion, and then invited him to go along. It sounded like a fun trip to make, to a place they both loved, and they had been seeing each other for a month now. Their connection was growing stronger.

During the car ride down to Seward, Maria asked Phil what he thought about alcoholics and alcoholism. His response was that he had several alcoholics in his family, but that he had never spent much time in the presence of someone who was a practicing drunk. He said that he thought that what was important was how long ago the person took his or her last drink. This was when Maria disclosed that she was a recovering alcoholic and that she was on her way to Seward to celebrate her twentieth Alcoholics Anonymous birthday. Phil said that twenty years sounded like a pretty good run of sobriety. He was still pretty ignorant about the details of what alcoholics are like and how they act, and found that he had little concern about spending time with someone who had not had a drink in twenty years.

They went on to Seward; Maria went to her birthday get-together while Phil went to visit the house he had built fifteen years earlier. The couple who had bought it had divorced and the woman still had the house. She had paid off her debt to Phil several years before this, and the large equity he had in the Seward house then enabled him to pay off his Anchorage house far ahead of schedule, which he had just done the month after he met Maria. Phil asked the woman who bought his Seward house if she planned to stay there for a long time, and she said that she was unsure, but that she would probably be there for a number of years yet. Phil got her to promise that he could have first bid on the house if she decided to sell it. He was looking ahead to retirement one day and still had a dream of finishing the house-building project he had enjoyed so much. She said okay, she would give him first chance, and Phil checked with her periodically for years after that. He loved Seward and always dreamed of returning there.

Maria and Phil spent their first night together in Seward, and having already determined that they loved being together, they found that they loved sleeping together, as well. They talked about whether or not this was a good idea, because they were both against casual sex and sleeping around, but it was clear that this relationship was growing and was going to be something important, so they went for it. Their fun, fantastic, and frequent lovemaking started then and there, and they are still each other's favorite people on earth. They became inseparable and had a wonderful summer, camping, hiking, exploring Alaska together, meeting each other's friends, and encountering each other at work. They began a practice of rushing home at lunch time for some noontime lovemaking, although the idea of sex in the office, which seems to be a popular topic in today's culture, did not occur to them.

People counsel against work place love affairs, but this is one that came out about as well as anybody could ever hope for. Phil and Maria worked at opposite ends of a very large office and had very little interaction in the tasks they performed, but they had lunch and breaks together and ran into each other fairly often at the copy machine and elsewhere, and being at work with someone you love can be terrific. Of course, it would not have been so good if things had not worked out for them, so the advice about avoiding love affairs at work is still valid. But for Maria and Phil, the story is a happy and wonderful one, and getting together with someone at work turned out great.

37

PARTNERS

Phil and Maria traveled separately but at the same time to the Rocky Mountain region in August of that summer, Maria to Utah, where she was born and raised, and Phil to Cheyenne to see his folks. Maria and Phil wanted to meet each other's families, because they were really getting serious about each other and felt the wish to share their happiness with their families. Maria was brought up as a Roman Catholic, had spent a lot of time as an adult exploring other Christian faiths, and had returned to the mother church during the last ten or so years. Phil learned that Maria had been married a bunch of times, four to be exact, and that she'd had a pretty troubled life.

Maria had a sister living in Grand Junction, Colorado, so they made plans for Phil to borrow his parents' car and drive from Cheyenne to Grand Junction, where he connected with Maria and met her sister and her sister's husband. Then Phil and Maria drove to several places in Utah, where Phil met Maria's mother, brother, and a bunch of other relatives. They then returned to Cheyenne, where Maria met Phil's family and friends.

One of Maria's two grown sons lived near Denver, Colorado, and Phil got to meet him during the trip to Grand Junction. He was a very handsome and personable young man of twenty-five, who Maria said was troubled and was the source of a lot of worry for her. The young man was unemployed and living alternately with his father, Maria's second ex-husband, and with his stepmother, the woman his dad had been married to after Maria. The two were separated and going through a divorce, but the son apparently was not divorcing the stepmom because he was staying at her house, at least part of the time. Maria's son's name was Cesar, he was as handsome as his mom was beautiful, and he seemed to Phil to be troubled.

Cesar had been born in Cheyenne and his parents divorced when he was about three. Maria married another man a couple of years later, and when Gus was eight and his older brother Allen was eleven, the four of them moved to Alaska. The family settled in Gakona, Alaska, and lived in a large log cabin that Maria's husband and the boys built near the Gulkana river, in a very rural setting. It was, in fact, outrageously rural, requiring them to negotiate six miles of terrible, unimproved dirt trail to get to Gakona, a small settlement where a few hundred people populated an area around a wide place in the highway. Life was very hard out there in such a dramatically rustic setting, and Maria's marriage to the man from Cheyenne could not withstand the pressure. When they split, Maria and the boys moved into the town of Glenallen, and the husband went back to the lower 48.

Before long, Maria was married to a neighbor in Glenallen who had two little girls, whom Maria found adorable; she dreamed of being a mother with daughters. It was starting to look like Maria would marry people because they applied for the job rather than because they were good husband material. By the time Phil met her, Maria had been split from the last one for a few years and was succeeding in making a go of it on her own, rather than marrying everyone. Phil appreciated the sense that she had, similar to his, that the growing culture of sleeping with everybody in sight was bad for individuals as well as for the society at large, and that the idea of promiscuity as a life-style was wrong. It seemed, however, that the mistake Maria was making was getting married so much to avoid getting a list of partners that was too long.

The trip that Phil and Maria took to the Rocky Mountain region was a big success, and Phil's parents fell in love with Maria. Her irrepressible cheerfulness wins over almost everyone, and Phil's parents, especially Loren, were enchanted by her. One of the best things that happened as the result of Phil's teaming up with Maria was that his dad started behaving himself when Phil came to town with her. Loren quit trying to start arguments with Phil when Maria was around. Loren was so nuts about Maria that he forgot to make trouble for Phil. Young love can happen at any age, even when the guy is past fifty, as Phil was, and the gal is approaching fifty, as Maria was.

Phil really fell for Maria's family, a bunch of warm and welcoming Latinos, who radiated the same kind of warmth and energy that Phil found so wonderful in Maria. Her brother Horacio was a hard-working biker-type, who spent a lot of his free time working as a leader in a biker group dedicated to preventing and stopping child abuse. He had a checkered past as something of an outlaw, but was atoning for the mistakes he made as a young man by doing genuine good for children who could not defend themselves. He worked in a steel mill and traveled the country as an ambassador for his anti-child-abuse organization. He had a personality that was a somewhat muted version of Maria's vigorous embrace of the whole world, and his friends were legion. Horacio's wife was a cheerful and fun-loving lady who spent a lot of time riding on the back of her husband's Harley-Davidson motorcycle.

Maria and her sister Alicia, who was six years younger, looked enough alike to be mistaken for twins, except for Maria's salt-and-pepper and Alicia's jet black hair. Alicia was a reformed hippy who had married when she was nearly forty to a kindly and hard-working Minnesotan who was near her in age, and they were very devoted to each other. They had decided not to start a family at their advanced ages and reserved all the love they would have given to children for one another.

Maria's father Joe had died ten years earlier, had worked as a coal miner when Maria was small, and had left the home when Maria was ten. She spoke lovingly about what a warm and caring dad Joe was and how fondly she remembered his cheerfulness and kind heart, characteristics that she inherited from him. He had been an alcoholic who, unlike Maria, had never succeeded in kicking his reliance on the bottle. He died of his addiction before reaching age seventy, and Maria had some sad stories to tell about the effect his drinking had on the lives of everyone in the family.

Maria's mother, who was eighty-four when Phil met her, had suffered a stroke about six months before Phil met Maria and was living in a rest home in Duchesne, Utah, where Maria grew up. The mom, whose name was Leonora, was still physically quite able and vigorous, but the stroke had removed her ability to speak coherently, and her reasoning abilities were severely damaged. When Phil met her, he could understand only a very small number of the words she said, but could get nothing in the way of meaning from her carrying on, which she did quite vigorously. Leonora seemed to like Phil quite a lot, which Maria, who could understand some of her speech, said appeared to be because he reminded Leonora of a favorite relative of hers who had passed on some years earlier.

Maria did not speak nearly as favorably about the kind of person her mother had been, even though the father was the one who was the alcoholic, and Phil began to hear stories of a very troubled and chaotic childhood, from which Maria had grown up to an equally chaotic adulthood. Maria said that her mother was the youngest of a large group of children and, rather than marry, had stayed home to care for her aging parents. The family had been relatively well-to-do, but there had been a lot of craziness and dysfunction that had contributed to a volatility and instability in Leonora that she exercised generously as she raised her children.

Leonora remained at home until her parents died within a couple of years of each other, both succumbing to painful and lingering cancers and subjecting Leonora to some very domineering, unappreciative, and unkind treatment in the process. The parents did not die until Leonora was well into her thirties, but she wasted little time in getting married to Joe, who was a hard-drinking coal miner. The marriage was in trouble before it started because Leonora was as difficult as her parents were and had a widespread reputation for being very troublesome to be around, and Joe just took refuge in booze to drink his troubles away. Joe lost an arm in a drunken accident before they married, but continued to work as a one-armed coal miner for years until the disability finally forced him to find another way to make a living.

By the time Maria was born, a year after her parents married, a pattern had emerged of a lot of screaming and fighting in the home, and Maria's most vivid memories of growing up were of being awakened in the middle of the night by her mother and rushing off in her pajamas to stay with relatives, who lived thirty miles away. There would be another terrible fight, and Leonora would run off for from a night or two to a few weeks. This happened so much that Maria grew up thinking of her cousins as brothers and sisters almost as much as her own brother and sister were. For some reason, Leonora would always take Maria and leave the other two children with Joe, whether he was sober or not.

Joe left the home for good when Maria was ten but remained a factor in his children's lives, paying his child support faithfully and holding the same custodian job for the next twenty-five years in a town seventy miles away from where his children continued to live with their mother. Leonora told the children that their father was a bum and that he never paid child support, but Joe saved all the documentation of the payments he made without fail over the years and showed them to Maria when she was an adult. Maria says that she was at odds with her mother throughout her adolescence and that Leonora repeatedly told her that she was as worthless as her father and would end up a no-account drunk just like he was. Maria considers herself to have been verbally and emotionally abused by her mother, but even so, says that she is grateful to her mother for having taught Maria to sew, which she still loves to do. It was how she made her living for a number of years before she moved to Alaska, and how she supplemented their existence when she and her third husband were eking out a living in Gakona.

Maria started drinking in high school, and most of her memories of having fun as a teenager include getting drunk. Maria left home when she was a senior and lived for a couple of months in Salt Lake City with a girlfriend who had moved there with her parents. A truant officer found Maria and persuaded her to come back home to finish high school, so she did, but Maria told her mother that as soon as she finished school she was leaving, and when she had that diploma, she left. Despite the hostile relationship with Leonora, Maria continued to be a loyal daughter, seeking a good relationship with her mother for as long as Leonora lived, but it never really happened.

Maria worked for various employers as a seamstress and demonstrated a real talent for the craft. She was a very fast worker and excelled with employers who paid piecework instead of hourly, because she could work faster than anyone. She partied a lot, but earned her living and started dating a nice young man from her hometown. They got engaged, he joined the Army, they got married, he went back to the Army without taking Maria with him, and after thirty days of marriage, half of it with no husband, Maria ended the marriage. She now says that the running away lessons she got from her mother became a code for living, and this was her first big demonstration of how she would do that. She says that the thirty-day husband was a decent and good person, and that, as time went on, she felt a lot of guilt about what she did to him.

A year or so after ending that first marriage, Maria had been working and partying and found a man ten years older than she who was a ladies' man and twice-divorced because he beat his wives. Knowing this, Maria chose to marry him and spent the next seven years getting punched around, leaving, returning, getting beaten some more, leaving, and so on. They moved from Utah to Cheyenne shortly after getting married, and that was where her two sons were born. Phil had long since left Cheyenne when Maria moved there, but she was there during the time he was stationed at Warren AFB while he was in the Navy. Cheyenne is a good sized town, however, and their paths never crossed.

Maria was hospitalized on a few occasions because of the abuse, and by the time she divorced her abuser, she had become a serious alcoholic, drinking every day, drinking at work, and driving while drunk as a matter of routine. She told Phil that her guilt for leaving her first husband after such a short time made her feel that the punishment she was getting was karma and that perhaps she deserved the suffering she was going through. She finally divorced the guy who knocked her around so much and, some time after doing so, committed a hit-and-run while drunk, for which she spent a night in jail. She joined Alcoholics Anonymous, worked the steps with sincerity and determination, and never took another drink. Maria's older son Allen witnessed and remembered seeing his mother get knocked around and, as an adult, had virtually no relationship with his father. The younger son Cesar was very young when Maria divorced his dad and did not remember the violence. He maintained a relationship with his father after he grew up.

Maria encountered a lot of men on the make in AA and said that she avoided the predators, but at some point she met a sincere and earnest man there, and they hooked up, eventually becoming married. She says she picked him because like her, he had a sincere devotion to getting free of the burden of alcoholism, and they had their dedication to sobriety as a shared value. That turned out not to be enough to keep them together, but it seemed like a good place to start. After a couple of years of life together in Cheyenne, they took Maria's boys and emigrated to Alaska, where that marriage failed from the stresses of living such a rugged frontier existence six miles up the river road in the wilderness of Gakona.

The next husband was a neighbor after Maria and the boys moved into Glenallen, and he wanted this gorgeous Latina to be a mother to his little daughters, which she wanted to do, so they got married. They had nothing else in common, and the marriage failed almost immediately. Then Maria got hired as a clerk by the Alaska Department of Labor, and after a year and a half of working there in Glenallen, she bid on a job in Seward, was selected, and moved with her sons to take her new job. She told her husband that he could do whatever he wanted, but she was leaving. They were apart for six or eight months, and that was appropriate because the marriage had truly failed right away. The husband decided to move to Seward with his girls anyway, and the marriage was rejoined. Unfortunately, it promptly resumed its failed status, and after a few more years of unhappiness, they split permanently.

By the time Maria met Phil, she had made the decision, because of all her bad choices, not to marry again. She had been single for two or three years, had dated very little, and had kept herself busy with a host of activities such as AA, church council, IAPES, neighborhood watch, Exercise for Long Life, and a few others, but she was so spectacular looking and had such a radiant personality she couldn't stay out of the dating game forever. When the Labor Department closed the Unemployment Insurance portion of the Seward office and transferred Maria to Eagle River, just outside Anchorage, then transferred her again, six months later, to the Anchorage office, her head was spinning with all the changes. Leaving Seward, which she had come to love very much, was extremely traumatic for her, but she was glad to have a job, so she tried to make the best of things.

On one of their first dates, Phil let Maria know that his value system was a traditional one. He had diverged from that by living for a few years, unwed, with someone he intended to marry, but that was not going to happen again. Maria took from this the idea that, at some point, marriage would be in Phil's plans. . Going out with someone who expressed this point of view was inconsistent with Maria's decision not to marry again, but she had shown her proclivity for getting married and this was not out of her frame of reference, decision or not, so she continued to see Phil.

Later on, after she and Phil had started getting serious, some behaviors of Maria's that were indicative of the unhappy upbringing she had gone through began to surface, and Phil began to see signs that the reasons she had been married so many times were not solely because the other parties caused all the trouble. Comparatively speaking, the fact that Darla believed that her father did not love her, and even with the mean and disrespectful way that Pop Oldburg treated his wife, Darla's home life had been a walk in the park compared to Maria's.

It is now clear that the old need in Phil to find someone difficult and high maintenance to rescue, which must have led him to Darla, was still operating in full force. His thinking at the time was that after being married to scoundrels, rats, and losers, which was how Maria viewed all but the first of the people she had married, being married to a peaceful and gentle, good guy like Phil would be such a wonderful thing for Maria that she would quickly love the peace and become like him, and they would live happily and peacefully ever after. It is said that good guys are often guilty of thinking like that.

The biggest difference between Darla and Maria in the way they regarded Phil was that Maria deeply and sincerely loved her father, believed that he deeply and sincerely loved her, and as a result, liked and appreciated men. Even after being beaten and abused by one husband and not well-treated by others, Maria still loves and embraces the human race, men just as much as women, and Phil recognized the fact that, difficult though she may have been, the enormous love she lived and demonstrated every day boded well for a relationship with a loving person like him.

Darla deserved credit for her efforts as an adult to love and relate to her father, but her belief as a child that he did not love her created the man-hater she became and destroyed any chance that she could ever succeed in relating to a man. Darla deserves a lot more demerits for the way she conducted her relationship with Phil, however, and her declaration to her children that she will never have another man close to her in her life shows that she recognizes that she is unable to relate to men, although she most likely believes it is their fault and not hers.

By the time Maria and Phil decided to marry and announced their engagement, Phil had become totally enchanted by this warm, loving, fun, exciting, beautiful, amazing person. Even though there were plenty of signs that life with her would not be a nonstop picnic, she was so delightful and fun that he was easily able to downgrade those signs and replace them with the belief that she would learn from him how to be peaceful and happy. They set the date of their wedding for December 7, 1996, and they were both sure that for them, at least, that date of "infamy" would from then on be a date of joy and wonder.

In November, Phil and Maria made a trip together to Washington, D.C., where Cole was attending the National War College as part of the Air Force's preparation of him for his duties as an officer. Phil introduced his beloved Maria to his beloved Cole, and they seemed to hit it off. Washington, D.C., is a wonderful place to visit, and Phil and Maria took in as much as they could. Maria's cousin Luke from Utah had been on the staff of Senator Orrin Hatch in the 1970s as a young college-age congressional intern and had stayed on in the Capitol, becoming over the years what is known as "a Washington insider," and helped them have an even better time in D.C. Luke exercised some connections and got Phil and Maria into a White House tour with one day's notice. Normally a White House tour has to be booked months in advance. Because of Phil's height, he even got to see President Clinton as the President moved out the rear door of the mansion, surrounded by a crowd of people. No one else in the tour group could see over the crowds and could not see the President. Phil thought Clinton was a low-life reprobate, albeit one with a great gift of gab, and disliked him enormously, but it was still fun for Phil to see the actual president. Luke took Phil and Maria to the Capitol building himself, and they ate lunch in the congressional lunch room, where they got to see the Senate majority leader and several other U.S. Senators having lunch.

They went to the Lincoln Memorial, the Vietnam War Memorial, the National Cathedral, Ford's Theater, the Iwo Jima Memorial, Arlington National Cemetery, and the grave of President Kennedy. They rented a car and drove up to Gettysburg, Pennsylvania, to see the Civil War battlefield there. That is one sobering place to visit. The death and carnage of that battle was beyond imagination. On the way back to D.C., they stopped at Harper's Ferry, West Virginia, where the great abolitionist John Brown attempted his anti-slavery revolt, for which he was hanged. Phil and Maria immersed themselves in the history of America, and this was a completely amazing trip for both of them.

38

WEDDING BELLS

Phil and Maria decided to have their wedding in Cheyenne because Phil's parents had come to believe that they were too old to travel and would not be able to attend such a ceremony anywhere else. Just as Phil was, his folks were thoroughly in love with Maria, and they were completely happy for Phil that he had found her. Phil wanted that spirit to be the underlying theme of the wedding, and so they set it up to take place in the very nice and quite expensive senior independent living retirement residence where they lived just outside Cheyenne. This facility had very roomy and nicely appointed gathering halls, which could easily accommodate a modest-sized wedding, and Cheyenne still had lots of Phil's relatives and friends to invite to be present. None of them had come to his first wedding in Seattle, and it felt wonderful to Phil to be able to share his long overdue happiness with so many important people.

Maria still had friends in Cheyenne as well, and learned that her younger son Cesar was again living somewhere in southern Wyoming or northern Colorado, although she was having trouble finding him to invite him to the festivities. Phil and Maria had seen him the previous August but he had moved to Oklahoma for several months just after they saw him, and then moved back to Wyoming a week or two before their wedding date, and was proving hard to locate.

The big day approached, and Phil and Maria flew from Alaska to Cheyenne a week or so early to get everything set up. They arranged for

287

Phil's old friend Lucca, whom Phil had known since he was six years old and who took the Denver Fire Department test the same day Phil did, to preside at their ceremony. Lucca had long been one of the people Phil liked most in the world because of Lucca's great personality; Phil also admired him because of his decency and integrity. Lucca is the kind of person you want doing the honors in anything that comes up, particularly a wedding. He had become a deacon in the Protestant church he attended and was living a life one would point to as an example to emulate.

When Phil and Lucca were kids growing up together, Lucca had a fierce wit, and to get into a "call-down contest" with him was to find yourself getting verbally slaughtered by someone who could not be bested by anyone. Phil learned very young that it was a mistake to get drawn into such competition with Lucca because there was no chance. Phil was never aggressive, troublesome, or clever, all of which were assets required if one were to be good at insult contests, and Lucca was all of those. He was one of the kids who used to go on stealing excursions that Phil wouldn't participate in as they were growing up, and there was some doubt that Lucca was going to be able to stay out of trouble as an adult. The boys were members of the same Cub Scout den in grade school, and Phil's mother did a stint as the den mother. She would have enjoyed her job as a mentor and guide to little boys, except that Lucca was there. Phil's mom was a kindly and gentle soul who sought to love everyone, but she hated to see old Lucca show up at the den meetings. She might even have hated him. Lucca was a hyperactive dynamo, was the source of 98 percent of the trouble Molly had to deal with in those meetings, and was probably why she quit the job. Phil's experience with Lucca was that while he could be the most fun, most engaging, and most interesting to observe of all the kids on their old home street in North Cheyenne, there was a dangerous side to him, as well. Lucca had a great gift for action, humor, and mischief and could be as entertaining as anybody on earth, but he could be as treacherous as a coyote, and getting too close to him was not safe.

But about the time the boys were juniors in high school, Phil's friend underwent a change, the source of which Phil never knew or understood, but which caused Lucca to quit stealing, quit causing trouble, and quit being untrustworthy, and which was as amazing a transformation as any Phil ever saw. Lucca continued to be fun and entertaining, but the dangerous part went away, and he has remained a truly fine and exemplary man for all the years since. Phil's parents came to love Lucca dearly, and Molly completely forgave him for what he put her through in Cub Scouts.

Lucca spent his career as a Denver fireman, and relationships among men who are together for twenty-four-hour shifts can have complications. He enjoyed good rapport with almost everyone at work during his thirty-plus years on the job, but the few people who did not like him for whatever reason learned not to screw with him in verbal contests. The kindly and friendly church elder whom Phil has enjoyed his whole life still has the ability to verbally rip people to shreds if it comes to that. Turning into a world-class nice guy doesn't mean you lose your innate talent for taking care of business.

Phil and his beautiful Maria had a wonderful time in Cheyenne getting ready for the wedding, arranging for food and flowers, getting the marriage license, setting up the way things would proceed at the ceremony, and relating happily to each other day by day. When the big day dawned, Phil was living the happiest day of his life, far more joyous for him than the day he got out of the Navy, and he knew with every fiber of his being that this was right and good. He wasn't even nervous. He was just happy. Phil said that he wished that everyone's wedding day could be as spectacularly perfect in every way for them as his was, at long, long last, for him. Phil and Maria wrote their own vows and exchanged them, pledging to love and honor each other for all their lives, pledged further to abide by the will of God, and enjoyed a heart-felt and beautiful wedding soliloquy by Lucca, devoted to love, and they were married.

All Phil's living cousins on his dad's side of the family, all of whom were around while Phil was growing up, were there. Phil's dearest friends from his youth who were still in Wyoming were there. In addition to Lucca and his wife, Jackie Warren was there with his wife. Jack recovered from their night in jail when he was sixteen and went on to enjoy a successful career as a police officer in Wyoming law enforcement. Jackie was as sure as Phil was that they didn't like jail. Jack's brother Dan was there with his wife. He also had become a career policeman in Wyoming, and after Phil left The Injectors band, Dan had continued with a part-time musical career as he led a professional band made up of mostly other musically inclined cops. Fritz Marsden was there with his wife. They flew down from Portland, much as Fritz had done when Phil bought the new Dodge pickup. Fritz was having a fine career with United Airlines and could go anyplace, anytime because of that. Ron Nevetz and his wife were there, and he and Phil had some fun remembering their times together when they were young. Ron was now a Colorado Springs, Colorado Fire Department captain and knew how much Phil loved firemen.

Old Mitch Mauro, who would always support a friend in a fight, was living in Washington, where he stayed after coming out to see Phil once when Phil was in college there. Mitch could not make it to the wedding but sent his warmest wishes. He had gone on to become the most raging alcoholic ever, had one of the craziest lives anybody ever heard of, then got sober and went on to build a pretty conventional American working life. Keith Strong was still working in engineering for Boeing Aircraft in Everett, Washington, where he hired on in the early 1980s after teaching junior high in Seattle. When a thirteen-year-old pulled a gun and threatened to kill him, and was then suspended by the school administration for THREE DAYS and let back in school, Keith said, "That's enough," and left teaching. Guns at school are taken more seriously now. Keith and Marcy sent their best wishes and were sorry they couldn't make the festivities.

Cole was Phil's best man and wore his Air Force uniform for the ceremony. Maria's sister Alicia was matron of honor. Phil's cousin Ron, who had helped when Loren's brother was causing trouble in his final binge, helped with the video recording of the event. God was in his heaven and all was right in the world for Maria and Phil. What a wonderful day that was.

Maria was unable to find her son Cesar, and what she heard from other sources was that he was angry at her for getting married again. This was understandable in view of how many times she had done it before, but was also an indication of the state of his mental health at the time. Not finding Cesar was a bit of a downer for Maria, but they figured that once the young man got to know Phil, Cesar would get over what was bothering him because Phil is a truly good guy, so happiness prevailed.

Phil and Maria honeymooned in Cancun, Mexico, and Mr. and Mrs. Temple had a wonderful time swimming, snorkeling, making love, visiting Mayan ruins, shopping, making love, sightseeing around the city, dining out, exercising, making ... etc., etc. It was a great honeymoon, and the all-embracing happiness that Phil experienced on his wedding day continued to rule the day in his heart. All those decades of loneliness, of feeling the unfairness of marriage to someone who had no idea of who Phil really is and who was incapable of relating to a good and decent man, of Phil's wrecking his own happiness because of an obsession with stuff from the past that no one can change, of Phil's trying to build a relationship with someone who would have liked to love him but could not, all that was over forever, and the new world of love and partnership with Maria was just beginning.

The round-trip to Cancun had begun in Cheyenne, so when the honeymoon was over, Phil and Maria flew back there and visited another day with his parents. Phil's dad was so nuts about Maria because of her fun, happy, outgoing personality, and because she massaged his hands, his feet, his neck, his arms, and his head, and having her around just buoyed him up. He never again, until just a few weeks before he died, said another mean or obstreperous thing to Phil. As far as Phil's relationship with his father went, the best thing Phil ever did was marry Maria.

Phil and Maria flew on back to Anchorage and started living their new life together as Mr. and Mrs. and went back to work at the Labor Department. About a month after the wedding, they threw a big reception at the Clarion Hotel in Anchorage to celebrate their nuptials in the presence of their Alaskan friends and coworkers. It was a wonderful party, with good music, lots of good food, dancing, singing, laughing, and fun as the order of the night, and Phil and Maria had another super kick-off for their life together. Maria had discovered that she had a bone spur on her heel when they did a serious lot of walking around Washington and Cancun, and she underwent foot surgery just before New Year's. She danced the night away at the reception two weeks later, contrary to doctor's advice, and spent the next three days trying to get over the pain in her repaired foot that had resulted from all the fun. Maria goes at life with such gusto that good sense and circumspection are sometimes not at the top of her list of ways to do things. They had a wonderful time, and Maria felt that a few days of discomfort was a small price to pay for celebrating the greatest happiness either of those two had ever known.

39

DEALING WITH SORROW AND FINDING HAPPINESS TOGETHER

Phil and Maria had been home just over a month, been married for six beautiful weeks, and one week had passed since their joyous reception party when, at 3 AM in the middle of a cold winter's night in January, the phone rang, and their lives would never be the same.

The caller was Allen, Maria's older son, and he said that he had just received word from Cheyenne that his brother Cesar, Maria's younger son, was dead. Cesar had been discovered in the living room of his soon-to-be ex-stepmother's house, with a large number of pain pills in his clothing and scattered around him, and it appeared that he had taken his own life. The post-mortem later established the pills as the cause of death. Maria was crushed, devastated, and overwhelmed by the magnitude of this news, and she went into a kind of shocked state of suspended response. It was as though this could not be real and the truth would soon come through and make things as they should be. Such colossal bad news is too much to take in and handle at first hearing. It just can't be true.

But the real truth had come and Cesar was gone. Phil and Maria flew to Cheyenne, from where they had departed just a few weeks earlier under such joyous circumstances. They now had to participate in the funeral and start dealing with this incredible tragedy. Maria's stunned state began, with the cold reality of the funeral and seeing his body, to transition into belief and the broken-hearted realization that her precious boy was really gone.

The funeral was a sad, sad occasion, with many young people who had been friends of Cesar's from around Cheyenne in attendance. Maria's brother and sister came over from Utah and Grand Junction, and Phil's parents, who had met Cesar the prior summer, were there. There were a large number of relatives from Cesar's dad's side of the family, as well. Little in this world is more tragic than the death of a twenty-five-year-old. The conditions surrounding this event were suspicious and odd enough that Maria was not convinced that the death was intentional suicide, but the official book was closed on the matter, so they headed back to Alaska to start the long road toward getting through this.

Phil and Maria went with Allen on a boat on Resurrection Bay, and Allen scattered Cesar's ashes at sea while the tears flowed. They acquired a site at the cemetery on the hill above Seward and erected a grave marker there so that they would have a place to go for commemorating the life of Maria's beautiful lost boy. What a sad time this was, but the love between Maria and Phil seemed to grow stronger in spite of it. In all the years since this happened, Maria has expressed to many people her gratitude that Phil was in her life at that awful time because of the love, support, and strength he brought to her when she needed it the most. There is no worse experience for a parent than the death of a beloved child, but humans are created to deal with what they have to deal with, and love is the greatest gift of all to help at such a time.

Phil and Maria went back to work, and although the magnitude of what had happened hung over them for a very long time, they handled it in an environment of love. Maria had her days of despair and broken-hearted suffering, but her fundamental zest for life and her brilliant spirit kept her head above water, and things got better, little by little. She went to counseling and underwent some hypnotherapy, all of which was helpful in teaching her ways to cope with what she was going through.

There were times when Maria's grief and sorrow, as well as the chaotic life she had lived in the past, gained the upper hand with her, and she was unkind in her treatment of Phil. He, having had all the unkind treatment he intended to ever deal with, and because he was no longer a hostage as a result of choosing to be there for children, insisted that they work on ways for Maria to deal with the terrible feelings that caused her to lash out at him. Maria went for counseling and training, from which she gained skill and knowledge that was of enormous value in the relationship. Maria consistently apologized to Phil when she got out of line, something that never happened, even once, in his nineteen years with Darla. What a beautiful thing to see happen after all that.

For Phil, even better than hearing apologies was his chance to witness the efforts of someone with Maria's sincere heart and loving spirit as she worked on developing the skills and processes needed to enhance the peacefulness of the Temple household. Phil was allowed to observe as this precious soul, who had been married four times before because she made bad choices and because she did a lot of lashing out at people who lashed back, learned how to live in peace with a peaceful man. It is a beautiful and inspiring thing to see and to be a part of.

Phil and Maria joined the movement known as Marriage Encounter and experienced the joy of associating with other couples who recognize that their marriages are the most important relationship they have, that their spouses are the most important people in the world to them, that having God in the marriage with them makes the marriage better, that love is a choice and love grows as partners choose to nurture and treasure it, and that getting together with couples who share similar values can be a boost to one and all. Phil had always known that this is how marriage could and should be conducted, with respect and tenderness, and yes, cherishing each other. How great it is for him to finally be with someone who is willing to be a part of that with him.

Maria and Phil bought a small motor home after a couple of years of tent-camping together and found that they really liked the added comfort of getting out into the Alaska wilderness in a style more suited to their age group. They bought motorcycles and rode together as their own civilized and law-abiding biker gang. Maria retired her own motorcycle a few years ago after a nearly disastrous mishap, and she now occasionally rides on the back of Phil's motorcycle. The two of them have traveled far and wide together and look forward to doing much more of that. They enjoy each other's company enormously and have more fun than one married couple should be allowed to have. Their lovemaking has declined some in frequency as the years have gone by and is no longer the amazing fireworks extravaganza that it once was, but they have an agreement to try for twice a week. It is rare that they actually manage to do that, but they love each other hugely no matter what, and life is wonderful.

Phil and Maria retired from their Labor Department jobs, and spend part of each winter in the mountains of Utah, where they can overlook the desert and be near Maria's extended family, whom they adore and love to interact with on a pretty much daily basis when they are there. Phil and Maria return to Alaska every spring and stay there until the holiday season, and absolutely love being grandparents to the three delightful children of Maria's older son Allen. They have one granddaughter and two grandsons, and they are true gems. Their little granddaughter reminds Phil a lot of his Sylvia when she was small. Her name is Maria, after her grandma, she is thoughtful and loving and adores her fabulous "Utah Grandma." Little Maria once told Phil that she hopes he lives to be a thousand years old because he is such a fun grandpa. What a wonderful thing for a little sweetie to say to her grandpa.

Phil and Maria love to entertain the grandchildren at their rural Alaska home, and everybody has great fun when the kids come to visit. Phil and Maria often go to where the grandkids live in Wasilla to watch them play basketball, football, and baseball; wrestle; sing in choir; perform karate; and whatever else they have going on. The grandfolks can root for the kids and admire what beautiful, talented, brave, and wonderful youngsters they are. Phil and Maria thank heaven for these precious children every day. The fact that they are not blood kin to Phil does not matter to them, and it does not matter to him. The little ones know their grandpa loves them, and he knows they love him, and that is all that counts. God is love, and love is the greatest force in the world for those who allow it to be, and this family does.

Maria introduced Phil to her Roman Catholic faith early in their marriage, and Phil found that he loves going to church and witnessing the rituals and sacraments as they take place. He likes to think that the peace and solace he experiences while there is due to the presence of the Holy Spirit. After he and Maria were married for about three years, Phil decided that, in order to be more fully able to share her faith with Maria, he would attend the Rite of Christian instruction taken by adults interested in learning more about the Catholic Church. Maria attended with him, and as a cradle Catholic, she learned a lot that she had forgotten or never knew about her faith. Phil and Maria enjoyed very much going through that together, and Phil became interested in getting baptized and becoming a Catholic. The skepticism Phil has about the classical religious view of God is something that is a part of him and cannot simply be overridden or extinguished, so he was not sure if he would be welcome in the Church, even though he loves going there.

Phil became good friends with a dear man named Father Ernie Muellerleile in Anchorage, and consulted with him about the possibility of becoming a Catholic and about Phil's persistent doubts and skepticism. After Phil went through a considerable amount of talking, sharing, visiting, and counseling with Father Ernie, the two came to the conclusion that Phil can embrace and profess the faith, and be welcomed into the Church and be a good Catholic, while just letting his doubts and concerns be what they are. Christ is someone Phil is proud to follow and emulate, and accept as his Lord, Savior, brother, friend, exemplar, and God. Phil honors Christ's beauty, his purity, his goodness, and his sacrifice. Phil's belief that God is love is in no way at variance from the dogma of the Church, and so he made the decision to become a Catholic. Phil has never been more content with any step he has taken in his life than he is with this choice. Phil was baptized, and he and Maria had their marriage consecrated in the Church at the same time. Father Ernie passed away a few years ago, and Phil cherishes the memory of his friendship with that dear man.

Phil and Maria both participate in ministries where they attend church in both Alaska and Utah, and they love to share the fulfillment and privilege of helping good people do more good in this old world. Spending time with virtuous folks who share their values is wonderful for Phil and Maria's marriage and adds to the sense that each new day is another opportunity for adventure, love, fun, inspiration, and joy. They thank God every day for the blessings they share.

40

SCHISM

One of the requirements for a convert to Catholicism who has been married before to be accepted into the Church is that a review of his or her prior marriage or marriages be done and a decision made as to whether such relationships can be considered null and void. After completion of the initiation procedure and this review, the applicant can be accepted into the body of the faithful. In order for those determinations to be made about prior relationships, the applicant has to write a history of his marriage or marriages and request that the review be done by Church authorities. The history that Phil prepared is the source of the final break between Phil and his son. Some of the narrative which Phil prepared for the Church of his life with Darla was used in constructing this story of Phil's life, and all that Phil disclosed to the church authorities is pure truth.

A tenet of the Alladist faith, to which Cole subscribes, is that backbiting is prohibited. Anyone who backbites is guilty of a grievous sin and is shunned by Alladist faithful. Phil's written work composed for the Catholic Church to describe his marriage to Darla would be considered by Alladists to be backbiting. Telling the truth is not allowed if it is unfavorable to the person described. Following that reasoning, testimony in court about the bad acts of people on trial is not permitted because it is backbiting. That would insure that justice never be accomplished because no one is allowed to say anything bad about anyone. That's absurd. The injustice against Phil of enduring all the years of abuse inflicted on him by Darla and the unfair judgment against Phil by his children defining Phil as unworthy to be their father cannot go undisputed.

Untrue or malicious storytelling about people is deeply wrong and should not be done. It is also true that gratuitously tattling, for no reason, on people who have erred is wrong and is bad for all concerned in relationships because the mistakes folks make are not all that defines them. Forgiveness is one of the most important acts that can be undertaken in the course of human events.

Also true, however, is that justice is important and injustice is wrong, and sometimes the only way to gain justice is to tell what happened, no matter how badly it may reflect on someone. One of the mistakes Phil made in his relationship with his son, after Sylvia decided that Phil was not good enough to be her father, was to think that Cole could persuade Sylvia to change if Cole could tell her the truth about why Phil left their mother, so Phil told Cole the truth. When Phil found after Cole's marriage that Cole was treating his dad just about like Sylvia had been doing, in an effort to get Cole to stop doing that, Phil told Cole's wife what marriage to Darla had been like. This was an attempt to engage her sympathy so that she could be an advocate for Phil.

Simply telling the truth is no guarantee of good results. Instead of responding with sympathy for Phil for what Darla put him through, both Cole and his wife reacted with anger and resentment, and chose not to believe what Phil said. At Cole's request, Phil stopped talking to him about what Cole's mother had done, and that agreement was working all right until the requirement came up for Phil to disclose to the Catholic church what had gone on in the marriage. Even though Phil was not giving Cole the information, the fact that he was giving it to anyone made Cole furious all over again. The choice Phil faced, as he saw it, was to be rejected and disrespected by his children because they wrongly believed him to be a disreputable person, something that he is not, or to be rejected by them because he told a truth they did not want to hear. Either way, Phil is toast, as far as they are concerned, so he might as well fight injustice and unfairness. That's a lot better than lying down and getting kicked without resisting.

Phil has told both his children that they owe their mother their complete love and respect for the good and well-meaning person she tries to be, despite the wrong she did in abusing him and destroying the marriage. Similarly, Phil has told them that they owe him their complete love and respect for the good and well-meaning person he is, despite the mistakes he has made. Their choice is to disregard that advice, to view their mother as a saint without blemish, to regard Phil as unworthy to be their father, and to treat him accordingly. Phil is unwilling to accept that as a set of circumstances in which he participates. The situation is therefore irresolvable.

That is what took place as the final break between Phil and his son. It's too bad, but Phil Temple continues to live a joyful and rewarding life in spite of misfortune, and there are good, strong reasons why his life fits that description. This story has a happy ending in spite of the negative part concerning the children. The reason this is true is that it is possible to live life so well, so fully, and so happily that the damage doesn't get done. That is what is going on here, and Phil's life continues to be a joyful adventure in love. How does one do that? There is a valid, effective, and genuine answer to that question.

41

HOW TO BE HAPPY DESPITE THE LOSS

Success at having a happy life is not related to material wealth, social status, family dynamics, fame, physical beauty, intelligence, or any other personal attribute or circumstance. Those things can add to the quality of life of a happy person, and lack or absence of these factors may, for some, add challenge to the business of being happy, but there is no rule saying they must. There are those who possess all those things at maximum levels and who are still not finding success at living. Just look at all the Hollywood types whose lives are wreckage or shameful spectacles. There are myriad examples out there of what awful lives people can experience. It is clear that there needs to be a better way for them. There is a better way.

The pursuit of happiness is an American right, and this fact is one of the reasons that it is a privilege to live in the United States. Sadly, there are a lot of Americans out there pursuing happiness like crazy but not finding it. There are lost and lonely rich people, and there are those of modest means who lead lives marked by joy and fulfillment. It's also possible to be rich and happy or poor and miserable. The truth is, success at living well and joyfully is a skill. Some people seem to be born with this skill in their DNA, and they can apply it without ever knowing that they are doing so. They just know they are happy. Others manage to learn the skill and make the conscious effort to have it work for them. Many get the information, then ignore it or fail to put it into action.

There exist any number of resources where a person can obtain information about developing the skill of successful living. These can include parents, friends, mentors, counselors, pastors, doctors, books, classes, seminars, twelve-step groups, and so on. The list can be very long of valid sources of this awareness. The amazing thing is that, with the absolute abundance of opportunities available for folks to get this information, there should be anyone left who does not have it. One look at all the misery and suffering out there is enough to make it obvious that people are passing up their chances aplenty. If you are missing the boat on happiness, read on. It's never too late. You can find out how wonderful life is and how to keep it that way.

What follows is a list of seventeen "Principles of Successful Living" that make up a very effective guide for staying happy, day by day. Seventeen is not a sacred number, that's just how it came out. It would be a simple matter to combine some of the principles and reduce the number, or divide some of the principles into more detailed presentation, and increase the number. None of that really matters. Producing a certain number of items just makes it simpler to organize the information for consumption by readers. That is why seventeen. The first is number one. If you internalize these principles, practice them, and make them a part of who you are and what you do, your life will be better. So, here goes.

Here is a succinct list of all seventeen principles. Expansion, amplification, and instruction concerning each one will follow.

1. Look for and focus on the goodness in others.
2. Focus on the goodness in yourself.
3. Forgive others.
4. Forgive yourself.
5. Learn and practice an affirmative approach.
6. Keep all your commitments.
7. Acknowledge your spiritual nature.
8. Believe that love is a force.
9. Be thankful.
10. Abide by the Golden Rule.
11. Seek personal growth and self-improvement.
12. Practice visualization.
13. Learn trust.
14. Take risks.
15. Be of service.

16. Seek and accept help.
17. Exercise and eat right.

This list is nothing new. It's not surprising, astonishing, amazing, earth shaking, or any other descriptive words one might think of to make a sale. Some words that absolutely describe this list include valid, true, effective, down-to-earth, on-the-money, real. Anyone who applies these straightforward principles consistently, every day, sincerely, long-term, will have a good life. Try it.

1. Look for and focus on the goodness in others. Replace complaints, gripes, and negative feelings with affirming, admiring appreciation of other people. Nobody is perfect. Almost everyone has something wonderful about them. Make that where you point your attention.

This appears as number one on the list because it is the most fun to do. Making a habit of looking for the good, the beauty, the wonder, the special gifts and talents, the uniqueness, and the miraculousness about each person you meet is a sweet way to live. At first, it takes determination and consistent effort just to remember to do this all the time. It becomes a subliminal process after you do it for a while so that the need to push yourself to do it eases, and it just comes naturally. That is only after you have trained yourself to do it. Once you have made this a part of your daily existence, you'll agree that it brightens your life from moment to moment, person to person, encounter to encounter, all day long, and eventually, all life long.

It's most important to focus on the positive things about the people closest to you. They are the ones who will share with you the greatest benefit of your application of this principle. They will see the twinkle in your eye as you make what you love about them, what you admire about them, what you treasure about them the center of your interaction with them. People who feel admired, appreciated, loved, and cherished are more positive, more loving, better to be around. You can cause this. Both your life and the lives of those around you will be better if you make this effort.

You will be the one who gets all the benefit of your looking for what is wonderful about strangers and people you encounter more casually and less intimately than those closest to you. The strangers and casually encountered people will most likely never know, never have the least idea of what you are doing, so they won't benefit much, except that getting treated with kindness and respect is never a bad thing. What happens inside of you is the greatest result of what you are doing. You will reach a point when getting together with people is such fun, not because of what they say or do, but because it feels so good inside of you to take inventory of the goodness and inner beauty of everybody you meet. If this is the only one of the seventeen principles you use and observe, your life will be better and more fun just because you do this one.

Adopt this, practice it, and make yourself do it until it is habitual. You'll love it and you'll be grateful for what it does for you. If you are trying to find a way to enjoy your life despite being estranged from or rejected by your children, this is a way of experiencing with everyone around you the love that would ordinarily go to your children. It's very healing. It's very effective. It's wonderful.

2. Look for, focus on, and believe in the goodness in yourself. Seek ways to confirm in your own mind what is good, admirable, and wonderful about yourself. Create goodness in yourself.

It is important to have a good opinion of yourself and a good self-image to have a happy life. You have already identified yourself in the course of reading this book as a loving, devoted, nurturing, guiding parent to your children. You are a responsible person, a good citizen, a loyal friend, a thoughtful neighbor, a loving child to your parents, a generous contributor to your church or your favorite charity, a sincere lover of mankind and Mother Nature, and so on. You have to acknowledge and appreciate all of these things about yourself. If you have difficulty doing that then first be sure that you are conducting yourself in ways that merit respect, both your own and that of other people. Then spend some time appreciating those admirable and positive characteristics in yourself. If there are people in your life who create trouble for you or undermine your affirmative sense of yourself, then bring that to an end by whatever lawful and ethical means may be at your disposal. It's harder to focus on the goodness in yourself when someone else is putting a lot of energy into tearing you down.

If your separation from your children is related to the treatment you received from someone tearing you down, then it is even more important for you to succeed in recognizing and focusing on the goodness in yourself. If you possess certainty in your soul that goodness and virtue are elemental to who you are, then you are on track to the life you want. Don't allow hateful, vengeful, angry thinking to overcome your goodness. Looking for the goodness in others makes it easier to find the goodness in yourself.

Those who do wrong, lie, cheat, steal, do harm to others, are irresponsible, regularly do things that are evil, dishonest, or negative, have very little chance at true happiness. Down deep, they know that they are doing wrong, and a soul engulfed in wrongdoing can never experience true self-respect or find true peace, which is fundamental to real happiness. If you are someone like that, stop it. Repent. Start doing right. Become a good person. If you can't or won't do that, then pitch this book, because there is no hope for you. If you acknowledge that a righteous life is essential to true happiness, then you're on the right track and you can do it.

Most people are basically good and don't have to make any big changes to be able to recognize their own virtue. If you are doing the right thing, then it is not such a big step to recognize it, admire it, be glad about it, and focus on enhancing, nurturing, and growing that part of yourself. Be thankful that such an important part of having a great life can be included in day-to-day living just by doing it.

In the story of Phil Temple, his life-long knowledge that the goodness inside of him is fundamental to who he is, and nineteen years of constantly being torn down and accused of evil was craziness of monumental proportions. He would have had a nicer life if he had left the person who was guilty of all that abuse, but that would have meant leaving his children. He stayed and had a pretty rough time, but his sense of his own goodness emerged intact. His relationship with his children now might or might not have been different than it is if he had left when they were little, and the negative religious influence that was present would likely have had its effect regardless of when he left, but his being around for longer was better for them, and their lives are better because he did. It was his duty, it was the right thing to do, and he would try to do it again, but this time he would put a stop to the abuse, with whatever result that engendered.

3. Forgive others. Free yourself of the poison of resentment by forgiving people for whatever mistakes they may have made. Carrying resentment does not hurt the person you resent nearly as much as it hurts you.

This principle is one of the most important of all of the items on the list and may also be the most difficult to bring to reality. If you have been rejected and wronged by your children, then the potential is very great for you to be harmed even more by harboring anger, vengeful thoughts, hateful feelings, and resentment. The more you stew about the wrong done to you, the more damage you do to yourself. If you go around hating and spending time focusing on how unfair it all is, you will never find peace and joy.

The descriptions in this book of Phil's life with Darla have been fairly graphic. That was done because telling the truth, as part of an effort to bring help and answers to people who have experienced the same kind of loss that Phil has, is a good thing. Providing aid to such folks is a righteous act, the character of which could be honorably chosen as a life's work. Writing about these events is also very therapeutic, much as journaling and diary-keeping can be, but focusing on them and suffering again and again about what happened is harmful to the person doing it, and should be avoided.

Phil has forgiven Darla for what she did, and when there is some reason for her to come to his mind, which is rare, he focuses on what he knows about her that is good. She is a sincerely motivated person who wishes to do good in this world and who intends to do what is right. She seeks to conform to God's will and wants to be remembered as a pure and virtuous person. It may be that she is being successful at that, and may God bless her for the good she does.

Darla deserves sympathy and even pity for the things that happened to her as she was growing up, which caused her so much emotional damage and rendered her incapable of adult behavior and of healthy relationships with men. She is to be pitied because she will never know the joy and wonder of a marriage with a true soul mate. Maybe her daughter has become a soul mate, which seems rather pathetic, but it may be a good thing. True love between humans is not something to condemn. One important factor in forgiving someone who did all that wrong to Phil is that he doesn't have to endure that ever again.

Phil has forgiven his children for the wrong they have done him. They were in a very tough spot, and choices against one parent, such as they made about their father, are pretty common. The children were misguided and harsh in what they decided to do, but they believe that what they did was right, and they most likely did not do it out of malice. Sylvia became so unpleasant and difficult to be around that there is nothing to miss about that, but the wonderful child she was is a happy memory always to be treasured. Peace reigns in Phil's heart about the way things are, and he still admires Sylvia for the strong and able person she grew up to be. He prays that she finds happiness.

Cole is a good American, is a good man, and is probably a good father. He is not a good son to his father, but that is not surprising, given the mother he had. It is fairly certain that he is a good son to her. God bless him for that, and his father forgives him for what he has done wrong. After his marriage, Cole's mother's influence on him compounded and redoubled, and he became very disagreeable to be around, which it is better not to experience. Because Phil and Cole were close before Cole married, and because they had some good times together, Phil's losing Cole was a tough adjustment, but when the choice is to endure more of the same ugliness that came from his mother, the adjustment is easier. The success Cole is having in his career is admirable and he is to be congratulated for it.

Should Phil's children reconsider their ways, he would be available to them for reconstruction of their relationships, but does not expect that; He doesn't even hope for that. His life without them is too sweet to hope for the kind of disruption they might bring. The love he offered them is now for others, most importantly his beloved Maria, and that is where he lives. Phil's children are forgiven and he has peace.

Your own journey in this regard is truly your own. Nobody can prescribe just how it has to be for you, but you must make the journey. Think lovingly about what is meritorious and positive about the people whom you must forgive in order to make your way to peace and joy, and if that is difficult, just remember them as babies and children. No matter how bad they may be as adults or how wrong they may be in the decisions they make concerning you, babies and children are all precious little gifts from God and are easy to forgive.

If you need help or advice about accomplishing forgiveness, seek it out. Reaching a place where you have fully forgiven can be a long process, and information about how best to accomplish it, day by day, can be invaluable. Get books, use counselors, ask friends and confidants, pray. It is very doable and you can do it, too.

4. Forgive yourself. Guilt is felt when a person does not forgive himself for mistakes made or wrongs committed. Guilt is the same thing as resentment, except that it is directed at you, by you. Acknowledge that everyone, including you, makes mistakes and needs forgiveness.

You have already made the determination to focus on what is good about yourself and to be sure that your conduct makes you deserve to be regarded as a good person. Nobody is without sins or errors in his or her history. We learn from our mistakes, and we become better people because we determine not to repeat them. That is what makes us worthy of our own forgiveness. Feeling guilt is possible only for people whose instincts are to do what is right and to avoid doing what is wrong. The mere fact that a person experiences guilt defines that person as someone with goodness inside. That is a great place to start forgiving yourself for mistakes you have made. Feeling guilt proves that you are a fundamentally good person. Resolving not to repeat the wrongs you have done defines you as repentant and worthy of another chance to do right.

People who can feel no guilt despite having done what they know is wrong are sociopaths. There are some wrongs that are so evil and heinous that forgiveness, either from others or from one's self, can be earned only by going to prison, being put to death, or some other extreme punishment. There are presumably no people who are responsible for such acts seeking the help available in this book because they were steered away in the introduction as deserving the rejection of their children. That leaves the rest of us who loved and cherished our children and did right by them, but who may have done things that would have been better left undone or done differently.

In the case of Phil Temple, taking up with a friend of his children's mother some months after he left the marriage may have been his biggest error. That was a mistake, but understandable and forgivable in light of what he was going though at the time. Phil is not sorry for leaving, but he is sorry for allowing things to proceed the way they did, and he apologized for it years ago. He has forgiven himself for doing it. He would not do it again. His guilt is gone.

Perhaps Phil should not have tried to persuade his son and daughter-in-law to stop treating Phil like a bum as Cole's mother and sister had done. This seemed a reasonable approach to what Phil was experiencing, and he did it with the positive intention to right a wrong. It did not work and should not have been tried, but Phil has forgiven himself for the error, and learned from the experience.

Maybe you feel guilt about something you did that was not quite so understandable or motivated by difficult circumstances. If you are sorry for what you did, if you have apologized and tried to make amends for doing it, and if you will never do it again, you have earned your own forgiveness, and you can give up your guilt. Even if others won't forgive you, you merit forgiveness and you can walk free.

You must do what it takes to forgive yourself and shed your guilt. A person walking around carrying a load of guilt cannot live a happy life. Do what it takes to remove that load.

5. Learn and practice an affirmative approach to living. Cause positive focus to be accustomed behavior. Avoid negativity. Develop satisfying diversions that can take you out of a period of negative thinking whenever it shows up. Recognize that negativity is the disease that afflicts this world more completely than any other malady. Fight it off.

Anyone who has experienced clinical depression knows what harm negative thinking and negative self-talk can do. What makes depression so awful and so difficult to overcome are the hopelessness, the despair, and the impenetrable conviction that nothing can come out right, that bad will follow bad indefinitely, and that there is no point to anything. People who are not depressed but who have a negative outlook experience negative self-talk in a way that is not a medical illness, but which is similar to depression in that the insidious character of negativism can eat away the happiness, the goodness, and the joy in life without the person even being aware of it.

The solution to the negativity that can wreck a life is to be able to recognize it, to be aware of the harm it can do, to take steps to eliminate it from one's mental patterns, and to substitute positive focus and affirmative thinking in its place.

The first four principles in this list of keys to successful living all include requirements that we practice positive focus. Looking for and focusing on the goodness and beauty in others, looking for and focusing on the goodness and beauty in ourselves, and looking for and focusing on reasons and ways to forgive ourselves and others are essential to living the best life we can. Making that positive focus an automatic response to everything that comes up is how we make it work for us. If we recognize negativity and smash it down every time it comes up, then replace it with a forced positive focus, the desired response becomes habitual and life is better. It works and it's worth doing.

6. Keep all your commitments. Never make a commitment that you can't or won't keep. Honor all your vows, pledges, promises, contracts, commitments, of whatever sort. Recognize yourself as someone who is true to his word. Conduct yourself so that everyone, including yourself,

knows that you are someone who always does what you say you will do.

Self-respect is an essential element in living happily. A person who lies, cheats, steals, and harms others is not worthy of respect and knows it. He knows that he is not worthy of the respect of others, which ensures that he will not respect himself. His spirit knows that he is dishonest and does bad things, and his punishment is the absence of self-respect. People without self-respect can never know true happiness.

For those who are not criminals or liars, the situation is more subtle. Otherwise decent, honest, truthful, law-abiding people who make promises they don't keep, take vows they don't honor, make pledges they don't follow through with, or fail to fulfill commitments they make are subject to the same law of inner responsibility. If you know it's true that when you make a promise you probably won't keep it, your heart is aware. If you made a promise and did not keep it, your heart remembers. If you make an appointment and know you'll probably be late for it, your heart is aware. If you're always late, your heart remembers. If you vowed to be faithful to a spouse but expect to dishonor that vow, if you pledge a donation but don't send it in, if you tell someone you'll help them move, then back out because you don't feel like it, if you set a goal to lose weight, then pig out, if you promise yourself to do the right thing, then don't do it (and the list goes on), your spirit is aware, it remembers, and it recognizes that you fall short. Your self-respect is diminished. Without self-respect, true peace at heart cannot be reached.

Begin today to keep every commitment you make, no matter how small or unimportant you think it is. Your inner being knows that all of your commitments are important because your self-respect depends on keeping them. Showing up late for an appointment is not such a big deal to the world, and few people are wracked with guilt about being a little late. They may not give it another thought. That tiny ledger inside is keeping track, however, and if your internal accountant knows that you are someone who fails to be punctual on a recurring basis, you have sabotaged yourself and you are downgrading your potential to be a happy person.

There are people who make promises just to get somebody off their back or who pledge to provide help in order to be thought of as a nice person, but then don't follow through. They may or may not have known from the start that they would renege, but either way, they made a commitment not kept and they are lesser persons for it, and the quality of their life is reduced. It would be better never to promise anything or never to take any vow about anything than to make commitments you don't keep. Then questions might come up about how much you care about your fellow humans or about how public spirited you are or how generous you are, but those are separate issues.

Never commit to anything you can't or won't follow through on, period. Once you have made a commitment, honor it fully and completely, period, no matter what. Once you establish this as a no-exceptions policy, you will be pleased at how it improves the quality of your life. If you have made promises to your estranged children that were not kept, fulfill them, regardless of the questions of reconciliation or retribution. You made a commitment, and it must be met. If your children made promises to you that they did not keep, forgive them, but also take notice, so as not to keep yourself vulnerable to disappointment and the failings of others.

The few times Phil Temple violated his marital vows while he was married to Darla were very unhappy experiences for him. He rationalized his behavior by believing that Darla deserved any disloyalty he might subject her to because of her awful treatment of him, but his spirit knew that, irrespective of what Darla might have deserved, Phil was bound by the vows he had taken and he was violating them. Because of all that, Phil would now never do such a thing again. Even if Phil's beloved Maria turned into Satan, an unlikely eventuality, Phil would honor his marital vows, no matter what. He would also take steps to get the situation resolved, but without dishonoring his commitment. It feels wonderful to Phil that his wife can trust him completely, and that she knows it.

7. Acknowledge your spiritual nature. Humans are spiritual beings. Seek ways to recognize, respect, affirm, and experience this. It is important.

The current trend in this country toward the secularization and coarsening of the culture is bad for all Americans, even though, for the short term, many of them think that they are enjoying what is happening. Activist, liberal judges have done great harm to America by fashioning, out of whole cloth, an environment in which pornography and birth control are available to eleven-year-old children; where sexuality among children is fostered and promoted; where vile criminals are regarded as victims of society and are allowed to practice their evil on victims who don't even know that our legal system has created this atmosphere that has loosed these predators on them; where vulgar and disgusting language is heard loud and clear, far and wide, everywhere, without remedy for decent people; and where the indiscriminate destruction of innocent human life is found to be a constitutional right instead of the ugly crime it truly is.

We are all the worse for living in a place where degenerate Hollywood smut merchants cause indecent and perverse behavior and speech to become acceptable and mainstream. We watch in horror and dismay as America becomes an increasingly disturbing place in which decent, law-abiding people who respect others and ask for respect in return have fewer and fewer places to turn in search of refuge from the public ugliness that is commonplace in what was once the land of the free and the home of the brave. News media, which once were reliable sources of truth and information to the public, are now propaganda organs dedicated to turning America into an imitation of Socialist Europe and from which truth is an unobtainable commodity. This is because many, if not most, of the leftist educated journalists who populate all the newsrooms now promote their secular agenda instead of informing the public.

In a former era, most Americans went to church or temple and decent, modest, respectable behavior was the norm. Once, schools and colleges were places where young people were educated and refined. Today those same educational institutions are dens of indoctrination where our young are being turned into libertines, progressives, and fools whose primary concerns are their personal rights and self-gratification. The "Californication," the "New Yorkification" and the "progressivication" of America is the death knell of what was truly the most virtuous country ever to have existed on the face of the earth, and it is a tragedy to watch. To be sure, traditional America was not without its flaws. Slavery and racism are two of the worst, but America's greatness is shown by the fact that slavery is long-since gone, and racism, once lawful and institutionalized, is a much different fact than it once was; it continues to die out, and we can look for the day when it will be all but nonexistent.

Traditional values have been pronounced dead by Democrat politicians. America has become a country populated in the majority by young people who would not answer the call that Americans responded to in World War II to save mankind. America is the sole reason Europe still exists in freedom. Europeans condemn America for being warlike, when, in fact, they should be on their knees thanking what this country formerly was for their very existence. Europe has become a place where no one is willing to fight for what is right or against evil. America is becoming the same, and when the change is complete, chaos, mayhem, and evil will prevail, worldwide.

A civilization that will not fight against evil and for what is right cannot long survive unprotected. America is crumbling as the world's final bulwark against evil and evil is strongly on the march because of the progressive cancer infecting America. Evil has always been on the march, but with America there to fight back against it, the world stood a chance. Now that our country is rapidly becoming a nation that refuses to stand against evil and in support of right and good, the outlook for mankind is bleak. Without America to resist the next Hitler, the next Soviet Union, the next efforts of Al Qaeda, the next Fidel Castro, the next Saddam Hussein, they will not be resisted and will not be overcome.

The decline of America as the bastion of courage and strength in the world coincides with the decline of spirituality and religion in America. The total collapse of America as the beacon of freedom and goodness on earth is well under way and will ultimately occur along with, and because of, the total collapse of spirituality and religion among its people. Go to church now, and you see mostly old people. Too many of the young are out getting stoned; getting laid; getting pierced; seeking fun, fun, fun; or complaining to each other about what a rotten country America is. Boundaries on personal behavior have been removed, so no individual conduct, no matter how reprehensible, can now be judged, and everything goes.

Unless we can turn the tide soon and reestablish spirituality and virtue as the norm, it will be too late. A godly and virtuous country is made up of godly and virtuous individuals. People who recognize that honesty, truthfulness, decency, charity, modesty, chastity, personal responsibility, and the courage to fight against evil are fundamental to a good life can, if present in sufficient numbers, create a nation where those values predominate. People who contemplate, meditate, and act on these values can have rewarding lives and give new life to a country where goodness and virtue are once again the rule.

Pray, meditate on philosophical and holy writings, seek God or your higher power or turn to Christ, go to church, temple, or other place of worship. Take part in charitable works. All of this will sweeten your life and give you new reasons to enjoy each day and love being you. Being a Christian is a beautiful thing. Being a Roman Catholic is a joy and a privilege., Going to church and partaking of the Eucharist and enjoying the wonderful people found at church are life enriching.. A great life is even greater because of belonging to the church and seeking to emphasize the spiritual aspect of life. As brothers and sisters of Christ, we learn that love and goodness are what matter. We can find refuge from what is happening to our country in a relationship with God, and be happy in spite of where America is headed. We can also find ways to change what is happening and fight against the decay we are witnessing. Go for it. Play the spirituality card. Life is better when you do. Phil met Maria after he started praying.

8. Believe that love is a force. Know that it can be the greatest force in the world if people will allow it to be. Exercise your love every chance you get.

Loving mankind is a worthy concept, but loving people, face to face, is what it's all about. As rough as Phil's experience was in the love department, spending twenty years married to a verbal abuser then being thrown aside by her equally sad-case children, one might think he should give up on the concept. But he has not, and will not. Just because giving love to some people ends up being futile, that is no indication that it won't be gloriously successful when tried again. The sweet contentment, satisfaction, and joy Phil has in his life make it all worth it. He has a sense that it is his reward for all the sincerity and loving effort that he put in over the years in loving the people whom God has put in his path. It's also high time for it to go right in view of all the junk he's had to deal with.

All the kindly, thoughtful, interesting, stimulating, and loving people in Phil's life today cause him to be nearly overcome with gratitude, pleasure, and elation that he should be so lucky as to have it come out this way after all the loss that has gone before. Because Phil spends so much time looking for what is good and beautiful about everyone, it becomes very easy to take the next step and love them. The fun part is focusing on the excellence in each person. The miracle and the joyful part comes in finding that love truly is the greatest force in the world, and that it is worth all the effort you can put into making it a factor in your daily life. Lists are good things to make. Here's a nifty list prepared by Phil Temple, an equal of which you can make from the people in your own life.

Maria T. My wonderful wife. She is a force of nature whose smile lights up my soul and my world. She spreads her loving spirit into every corner of every place she goes and is the greatest joy of my life. I love her so much.

Loren T. My dad. A more honorable, loving, and decent man never lived. As hard as he was to deal with sometimes, I was lucky to have him for my father, and I honor his memory with all my might. I love him dearly. God rest his dear soul.

Molly T. My mom. Her sweet, gentle spirit lives on in my heart, and I'm proud that it was she who gave birth to me. My love for her is forever.

Our three grandkids. They are so wonderful and fun, and their old Grandpa, yours truly, loves them more than they can imagine.

Lucca B. and his wife Josie. I love them.
Keith S. and his wife Marcy. I love them.
Ron S. and his wife Dotty. I love them.
Abe A. and his wife Linda. I love them.
Celso M. and his wife Kim. I love them.
Larry H. and his wife Lilly. I love them.
Ron N. and his wife Lexy. I love them.
Mitch M. and his wife Barbara. I love them.
Dan W. and his wife Trudy. I love them.
Fritz M. and his wife Pam R. I love them.
Bud M. and his wife Kate. I love them.
Jack W. and his wife Sue. I love them.
Zoltan G. and his wife Cathy. I love them.
Erin S. and his wife Jackie. I love them.
Clarence C. and his wife Marilyn. I love them.
Mark W. and his wife Alicia. I love them.
Horacio M. and his wife Pat. I love them.
Allen M. and his ex-wife Jackie C. I love them.
Allen H. and his wife Michelle G. I love them.
Mark, Merlinda, Celina, Lupe, Marcella, Melissa, Adam, Mason, Mckai, Maddox, Matthew, Michael, Barbara, Nick, Zoë, George, Tom, Gene, Ken, Albert, Chucky, Sundra, Mike, Steven, Byron, Tony, Gabriel, Henry, Dodie, Larisa, Cora, Eldon, Jerry, Sandy, Jesse, Pat, Kate, Ernie, Andy, Tony, Joe, Job, Denise, Jamen, Destiny, Marcie, Sophie, Jennifer, Damien, Jeremy, Loretta, Beni, Debby, Steven, Tom, Carol, Theresa, Michelle, Desi, Rebecca, Michael, Arturo, Euphemia, Stephan, Leo, Sharan, Joe, John, Frances, Gordie, Marcia, Paul, Pam, George, Misty,

Pam, Eddie, Lydia, Merlynn, Eddie, Margit, Joyce, Evelyn, Joe, Maureen, Judy, Debbie, Jackie, Marilyn, Andy, Joe, Roger. I love them all.

Make your own list. Make it true. It's great.

9. Be thankful for all the beauty in your life, and there is plenty, if you just learn to focus on it. Maintain an attitude of gratitude.

If you can't think of anything in your life to be grateful for, you aren't trying. If you can't make a list of things that you can be thankful about, it's because you don't want to. There is no one who is utterly without cause for gratitude. If you want to be happy and enjoy your life, focus on those things for which you ought to be grateful, and cultivate your sense of appreciation for your blessings.

It is a matter of simple common sense to realize that what you place your focus on and what you direct your energy toward is what your life is going to be about. If, in your thinking, you emphasize complaints, objections, dissatisfaction, unfairness, failures, and faults, then that is where you live, and happiness is elusive, at best. If, on the other hand, your focus is appreciative, positive, and uplifting, then that is how your life is. It just makes sense.

Here again, we are talking about mental habits. Negative habits take time and energy to get established, and they take time to break, dismantle, and replace with positive habits. Nobody can do it for you but you, and the habits won't change themselves. You have to do it. Start today. If you can, find a friend or partner who will work with you in a project of developing new thinking patterns and techniques of positive focus. If you can't find someone to do it with you, do it by yourself. Set aside appointment times where you just sit down, either with your project partner or alone, and think about, write about, or discuss all the things you have to be grateful for. Make lists. Compete to see who can show the most gratitude or find the most reasons to be thankful. Teach yourself or teach each other how to direct your personal power into this elevating and uplifting way of living.

If you have habits, proclivities, addictions, tendencies, or obsessions that prevent you from focusing on reasons to be thankful and happy, stop them, change them, get treatment for them, obtain counseling for them, undergo rehab for them, do whatever it takes to achieve the growth necessary to accomplish alterations in how you do things so that you can become the grateful, happy person you want to be. When you go around feeling grateful for everything you should be grateful for, you'll even end up being grateful for all your gratitude because it makes your life better.

10. Be careful about what you say to others. Do not be a source of pain. Observe the Golden Rule. If you would not want it done or said to you, don't do it or say it to anyone else.

This is a very big one. Phil Temple spent many years living with someone who exercised almost no control over what came out of her mouth. The term is almost, because Darla virtually never swore. That indicates that the awful things she said without cussing were by choice, not because she was without the ability to be in charge of her utterances. She may not have been in control of the feelings of rage that she experienced over such minor stuff, and that is what therapy and counseling are for. But she could have been in better charge of what she said when those feelings came up, and she chose not to be. What she ended up saying, time and again, was bad enough and hurtful enough do to enormous damage, profanity or not. The meanness in her was no doubt the result of the mean treatment she got growing up, but even people who enter the world under those conditions are responsible for harm they do by what they say. Bad treatment growing up might be a reason, but it is not an excuse.

It is a most amazing thing that there are people who are very sensitive and whose feelings are easily hurt by what others say, but who let 'er rip and are perfectly okay with verbally brutalizing others. That's crazy and it is a mystery why such people can't empathize enough with their fellow humans to ease up on how they talk when displeased. Phil's dear Maria spent most of her life having terrible stuff said to her and saying terrible stuff to others, and she had a pretty awful time of it as a result. Ask her now which she prefers, living in a peaceful relationship where both partners are careful and thoughtful about what they say to each other, even when disagreeing or problem-solving, or living in households where there are no limits on the offensive things people say to each other. Maria prefers the former and has learned a better way. You can accomplish the same.

If you are like Phil, without a mean bone in your body, but you live with someone who is mean and says terrible stuff to you, put a stop to it. The mistake Phil made was allowing it to go on from Darla because he wanted to stay for his children. None of the trouble in that marriage was because of meanness on Phil's part, and that same lack of meanness and the presence of a sincere heart are now largely responsible for the success of his present marriage. It is possible to refuse to tolerate meanness without being mean yourself and that is what is recommended.

If you are inclined to say ugly things to others, curb your tongue. If you are having trouble finding happiness and you don't limit the verbal punishment you dish out, then you are causing your own problems. If you need counseling, training, or therapy to learn how to control your mouth, then get it. If you verbally abused your children, then you probably earned their rejection of you, and it may be that you owe more atonement to them for the bad things you made them listen to. The Golden Rule of treating others as you would wish to be treated is truly golden. Abide by it. Your success as a person depends on it.

11. Seek personal growth and self-improvement. Know that happiness and successful living are skills that can be achieved. Set goals, read books on personal growth, take courses, attend retreats and meetings. Surround yourself with people who are happy and who know why that is true. Acquire for yourself the mastery of living happily.

One of the most important features of participatory seminars is the practical exercises that they offer for the purpose of teaching those taking part what it feels like to experience the principles being taught. You can actually find out what it's like to look for the beauty in other people, to trust a stranger, to love and forgive one's self, to forgive others, to keep commitments, and all the other principles contained here. For that reason, attending such seminars is highly recommended. They can give you eye-opening experiences that will make all these factors real for you and allow you to truly internalize the concepts in ways that just reading books will not necessarily do.

Review this list of principles daily, either as a written checklist, or mentally, so that making use of the list becomes second nature. When you are continually checking up on yourself, you will be able to detect slippage in your performance, and redouble your efforts to keep doing what it takes. Being happy and loving the life you are living is worth all the effort you can put into it. Be an active seeker of authentic ways to make the most of your time on this earth.

12. Practice visualization. Picture beauty in your life. Endeavor in a loving, spiritual, and affirming way to achieve beauty in your life.

Review regularly that which you have learned about living well and keep it fresh.

Imagine the people, circumstances, and things in your life that you believe would contribute most to your true happiness, set the goals of achieving or acquiring what you have imagined, and then get busy making it all happen. It is amazing at how the things people visualize in their lives end up coming true. One can visualize jobs, people, circumstances, and material possessions and see them come to realization. It happens all the time. It's also necessary to do what it takes to bring to reality, but picturing what you want makes it easier to focus on creating the actuality that you want.

Phil always had the capacity to be a partner in a loving, joyful, rewarding partnership of marriage, and always had an image in his mind of how that would be and what it would feel like. He now has such a marriage, and carrying that vision around in his mind for all those years helped him bring it to reality. Praying helped, as well.

After Phil quit that awful cannery job and while he was looking for work in Anchorage, one of the stops he made on a regular basis was at the Unemployment and Job Service office. Phil was impressed with what a positive and pleasant environment there seemed to be for the staff, and found himself thinking that he would be good at helping people like him who were looking for work. He began imagining himself working there, and even when he had another job, there was this snapshot in his mind of having a job there. Within about eight months, he was hired by the agency that operated that office. Two years later, he was actually working in that very office.

Phil took time to observe the way different people went on with life after they retired, and developed his own view of what kind of life he would like to lead following retirement. After he married Maria, Phil shared his dream with her, and then they looked forward together. Phil wanted to continue living in Alaska, because he loved that place so much, but he also wanted to spend time in the lower forty-eight so that he would not have to live so fast and furious during the Alaska summer, in anticipation of the approaching winter. Phil and Maria now live a few months in Utah during the depth of the Alaska winter, and actually get to experience more weather that is similar to Alaska's spectacular summer. Springtime in Utah is much like summer in Alaska. When winter is at its deepest in Utah, they go to Las Vegas, Arizona, California, or Hawaii, and winter in those places is a lot like summer in Alaska. Retirement for them is just like Phil envisioned it. It is true that planning, budgeting, and long-term projection have also been part of creating what they have now, but it is undeniable that visualization played a role in their getting this life.

Picture yourself and your spouse or partner in the beautiful, loving, joyful relationship you want. If you don't have a partner, visualize the partner who could create that wonderful relationship with you. Imagine yourself in the job you want. Picture the home you want. Picture the life you want. Envision the retirement life you want. Then set about making them all come true. If you know what you want, then get busy doing what it will take to make it happen. If you are old enough to be dealing with estrangement from your adult children, then a dream job or a new life partner may not be what your visualization would be about, but visualizing a happy, joyful, rewarding life makes perfect sense for anyone. What you visualize should be possible and within the realm of reality. Pipe-dreaming the impossible makes no sense, but a happy life is possible for anyone, and envisioning that is a great idea.

You may even visualize a reconstituted relationship with your children, which may make sense or not, depending on the facts of each case. In many instances, such a thing is not possible, so keeping one's hopes up about the hopeless is unwise. We have no power to change other people, and big changes in people are often what would be required for reconciliation to take place. Working toward the changes needed in the lives of others is just not reality. It doesn't hurt to have a picture in mind of how beautiful and sweet reconciliation could be, but betting anything on impossible people is foolishness. If you can create a picture of a renewed relationship in your mind without allowing sadness, regret, or sorrow to accompany the image, then it's fine. If the hopelessness gets you, then stay away from such images. Life is about being happy, and if thinking about lost people makes you unhappy, don't do it. Stick to the possible, the attainable, and the beautiful. Visualization has real value if you keep it positive.

13. Learn trust; make it a way of life. Trust and believe in others. Trust and believe in yourself. Be sure that others can safely trust you. When you learn that someone cannot be trusted, arrange circumstances so that you are not vulnerable to their lack of trustworthiness.

The most difficult thing in the world for someone who cannot be trusted is to believe that someone else can be trusted. It is part of human nature to regard other people as beings who tend to think and to do things in much same way that we ourselves do. For a person who is accustomed to lying, breaking promises, dishonoring vows and breaching contracts, presuming that others will honor their agreements is almost impossible. The nearest someone like that can come to trusting others is to rely on their dishonesty. Believing that nobody will tell the truth, that nobody will keep promises, that nobody will honor vows, and that nobody with abide by agreements allows such a person to protect himself from being disappointed by those shortcomings. Being able to make oneself immune to the untrustworthiness of others certainly has value, but if that's all you've got going on, oh my, what a lousy way to live.

The most vital component in a happy relationship, marriage or otherwise, is trust. The knowledge that the person who has vowed to love, honor, and be faithful to you will without fail, do exactly what he or she has promised to do is a jewel beyond price, and without it a relationship cannot succeed. It might continue to pass time on the calendar without trust, but that is not success. That is just tolerating failure.

The biggest difficulty that Maria and Phil had when they started out was Maria's inability to trust. She had been in relationships with men who were dishonest, deceitful, disloyal, and unfaithful, and she had learned to expect that as normal. She herself was trustworthy, so Phil believed that she could learn that a man could be trusted. He hoped that she could accept and believe in his integrity because, even though relying upon men had been a mistake for her in the past, she could come to know the real Phil and learn to feel safe. That is exactly what has happened, and their relationship prospers because complete trust is at its heart. What a great way to live.

The earlier discussion of the principle that a successful and happy person keeps all his promises, honors all his commitments, and abides by all his agreements relates directly to the issue of trust. If you make a point of keeping all your promises and never make commitments you can't or won't keep, then you will become accustomed to living your life as a trustworthy person, and you will find it easier to trust others. The key is keeping your word.

There are people who cannot be trusted or who prove through your experience with them that trusting them is a mistake. That is great information, and associating with untrustworthy people need not be a source of trouble for you. Making yourself vulnerable to people who are truly trustworthy is safe and can be very rewarding. Maintaining your distance from untrustworthy or dangerous people is just good sense. You can love them and appreciate them without making yourself a potential victim of their treachery. This applies to estranged children as much as anyone. If what you know about them is that they are dangerous to you, then it may be your good fortune to have them out of your life.

Focus on the people on whom you can rely to look out for your best interest. Let the others be. Make sure everyone can trust you, whether you can trust them or not. Your own integrity is too important to the quality of your life for you to be any other way.

14. Take risks. Be willing to extend yourself beyond your comfort zone. Be open to new concepts and ways of being. Don't be closed to new possibilities in life. Show courage in trying new things and meeting new challenges. Stretch yourself. The world is a richer and more rewarding place when you do.

A lament heard from bored people and from those leading unfulfilling lives is that they are in a rut. Those who are living in a rut are not making the most of their lives and are not experiencing success at living. A terrific way to make life interesting, challenging, and rewarding is to get brave and push yourself into arenas and activities beyond what you are accustomed to. This is not to say that we should do foolish, dangerous, or unwise things to find happiness. Taking risks to live a better life is different from living a danger-filled life. Get yourself out there in healthy, constructive, affirming ways, and you'll be glad you did.

If speaking in front of groups of people is uncomfortable for you, try joining a theater group, audition for a part in a play, or volunteer to be a lector at church. If meeting new people is a stretch for you, become a Big Brother or Big Sister to a youngster who needs a mentor or visit shut-ins or the immobile at hospitals, in retirement centers, or in their homes. Be an aide or foster grandparent at your local school.

If trying new things makes you uneasy, overcome that unease by taking an art class or a creative writing class, painting pictures, sculpting statues, or writing books. Teach a class in an art, craft, or skill that you can do well. Join your small-town fire department and take training as a firefighter or EMT. Join the police auxiliary and support your local police. Become active in a professional or labor organization where your experience, skills, or knowledge can be useful to others. Become active in a political party or movement that shares your values. Join a book club or discussion group. Try a new hobby. Think up your own original ways to step outside your comfort zone, challenge yourself, and take good risks.

There are a million and one possible ways to expand your horizons. Innumerable interesting, worthwhile, useful, beneficial, fun, educational, spiritually uplifting opportunities exist out there and await your decision to get involved. Principle number five in this list, "Learn and Practice an Affirmative Approach," is a key element in this portion of your campaign to improve your life. If you get involved in a pro-life movement, make it because you love mankind and believe in preservation of each individual life, not because you hate abortion or abortionists. If you become a Democrat party activist, do it because you believe in what the party stands for and what they want to achieve, not because you hate Republicans or despise conservatism. Focus your thinking so that what you are doing is devoted to bringing about good, creating benefit, achieving improvement, providing help.

If you experience negative thinking or depression because you are in a rut or because your children are out of your life, directing your energy in these new fields of endeavor and stretching yourself to experience life in new ways will provide great help in overcoming those tendencies to be negative and self-damaging. You will have things to look forward to, to be proud of, to be busy attending to, and your negative feelings will be overcome. Even when you find yourself experiencing stage-fright, nervousness, performance jitters, or other uncertainty about what you are undertaking, you will learn that these feelings can be made to work for you to improve your performance, enhance your preparation, motivate you to try harder, and in the end, be to your benefit. Instead of dreading the butterflies, you will learn to welcome them because of the rewards they help to bring when you have completed your task and are feeling good that you have done it.

Start looking now for ways to challenge and stretch yourself. Get outside that comfort zone. Fill in that rut by taking a chance.

15. Be of service. Volunteer, help out, give of your time, talent, and treasure. Do good things for others, without recognition, if you can. Give. Do good works.

This is especially important for persons whose children are no longer in their lives. For Phil, one of the best parts of being a parent was how he found himself truly overcome by the unconditional character and utter selflessness of the love he felt for his children. It was sweet beyond words to care about those little ones so much that Phil would not have hesitated to give his life for their benefit and would have been happy to do it. In one sense, that is exactly what Phil did, at least from the standpoint of enduring Darla's abuse so that they would have a loving father in the house. Phil's love for his children was his motivation for staying, for had they not been born, he would have left at least a dozen years before he did.

A strong sense of doing good for others without regard for his own benefit was the direct result of Phil's staying, and that feeling helped counteract the loneliness and dissatisfaction that was a daily feature for him of living with Darla. The sense of meaning that he derived from doing something this meritorious and sacrificial was what Phil lived on for most of the years before his children became teenagers. Between loving them with all the power that was in him, carrying around the sense of doing something holy and godly for their benefit, and distracting himself with interesting and enjoyable activities, Phil was pretty successful in having a pleasant life until things got so bad that he had to leave.

For those who have come to rely on the satisfaction that comes from doing good things for their children and who have then lost those children, substituting doing good for others in place of doing good for their children can do great things in reconstituting that essential sense of happiness and contentment that comes from dedicated parenthood.

There is an endless number available to you of worthwhile, productive, useful, helpful, and rewarding volunteer activities. Choose one or a few of these, and get into them. American society has become so obsessed with self-gratification and personal rights that a large fraction of the citizenry of this country is without any knowledge of the enormous value to the individual of service to others. Anyone old enough to be concerned with estrangement from their adult children is old enough to have had at least some exposure to the America that used to exist, in which service to God, country, and others was honored and respected by most people and practiced by great numbers of Americans. In the old America, service to others was integral to the national fabric and was a part of our culture. Service to one's own gratification or one's own prejudices is what this country has come to be about for too many, but that has not eliminated the possibility for anyone to take advantage of the uplifting, heart-expanding value of doing good works and serving others. Do it.

16. Avail yourself of help and knowledge that others can provide. There is an abundance of counseling, assistance, friendship, love, advice, and help out there that can be yours just for the asking. Don't assume that answers will just come to you. Don't just go it alone. Seek guidance through prayer.

There is an old saying that you can't pick your family but you can pick your friends. A good friend is a far better feature in your life than a cruel, disloyal, or treacherous relative. Seek out your friends. Rekindle old friendships, make new friends. Spend time with them. Share yourself with them. Be an asset in their lives. The older one gets, the more priceless good friends become. Most of the time, they can just be there for companionship, good times, and enjoyment. Other times, they can provide advice, caring, and wisdom to help us get through tough situations. Recognize the value of good friends and cultivate friendship. Don't become isolated.

Professional counselors are sometimes characterized as people whom you pay to be your friend. At times when the help and advice of untrained and nonprofessional friends doesn't quite fill the bill in solving problems, overcoming difficulties, or dealing with troublesome feelings, taking advantage of the training, experience, expertise, and knowledge of licensed professionals in dealing with problems can be exactly the right approach. It may be that we are all a little bit crazy and, at times, may all need professional help. It is certain that this list of principles for successful living, when sincerely and consistently applied, can do what it takes to ensure an enjoyable and happy life, and if you apply the list diligently, you'll have little need for counseling. The ideas and approaches presented here are very much like what you will get from counselors, so most of what they provide to you, if you are regularly applying this material in your daily life, will be more detail about how to make these ideas work in your distinct situation. Sometimes distractions or misfortune can get so big that, even for the most joyful among us, additional, trained help can be what is needed. Be aware that professional help can be a good thing, and use it when the need is there.

Members of the clergy are often good resources for loving assistance, advice, and counseling, and probably won't cost as much as shrinks. Some of the dearest and most wonderful people in the world are those you can find at church, and anyone who has dedicated him or herself to the service of God and humanity, which is what pastors, ministers, priests, rabbis, deacons, and nuns have done, deserves respect and stands a good chance of being skilled at helping people with problems.

Some of the finest and most purely good people who ever lived have been members of the clergy, and there should be no hesitation in turning to such people in times of need. Just like with anyone else, including relatives, you must determine the fitness of any particular person to play a role in your life, and there are scoundrels among church people just as there can be troublemakers in our own families. Find out about reputations and track records before relying upon people who are new to you. Once you have satisfied yourself that a counselor, pastor, sponsor, or other designated member of a helper category meets requirements for integrity and skill, take advantage of the good they can do for you. There are many great resources at our disposal when we need help. Let's use them.

17. Exercise regularly and eat healthful food. Honor your body.

Most people have heard about endorphins. In response to a variety of stimuli, our bodies produce these peptide compounds which, in turn, bring to us feelings of well-being, pleasure, satisfaction, contentment, and peace. This can happen whether or not other factors in our lives are at work at that moment to cause the same sorts of feelings. One of the things that can stimulate our bodies to produce these compounds is exercise. That explains why some people become such enthusiastic participants in exercise programs. They love the good feelings they get from working out, whatever form that may take.

Exercise has important effects beyond just feeling good for the moment, as well. People who exercise regularly are well known to be healthier than people who do not exercise. It's a simple matter of common sense that the healthier you are, the better you feel. The better you feel, the better able you are to do what it takes to live happily and to enjoy all the opportunities that come your way to enjoy being you.

Eating healthful food is a simple and economical way to make life better. Fresh fruits and vegetables are cheaper and much better for us than packaged and prepared foods. Fast food consumption continues to increase in America and the health consequences to all our fat children is a time bomb that will, in the future, compound the critical problems of health care accessibility and cost that already plague this country. You can reduce the impact on yourself of this national crisis, as well as enjoy life more, just by eating right and exercising regularly.

If you will persistently use the other sixteen principles on this list, it is a certainty that your life will be good. If you also honor your body with healthful food and regular exercise, life will be even that much better. Who would not want to do it? Go for the gold.

42

WRAP IT UP

There you have it, the story of the life of Phillip Temple and the reasons that, even with the unfortunate loss of his children, a good, happy, rewarding, and wonderful life it is. Reflecting upon what has transpired over these years, One cannot help but feel a sense of amazement at how, despite all the best intentions that existed in Phil's heart, and despite all the sincere efforts he has made, and continues to make, to be a good and loving person, this estrangement exists between himself and the two people whom, for many years, he loved more than anyone else on earth. Knowing what is known about the thoughts, feelings, and beliefs that exist inside of Phil Temple, and knowing about the enormous effort he makes every day to be thoughtful, fair, considerate, understanding, forgiving, and kind to everyone he encounters, one would have thought that he would not have an enemy in the world. The truth is, that except for his children, their mother, and his sister, Phil has exactly that: not an enemy in the world. There are those who would disagree with him politically or morally who might consider him to be their enemy. But another of the beautiful things about what America can be if we save it from the progressives is that people can disagree without being hateful or vicious. The enmity part is their choice. To be frank, those who are destroying America with their ugliness probably are Phil's enemies, at least from a theoretical point of view. But he is willing to sit down with them and look for the good in them while they all discuss, with civility, how not to destroy America.

Sad to say, there are many just like Phil, decent, loving, good people, who, for reasons outside their ability to control, have these disagreeable things to contend with in their lives. Phil takes full responsibility for what he has done and acknowledges that, like everyone, he has made mistakes, but someone as sincerely well-meaning and harmless as he is would normally be expected to have very little or none at all in the way of enmity or hatred directed at him. Fairness is not part of the equation in much of God's creation, however, and to wither away and suffer, resent the unfairness, and be bitter about what has gone on is self-destructive and of no value. Life is about recognizing, appreciating, and enjoying all the wonder, the beauty, and the goodness there is around us, and about trying to help others get that same value from this world. Phil had no way to know in the beginning about whatever it was that existed in the mother of his children, which led to the verbal and emotional abuse she inflicted upon him throughout their marriage. Phil had no way of knowing that some unseen force would turn his angelic little daughter into a surly, angry creature with no discernible heart, who would gladly reject her loving father with no regret or second thoughts at all. Phil had no way to know that the religion that the children's mother adopted and into which she led them would be one that they would believe supported rejection and damnation of their devoted, loving, and honorable father. There is nothing fair about any of that.

If, however, Phil allows all that stuff to overcome him, defeat him, and take him down, then that is on him. There are many in this world who have suffered much worse cruelty or catastrophe than Phil Temple has had to endure, and they have come through and prevailed. He asks no less of himself. Phil denies the misfortune that he has experienced the power to define him or the power to win, and his determination is working very well for him.

It may be that Phil has the good luck to have a Pollyanna-type personality with a sunshiny brain chemistry, which allows him to imagine that his world is a beautiful place with a vast array of reasons to be grateful, hopeful, optimistic, upbeat, loving, forgiving, joyful, and happy. What is actually true, however, is that Pollyanna-ism has nothing to do with Phil. He knows what to do, with God's help, to make his life one in which it is possible for him to recognize or create all of those positive things and to be happy. To repeat, HE KNOWS WHAT TO DO. You can do the same.

Lord knows, Phil has enough experience at the other end of the spectrum, with the deep depression he went through all those years ago, for him to be able to declare that he is not an automatically happy goofball with no grasp of reality. He is somebody who beat that situational sickness with appropriate measures and built a happy life using valid and effective principles, about which you have just read. This is why this book can be of great value to the many that walk in Phil's shoes. Do the work, practice the principles, learn the techniques, get the help, take the advice, and you too can be victorious and enjoy the wonderful gift of your life. Do it.

When the 9/11/2001 attacks took place, Phil's sister, she of Boulder, Colorado, and San Francisco values, made the observation that America was getting what it deserved. It is hard for Phil to believe that he grew up in the same house with someone who thinks like that. America is now, in 2010, being run by people who agree with that view of things and who seek to change this country into something that bears no resemblance to the great nation that saved the world in World War II, which rebuilt Europe and Japan from the destruction of that war, and which has shed more of her own blood and expended more of her own treasure than any other nation that ever existed, all for the purpose of freeing and saving others. America has kept almost none of the land it captured in those virtuous pursuits and has given it all back to the people who live there, so that they may follow their own dreams and make their own way. It is a privilege and a source of great pride to be a citizen of such a country, and it is scary to think what people like Phil's sister are trying to turn it into (apparently successfully). As frightening as that is, there can still be hope that Americans will come to their senses and reject the decline of our homeland into the pornography-loving, abortion-embracing, drug-devouring, traditional values-hating America of the Greatest Generation-rejecting, government-controlled paradise that the progressives are taking us into.

Despite all that, and as bad as what may happen will be if the progressives are not stopped, those of us can succeed who continue to practice what is presented here, as far as keeping our personal lives positive, joyful, and rewarding. Even if the government begins to employ the hateful and ugly tactics of today's far left, which at this point seems like a possibility but not a certainty, individual happiness should still be possible. Even under totalitarian regimes, an individual who lives according to the Seventeen Principles for Successful Living that are presented here can still lead a happy life, limited though it might be by government excesses.

The big challenge that the future may hold for Phil would appear to be related to the autoimmune disease, primary sclerosing cholangitis, with which he has been diagnosed, which he has had for twenty years, and which is disclosed in the story of his the life. What he means to have happen, and hopes that he is able to bring off, is that his healthy, positive, and joyful approach to living will continue to stand him in good stead with respect to the progress of this disease, and that he will live out a long and vigorous life, unaffected by the disease. His intention is that the malady, having been stopped in its tracks by daily joy, will remain a nonfactor in his life, and that he never has to deal with the liver-transplant-or-death choice faced by most of the people who contract this condition.

If, on the other hand, time catches up with Phil Temple, and despite all the joy and appreciation of life he can muster, the condition progresses, and he is faced with a grim reality, he hopes and intends to be as joyful and positive in facing death or transplant as he is while enjoying good health. If government intervention has, by that time, reached the point of rationing health care, and people of retirement age are deemed by the government not to be worth the cost of keeping them alive, then Phil may not get the chance for a transplant. Even then, he expects to be focused on the gratitude he feels for the wonderful life he has had and to go gracefully. Check him out. He hopes to be able to measure up to his own expectations. He wants to go out just as happy as he is while still here. That sounds like setting the bar pretty high for himself, but he thinks, hopes, prays, and believes that he can do it.

In the meantime, every new day presents a wonderful new opportunity for Phil Temple, or for anyone, to look for the beauty in others, to be forgiving, to rejoice in the love to be shared with those closest to us, to enjoy friends and family, keep promises, and do all the other things on the list that lead to happy living. Today was a wonderful, glorious day, and tomorrow will be yet another. The sweet taste of this beautiful life of love and joy is one that it is so wonderful to be sharing with the whole world. This book, in addition to being an effort to get a fair hearing concerning a sad family rupture, is an attempt to spread that joy.

Many believe that every life lived is a story worth telling. All that is required is someone to tell it. It is hoped that this story has struck a chord with you and that you can gain from this effort to be helpful to others who walk in the same shoes. If your adult children are lost to you, a beautiful life is still eminently possible and you can live it to the fullest. May God grant that what is offered here will be helpful to you.

The End